D1557982

# THE FEAR
# OF COOKING

# THE FEAR OF COOKING

*The Absolutely Foolproof Cookbook
for Beginners (and Everyone Else)
by BOB SCHER*

*Illustrated by Barbara Remington*

*HOUGHTON MIFFLIN COMPANY BOSTON 1984*

*Library of Congress Cataloging in Publication Data*

Scher, Bob.
The fear of cooking.

Includes index.
1. Cookery. I. Title.
TX715.S2964   1984     641.5     83-22535
ISBN 0-395-32216-2 (pbk.)

Printed in the United States of America

V 10 9 8 7 6 5 4 3 2 1

*To my parents,*
*and the memory of meals*
*that were lovingly prepared*

# Acknowledgments

So many people helped with the preparation of this book that I could not possibly acknowledge them all here.

I want to give special thanks to Brad and Susan Green for their generous hospitality; to my wise editor, Gerard Van der Leun, who caught me falling overboard on numerous occasions; and to Marlene Gabriel, my accomplished agent, who stuck with me from the title to the end; and to O'Brien Young, Enid Young, Belina Wagner, Anita Treash, Andrea Treash, Mark Theaman, Jennifer Tayloe, Pearl Sofaer, Suzy Sharp, Carol Schoneberg, Mary St. Thomas, Fredrica Parlett, Richard Owens, Charles Nilan, Carol Murphy, Marjorie Lambert, Mary Ellen Klee, Brenda Joynson, Cythea Homitz, Marsha Hart, Donna Harris, Gary Gunn, Karen Graf, Marilyn Gerber, Hank Gabriel, Nancy Fish, Marilyn Felber, Joe and Daraugh Forakis, Luise Erdmann, Pam Eccles, Robert Cameron, Felicia Brock, Donna Boss, Bruce Bixler, Teresa Baity, Joy Anderson, the Recipe Demon, the Mess God, and the Cooking Monster.

# Contents

**Part One / Getting Ready**

  1. Is This Cookbook Really Different?   3
  2. Secrets   4

**Part Two / Jump In**

  3. On Your Feet   11
  4. Action   31

**Part Three / Breakfast — A Good Way to Begin**

  5. Lucifer Toast   39
  6. Eggs Guinevere (and Toast Butterfield)   40
  7. Scrimbled, Scrambled, Scrumbled Eggs   46
  8. The Omelet Myth   53
  9. Lists Are as Odious as Comparisons   60
  10. French Toast   64
  11. Making More Than Adequate Coffee   67

**Part Four / Cooking on Both Sides**

  12. Tales of Kitchen Terror   73
  13. What Makes Cooking Go   85
  14. The Cornstarch Adventure   99
  15. The Other Side of Things   101
  16. Grendel's Law of Mess   105
  17. How to Invent Food: Herb Lore   108
  18. Sauce Making   122

19. Trout with Clout    141
20. The Overall Three    161

**Part Five / Focusing In**

21. Cooking Vegetables    167
22. The Artful Use of Nuts and Seeds    190
23. Salad    193
24. The Store    206
25. Meat    211
26. Cheese    229
27. Grains    237
28. Primo Pasta    245

**Part Six / Blending**

29. How to Invent Food: Innovative Cookery    253
30. Deep Soup    260
31. Casseroles, Beans, Stews, and Soups vs. Casserstews, Beanseroles, and Stewoups    279
32. Special Finishing Tools    295

**Part Seven / The Call from Childhood Through the Ages**

33. Baking    305
34. We Won't Dessert a Chapter on Need    331

**Overview**

35. Vital Aspects    339
36. How to Invent Food: The ABC's of Cooking    344
37. How to Sightread Cookbooks    349
38. The Boundaries of Cooking    353
Conclusion. At the End, the Beginning    363

Appendix I. On Owning Cookbooks    367
Appendix II. Additional Guides    372
Appendix III. Survey/Review    384
Index    386

# Don't Skip This
# (It's Not a Foreword)

The Fear of Cooking is a paralyzing reality for thousands of otherwise perfectly normal human beings. Are you one of those who cooks only scrambled eggs, or has never cooked anything at all? Perhaps you produce the same ten or twelve dishes month after month, year after year. Perhaps you've never been able to cook without a recipe in front of you. If so, take this book to heart. It is yours.

Surely you know at least one excellent cook who works largely without measuring, without being hemmed in by recipes, and without putting on airs. I do. She reads recipes, only not the part about how to put the ingredients together or how much of each one to put in. She just looks at the ingredients because, for her, they say almost everything she needs to know.

If you are going to cook, you must know something about ingredients — how they are combined, baked, broiled, or whatever, and what you can do to help these processes along. This book has been created and tested to help you *cook*, not just to get on with some tedious kitchen procedures. Its aim is to help you

learn not only basic methods of food preparation, but also how to vary them without recipes — even using only what you have on hand — without having to fumble nervously through a book while the fish is broiling.

see a process through without "knowing" anything — and learn something from it.

discover that you can cook creatively without having to wait to be reborn as a temperamental artist — in fact, without even having to be "creative"!

incorporate into the actual process of cooking vital aspects that, even if acknowledged, are seldom given much emphasis in other cookbooks.

understand that the *shortcut* to real cooking is not to avoid the drama. *The Fear of Cooking* will pamper you when necessary, but, when the times are ripe, will arrange to have you pitched overboard into an exhilarating world that you should have discovered long ago. (There are life preservers everywhere.) The most natural way to carefree, knowledgeable cooking.

### How to Use This Book

*The Fear* has been designed both to read through and to serve as a reference — and primarily for those in need, as a friend to work with. As your horizons widen, it may become a companion to other cookbooks or a gentle support, like an old friend, as you create your own fine meals.

One feature of this book is repetition. It will become evident that I have overemphasized certain useful ingredients (you will discover which ones as you proceed) because I have found, especially for the beginner, that this builds confidence and gives a sense of a solid base from which to expand. This is far better, it seems to me, than trying to assimilate too much information.

Above all, *The Fear of Cooking* demonstrates that you really can learn things *while trying them*, which is how most of us actually learned. And contrary to the assumptions of the clinical approach that is so fashionable today, if you're a little uneasy, a little apprehensive, or, let's face it, a little scared, you'll probably get the best results.

# PART ONE

# GETTING READY

# 1
# Is This Cookbook Really Different?

Does anybody need still another kind of cookbook? Haven't we got sophisticated ones, plain ones, comprehensive ones, ones for every palate, for every style of person who likes to cook or loves to cook — or even hates to cook — masterly productions that rise to gastronomical heights, and those that are just re-assuring or expedient?

Is this cookbook really different from all these?

You bet it is.

First of all, this book abounds in *contradictions*. It's going to contradict everything you thought were the fundamentals of cooking (if you ever thought that such things were spelled out in cookbooks).

Second, this book takes into account *vital aspects* of cooking that other cookbooks hardly, if ever, even admit are relevant.

Third, this book is about *the fear,* but it's also about *the wonder of cooking,* and not just the fun of cooking, no matter how exhilarating it is.

The aim of this manual is to help you jump in, yet without violating the principles and techniques of the cooking art that have been cultivated through centuries — from grandmas to gourmands, from the gourmet to the everyday.

This cookbook really is different.

This cookbook is also full of *secrets.*

# 2
# *Secrets*

Apple seller: You sound like you're the first lad who
ever saw an apple fall down.
Newton: You don't understand. The apple fell
*down.*
Apple seller: Boy, are you dumb. How else would an
apple fall?

This book reveals a multitude of medium, small, and even microsecrets, all of which are retroactively indispensable. That is, once you know about them you can't imagine having done without them. If you're a beginner, you're lucky.

No matter who "owns" a secret, you can be sure that all of them — and scores of others that you and I know nothing about — have been used and passed down through eons of cooking. Naturally you are bound to find some of them scattered here and there in cookbooks, but often, to your frustration, only half the secret is given. (They tell you to beat, but they don't tell you to beat *hard.*)

With some notable exceptions, it is not "the secret recipe" that merits a place in the upper echelons of secrets (although you may discover such recipes in this book). What are most significant are those directions that have more general application, like the use of salt, lemon, garlic, butter, etc., each of which is an important cooking substance — secrets that enable you to do things better or quicker.

Example. Maybe you were one of those who liked hot cereal when you were a kid, but you don't like it now. Why? Because once or twice you tried cooking it up for yourself, or someone else did, and it tasted like mushy pebbles. You know why? Because when you were a spunky little kid and your mom called you to breakfast, you were always horsing around with something, and when you finally made it to the table, the cooked cereal *had been sitting for at least 10 or 15 minutes —* not "a few minutes," like it says on the package.

That's the secret of good hot cereal. How many cookbooks, how many cereal boxes, tell you this? (Many don't even tell you to let it stand at all.) Something interesting happens to all grains in that short period *after* they're cooked up. Don't ask me exactly what. (After such a mind-boggling experience as being cooked, maybe the grains need some peace and quiet in order to settle down and taste the way they should.)

The difference in taste is not subtle. You can do a test if you like on what might have been your favorite cereal. I mean something like oatmeal or Wheatena or Zoom, cereal in which there is some notification that real grain, intact, was involved in the making of it.

Another "secret" about cereal, especially oatmeal: If you like it rich and creamy, instead of following those package directions, try putting it in when the water is cold, heat it up to a boil, and cook it the way they tell you to over moderate heat for 2 minutes; then cover the pot with a tight lid (a dishtowel between the lid and the pot will give you a tight seal and, by absorbing some of the excess steam, gives a nice finish to the oats), *remove it from the heat, and let it stand for at least 8 to 10 minutes.* Or longer.

If you don't like it especially creamy, then begin by stirring the oats into briskly boiling water, cook for about 3 minutes, then follow the above directions.

Of course, there are still other methods. The main point is that this more gentle way of cooking cereal is worth trying and takes only a few minutes longer.

There are also secrets so obvious (to a cook) that they are often not put so that a beginning reader can take them in. When you get to know these particular secrets, they reveal which things in a recipe are more or less unchangeable and which are variable, depending on personal or other factors —

such as the availability and quality of the ingredients, the season, the weather, the cook's taste buds, and what's left over from yesterday. As your knowledge of cooking grows, you will also learn what you can't tamper with; that is, what is crucial across a wide range of results. For example, if both cooking oil and honey are going into the granola, you should mix them together before you put them in.

. . . . . . . . . . . . . . . . . . . . . . . . . . . . . . . . . . . . . . . . . . . . . . . . . . . . .

GUIDE TO
**Great Granola**

Preheat the oven to 350°.

UNCOOKED ROLLED OATS to which you add very roughly a fourth as much ALMONDS, CASHEWS, COCONUT (shredded), SESAME SEEDS. Optional: SUNFLOWER SEEDS, RAISINS, even DRIED APPLES.

After you make it the first time, you will adjust according to your own taste.

In this granola there is no vegetable oil or honey: just BROWN SUGAR, enough to make it sweet enough for you (add to the dry ingredients above), and BUTTER (melted slowly over low heat just before putting in the oven), enough to pour over everything without drenching too much. (Yes, you can use vegetable oil and honey, but it may not be as Great.)

Put it into the oven on a cookie sheet for about 10 minutes — maybe a little longer — stirring and turning things over frequently with a spatula and *watching carefully* to avoid burning. The crispness will set in when cool.

On putting our own sugar on cereal: Even so-called health food granola often insults us with added sugar, as if someone else knew better how much sugar or honey we'd like to have. Putting on our own is not an extra bother; it's a personal touch we can give to our food.

. . . . . . . . . . . . . . . . . . . . . . . . . . . . . . . . . . . . . . . . . . . . . . . . . . . . .

And here's another secret, a secret that could teach you to cook wonderful gourmet dishes in practically any situation without reference books. Are you ready for this?

This secret is hunger.

Hunger reminds us of how *basic* cooking is. I mean, would God have put us down here on Earth and made us hungry and not provided some simple way of letting us eat? Of course not.

When you're hungry (not starving; that's different), it's not just for the food, but for the taste, the texture, the aroma, and even the atmosphere around cooking, serving, and eating. Something wonderful happens when you're hungry. You can taste better, smell better — you can even *see* better — and therefore you can cook better.

You can get recipes from almost anywhere, but no one else can eat or appreciate food for you. We've been given the gifts, the means to partake and enjoy, but we have to use them, to exercise them. And cooking does that. When the interest is there, the readiness, the *hunger*, recipes appear out of the *atmosphere* the way soup appears out of the stock.

Hunger inspires the cook. As we'll see in the chapters "How to Invent Food," the harmonious urgings of hunger provide an inexhaustible source of energy for creating those dishes that are pleasing to us and to the people for whom we cook.

Cooking is much bigger than any of us. Its laws were not invented by people; its workings are still largely a mystery. We have to trust that the vegetables will cook. In this, and in myriad other ways, we discover that food is not a hostile substance.

You may be afraid to do something in the kitchen, like cutting fat off slimy meat or cooking three things at once, but you can go through this fear if you remember what my grandma Jessie said — and maybe your grandma said it too:

"I could cook before I could read." It's that simple.

Are you ready for *more* secrets? Well, just turn the page and . . .

# PART TWO

# JUMP IN

# 3
# *On Your Feet*

A human being is an animal that cooks.

Let's face a few basic but monumental requirements:
1. You do have to have *some* kitchen equipment (not very much).
2. You do have to spend *some* time in your kitchen (probably less than you think).
3. You do need *some* guidance (it follows).

Example of Some Guidance:

You'll be going to the store a lot because food tastes best when it's fresh. **Don't fool around in there. Get out of there as fast as you can because cooking begins in the store.**

Naturally there are exceptions to the no-dawdling rule, but if you get bogged down at the market, your energy level can sink to that of a slug. Have you ever seen a slug prepare food? No, you haven't. And now that I've got your attention, I want you to know that the following statement in some form or other abounds in the cookbooks of today:

"Follow each recipe to the letter. Only an experienced cook can take liberties with or make changes in a recipe" (*The New McCall's Cookbook*).

This, of course, is nonsense. The actual situation is quite the opposite. Only an experienced cook can really follow a recipe. And often the so-called recipes, whose compilers subtly threaten you with unimaginable catastrophes if you don't follow them to the letter, are three or five or even fifty-five generations removed from the original. So what you are getting is someone's favorite *deviation*.

There's nothing wrong with this. It's one of the traditional ways that something alive, like cooking, develops and changes. In fact, one of the aims of this book is to prepare the reader, through direct experience with the materials of cooking, to follow a recipe (or a deviation from a recipe) the way it was intended to be followed.

It doesn't mean that you can do *anything* in the kitchen and get satisfying results. Precision is desirable; but to be precise means you have to include being precise about how much *latitude* there is. And there's much more latitude in cooking than one may think. Sometimes you can add, sometimes subtract. The whole point is to know when. This is a very important concept. If you didn't get it, read this paragraph again.

With this one idea alone, after you get the hang of it, you could be tossing the parsley into the rice like Julia Child without the slightest worry that it's too much or too little.

It's not a fault of any one of these cookbooks, many of which are excellent; it's only a fashion of modern education that we are instructed to learn such things through these rigid forms. I suppose that sooner or later everyone who goes on needs to acquire a repertoire of such forms, but it may be a question of temperament as to how someone approaches "learning to cook" in the first place. No matter how much inborn talent or flair they may have, beginning with eyes glued to a recipe, for some, is not only irksome but an insurmountable obstacle.

However you start, sooner or later, if you go on, you have to be able to cook with "goodness" and sense, so that people love your food and don't just admire it, and so that no matter what ingredients you are lacking, or what conditions (within reason) you are cooking in, you can carry through to the "goodness."

And that's the heart of it all.

### The Fear of Lists

You have to start with some implements, so here is a list of what to get. But if you just go out and get a lot of items on a list, without any thought or concern about what they are, it's confusing and discouraging, especially if you haven't cooked much before. Utensils and containers just sit there, blocking your view.

That's why I've taken the usual bald list and unraveled it a little. You can really do wonders with much less than I'm suggesting, but even so, my setup is austere compared with most cookbooks. Most authors assume that you are going to cook every single dish in their book and that you are going to use just what they use — or what they tell you they use. Nevertheless, there are thousands of superb cooks who use hardly much more than is set forth here. As a prelude to the main list, here is an even more basic array, *The Secret List of Naked Truths.*

### The Secret List of Naked Truths
Billions of delectable dishes of every description have been cooked with a few modest utensils like these:

*A chef's knife*
*A chopping board*
*A heavy skillet with cover*
*A pot with cover*
*A casserole with cover* (unless your skillet is big enough and has an oven-proof handle)
*A pretty big wooden spoon*
*A big metal spoon with holes or slots*
*A spatula*
*A strainer or colander*
*Bowl(s)*
*A screw-top jar* for shaking things up
*A dishtowel* (use, folded, as a potholder)
*Herbs and spices*
*Cups, plates, forks, etc.*

*Optional*
*A coffee maker* (unless you use a plain pot, campfire style)
*A grater* (but you can use a knife)
*A rubber spatula*
*A vegetable peeler* (or knife)
*A wire whisk*

### Back to the Main List as if Nothing Happened

Some things are more essential than others, depending on your style or on how your style develops. If you don't have something, improvise. Prop things up with forks, drain things in baskets, pound things with plates.

Only cookbooks (including this one) — and manufacturers — will tell you to get all kinds of stuff in the beginning that you don't really need and that you never may need. To some extent, it all depends on the scope of the cooking you plan to undertake. Once you have some basics, the principle is not to get something that costs a lot or that takes up your valuable kitchen space just because it's on a list or on TV. If you really need something, like a Cuisinart or a V rack or a copper mixing bowl, and you can afford it, then go get it — but *after* you finish this book. If you develop your kitchen at the pace you develop your cooking, you'll get only the things you really will use.

The very best utensils are your hands, but good knives are probably the most important items to purchase; sturdy pots and pans with tight lids, the next.

Since most lists are suspect as well as tedious, I hope the practical hints make this one a little more palatable.

### Knives

If you've never done much cooking, by all means get a CHEF'S KNIFE WITH AT LEAST AN 8-INCH TRIANGULAR BLADE. Almost magically, this will give you an instant rapport with cooking (along with the cast-iron skillet mentioned below).

However, you should know that there are plenty of excellent cooks who use only a STAINLESS STEEL KNIFE WITH A 5-INCH TRIANGULAR BLADE for all their chopping, slicing, mincing, whatever. (If you have small hands, you may prefer the 5-inch.) And you should have a carving knife, though you *can* use the 8-inch chef's knife for carving even though its blade is thicker and less effective. So unless you've already got knives, get the chef's knife and the smaller 5-inch job.

Obtain a rod-shaped sharpening steel and *keep your knives sharp.* This will help your arm and hand movements to be quicker, more enjoyable, and more precise. A dull knife, which can more easily slip, is actually more dangerous.

Right at the outset, inculcate this habit: Each time you use your knife (or every other time) stroke it on the steel a few times, pulling it along each side of the whole length of the blade to keep the edge true. (This should produce in you an affirmative sense of *wielding*.) Much controversy exists as to the angle of the stroke — from 15 to 30 degrees, depending on whom you consult. (I use about 20 degrees.) More important is that the angle be more or less consistent, and the easiest way is for the same person always to do the stroking. But even more important is that it be consistently done.

The unglazed bottom of a porcelain vase also works.

Pages packed with real information about the ups and downs of various knives can be written. But here are the practical essentials: The best knives are carbon steel. They are the sharpest, which makes them the easiest and most deft to use. They also hold their edge well, and if cared for properly, they resharpen easily. A good one will outlive you, even though, after years, you may have to replace the handle (because you kept getting it wet).

But carbon steel unquestionably requires more careful treatment than a good stainless blade. It also has a discoloring effect on acidic foods; for example, it turns red cabbage purple. It will rust easily, especially if you live near the ocean or in a very humid climate.

A good stainless steel knife is durable and has a tough edge — but never as good as carbon steel; once dull, it is difficult to bring back its original edge. Still, a good stainless knife lasts many years and is easy to care for. It is chemically inert and will not discolor acid foods.

Every so often, your knives need to be sharpened on a honing stone, or take them to your butcher (really, you can), and for a price he will send them out with his own knives to a professional sharpener.

Also get a BREAD KNIFE — *stainless steel.*

KNIFE RACK. Do not mix up your knives in a drawer (or a drainer) with other things. Just wipe them dry with a damp towel right after using and put them back in the rack. This is obligatory.

CHOPPING BOARD. I always think I need *two* boards, but I still

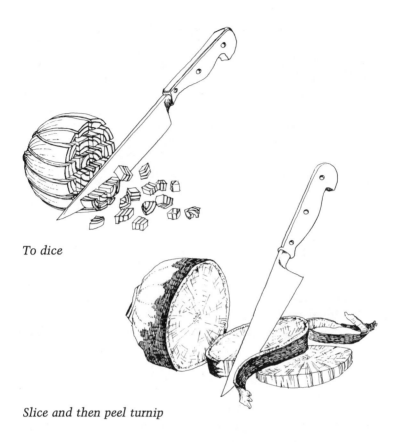

*To dice*

*Slice and then peel turnip*

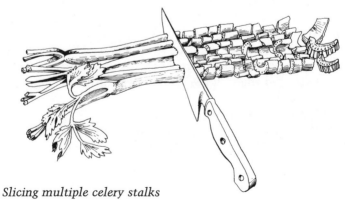

*Slicing multiple celery stalks*

have only one (I admit it's large enough for two). There may be an important principle here. Almost all cooks genially complain about not having some inexpensive piece of equipment, and they never get it.

A SMALL KNIFE WITH SERRATED EDGES *(optional).* For cutting tomatoes and soft fruit.

### Cutting Up

We'd best talk now about this very important subject. But briefly, or you may develop the Fear of Trying.

Take your chef's knife. Give it a couple of scrapes on your sharpening rod (or on the unglazed bottom of your porcelain vase). Put the tip of the blade on the cutting board and leave it there the whole time. (Notice that your feet are on the floor.) Move the other end up and down — but just high enough to slice — while with your left hand (your right hand if you are left-handed) you steadily move whatever it is you wish to chop into the line of the up-and-down-moving blade. Or, with your cutting hand guiding the *blade,* move the knife in an arc across the food, chopping as you go. Sounds dangerous, I know, but it's not. Another way, great for mincing parsley: hold the blade on top with *both* hands and go chop-chop, up and down all over. You'll have no difficulty learning to do it if you become even a little interested in what you're doing and what is happening to the food that you're working on instead of considering the whole business an obligatory annoyance. Relax. Know that untold krillions of beings all over the cosmos (some possibly even klutzier than we) have gotten the hang of it, or of some equivalent procedure.

You can mince or chop. You can slice crossways, lengthwise, or diagonally. You can dice into cubes. You can set pieces next to each other and chop more than one at a time. Watch other cooks when you get the chance. You'll observe that no matter how any book tells you to chop something, there's somebody who does it a little differently — and just as effectively.

*Take note:* Knives that are sharp are not only *less* dangerous (they don't slip), but they also preserve more nutrients! That's because they cause less damage to the tissue of the food.

A sharp knife is your best friend in the kitchen.

### Skillets

LARGE SKILLET, at least 10 inches across.

MEDIUM SKILLET, about 7 or 8 inches across.

You could start out with an enamel-coated cast-iron pan or one of stainless steel that has an aluminum or copper-reinforced bottom for better heat conductivity — both with tight lids and heavy bottoms. If you're fairly new at cooking, one of your skillets should definitely be *uncoated cast iron*. These are wonderful to cook with — and *cheap*. In fact, the cheap ones are usually the *best* ones. It doesn't matter if they're all scarred and ugly. (Most stores hide them on the lower shelves.)

One of the secrets known by all cooks who use them, but not always included in the instructions that come with the skillets, is a simple way to season one for use. First, scour it with steel wool and get all the rust out. *Rinse thoroughly.* Dry over low heat and wipe with a paper towel. Then put cooking oil in it (I use pure olive oil for this), enough to coat the bottom of the pan, and heat it slowly on the burner just until it smokes, rotating the pan to coat the sides.

Some people like to put the oiled pan in a moderate oven for about half an hour to bake the oil in. Either way, from then on you never have to wash, scrub, or scour your skillet. A properly seasoned skillet never needs anything but a wipe. (And the *sooner* you wipe it after you use it, the easier it will be to get clean.)

The first dozen or so times you cook with it, make sure there's some oil on it both *before* and *after* use. From then on, to avoid any buildup of rust and for good nonstick cooking, you can rub a few drops of oil in the pan after each use. This is only necessary when you haven't used oil in the cooking. It all depends upon the "micro-climate" in your particular kitchen — the humidity, the vapors, the temperature flux — which is one reason various cooks disagree about how to maintain their pans. Some people never have to do this.

If you *do* need to scrub your skillet (you see how we authors fudge), here's a more closely held secret: Add a little oil, then rub, preferably with a coarse cloth like burlap (but paper towels will work almost as well). Some find that coarse salt — that is, kosher or sea salt, which is, paradoxically, not as abrasive as so-called regular salt — will clean things up. But regular salt works, too. Afterward, rub some oil in with a paper towel. (When in doubt, always rub a few drops of oil in.)

But only use the salt treatment *after* your skillet has been fully seasoned (at least ten or twelve cookings). Otherwise, you may pit the surface.

If, for some reason, a gummy deposit starts to build up, here's even more closely guarded information: Get the pan good and hot with some oil in it. Then pour some *boiling water* into the pan. (Be careful, though. Steam!) It cleans like whisssk!! Then coat with oil, etc.

If none of the above works, or if you left water sitting in it and it got rusty, as long as your pan has acquired a good seasoning you can — guess what? — clean it with mild soap, warm water, and a pad or sponge, as long as you give it a final drying over low heat. (However, if rust should find its way into the pores of the metal, dump it.)

The whole business is actually very simple. The pleasure of owning a properly seasoned skillet can't be fully appreciated except by having one you've prepared yourself. It's great for helping you get a feeling for cooking. (Bonus: no washing!) And every time you cook with oil, it "helps" the pan.

But let's be realistic. Eventually you may get tired of watching over your seasoned skillet, but by then you're probably a seasoned cook! Okay. Then go out and get an enamel-coated cast iron or stainless steel pan, whichever you didn't get before.

### Pots and Such

Mainly, no flimsy, dinky pots! Get good heavy stuff. They heat better, they keep what's inside warmer longer, and they don't tend to get hot spots or burn the food. The stainless steel ones with aluminum or copper-reinforced bottoms are good, and so are enameled cast iron. People often acquire pots from here and there, so what I'm recommending is only if you have nothing, or next to nothing. If you already have pots, check them out. Make sure they're sturdy with lids that fit closely. Sure, you can fix food in almost anything that won't burn up, but what you actually do cook in, day after day, is important.

Every kind of material *cooks food differently*. Even the *shape* of a pot affects the cooking. Often — but not always — these differences are subtle; in any case, they depend on the kind of food being cooked and its reaction to the pan. Cast iron, for instance, can turn asparagus rather gray (although it's not bad for you). Eggs cooked in stainless steel or cast iron pans have a sharper flavor than those cooked in enameled pans. Differences in equipment are only *one* of the reasons why recipes are just guides. The author isn't cooking with *your* pots and pans on *your* stove, in *your* climate. When you get the real hang of cooking, you can cook anywhere. Because you're cooking by *being there* and by *watching and tasting and smelling and touching,* not just by copying someone else's description of how they say they do it.

You will want:

ONE OR TWO 2-QUART POTS and a 4-QUART, all with tight covers, and ONE BIG, TALL POT with a domed lid and handles. In

it you can make soup, lots of pasta, and almost any other thing imaginable.

A 1-QUART SAUCEPAN OR SMALL SKILLET. Not absolutely essential if you've got some 2-quart pots, but for making a sauce and melting butter and such, it's very nice to have.

A CASSEROLE. A shallow baking dish with a cover.

A SET OF NESTED MIXING BOWLS. Earthenware or glass.

A LARGE SALAD BOWL. It *doesn't* have to be wood (some think it's much better if it *isn't*, but there are just as many others who are positive that it should be). If you start out with a nice, big, earthenware bowl, which I think is a must somewhere along the line, you can use it for mixing dough as well. Get a wooden salad bowl later, or wait for someone to give you one for your birthday.

TWO STRAINERS. Fine and coarse.

A ROASTING PAN. The sides need not be deep; 3 inches is enough. Officially, you're supposed to have a V rack or a pan that lets the juices drip down below the meat. There are untold numbers of excellent cooks who have never owned either of these. A Greek butcher once told me: "Is American Mickey Mouse, these racks." However, since I'm an American, I got a simple trivet, like a cake rack, and it does the job.

AN OVEN THERMOMETER. This fits inside your oven. Sometimes it is more reliable than the dial setting on the outside. But even if your dial is calibrated properly, it can't tell you what's really going on inside as the oven heats up, cools down, or is loaded up with things cooking in there.

POTHOLDERS. Get at least two — one will always be missing.

SOME EXTRA PLATTERS AND BOWLS. Always welcome, including some very small ones for serving special things.

A COLANDER. A firm metal sieve with large holes for draining. Such a modest piece of equipment, so enjoyable to use.

A STEAMER. A useful and inexpensive device for steam-cooking vegetables and other more or less delicate things. It opens and closes like a steel flower and fits, within reason, into any size pot.

A JUICE SQUEEZER. I prefer the simple glass hand squeezers, but for lemons, limes, and *onions*, a small metal one is good. However, I'm a bit fanatical about doing things by hand. A mechanical juicer is fine, too.

A TEAKETTLE. For boiling water. If you're a stranger in the kitchen, you may not realize that it takes at least twice as long to boil a large amount of water than you think (or than you would like).

A COFFEE MAKER. Some sort of drip pot is best — even Brillat-Savarin (the nineteenth-century French gastronome) said so. The current fashion favors those using disposable paper for filtering the grounds; this is encouraged, no doubt, by the manufacturers of filter paper. Grounds can be filtered with many (nonchemically treated) cotton materials like flannel or linen, which are cleanable and reusable. I often use an old-fashioned drip pot with a perforated metal basket for the grounds. It tastes so full-bodied that before my friends find out what I used, they think I've discovered some especially good filter paper.

Much more important is the grind of your coffee, the water,

and you — because you are the real coffee maker. You can actually make very acceptable coffee in a plain pot, campfire style. (Ask your grandfather.)

A TOASTER. Certainly you can exist without a toaster. But you won't.

REFRIGERATOR CONTAINERS AND WIDE-MOUTHED JARS WITH LIDS (a few different sizes).

### Utensils (All of Which Can Fit Inside One Decent-sized Drawer or Be Hung on a Wall)

WOODEN SPOONS. At least three or four of various lengths and a couple of different shapes. A short spatula-shaped one is very useful. These constant companions, in my opinion, should never go into a drawer. They should be placed in their own container on a counter near the stove, always handy. This is pure folk wisdom.

TWO BIG METAL SPOONS. One with holes or slots for taking food out of liquid and one without holes that I think should be used strictly for basting. Use wooden spoons for everything else because when metal is used to cook with in a metal pan, it *scratches*. So just when you need to push at something or move something up from the bottom of the pan, you instinctively pull back because the two metals are not compatible. And that's when you burn the food. Of course, if you like using metal spoons in metal pans (and you don't burn the food), ignore what I said.

The following is a small selection from the vast assortment of ingenious and often bizarre-looking utensils that you can peruse in markets and cooking supply stores and that have been invented to go with various Arm and Hand Movements:

A METAL SPATULA. You'll use it a lot, and for lots of things besides turning pancakes.

A RUBBER SPATULA. Good for getting all the juices out of a pan (and other things).

A VEGETABLE PEELER. If you occasionally allow "guest cooks" to join you in the kitchen, get an extra one. Polite (or scared) guests usually like to help peel.

A CAN OPENER; CORKSCREW.

A GRATER. Make sure it grates nutmeg, too.

TONGS. You *can* do without tongs, but once you have them, you need them. So get them. (Otherwise, poke your food up with *a big fork*.)

A WIRE WHISK. An inexpensive way to feel like a gourmet cook. Very useful, but you know what? You can still be a gourmet cook without one. Nevertheless, get one!

AN EGG (AND CREAM) BEATER. The basic hand models with *double* "whirrers," each rotating in the opposite direction, are not only fascinating to play with, they are very efficient.

A SALT/PEPPER MILL. *Always* grind your own pepper as y⌟u use it.

AN APRON WITH A TOWEL HANGING FROM IT SOMEWHERE. You'll thank me for this, especially for the towel, which is for drying your hands, not for sopping up goop. Well, sometimes it does sop goop.

### Cleaning Up

WRAPS AND ROLLS. Paper towels (*get good quality*); aluminum foil; waxed paper; Saran wrap (or a similar plastic wrap); freezer wrap. Here is a statement that some will find difficult to believe: Some cooks *never* use paper towels! But I'm still self-indulgent.

A PLASTIC OR NYLON SCOURER (a Tuffy, for example). These are mild.

SCOURING CLOTHS OR PADS. These are abrasive.

A VEGETABLE BRUSH. Many get along without, but there are times . . .

CHORE AIDS. A dishrack; detergent; cleanser.

SEVERAL SPONGES (OR WET DISHCLOTHS, which Grandma always used and which last longer). Different ones for *counters* than for *floors*. YOU CAN NEVER WIPE COUNTERS OFTEN ENOUGH, so don't get nervous about it.

### Not Quite Essential, but Helpful

TWO BUTTER DISHES WITH COVERS. One for cooking and one for the table. I put these down as optional only because you probably wouldn't believe me if I said that such trivial-sounding things were important to have. But exposed butter quickly absorbs icebox odors, and butter (or one of its substitutes) happens to be a major factor in cooking. And while we're on the all-important subject of keeping butter, here's a tip:

If you cook regularly — say, at least once a day — then keep a day or two's worth of butter *out* of the refrigerator in a dish with a lightproof cover (butter goes bad more quickly when exposed to light). This way you will always have butter at room temperature for spreading (you'll use less), for baking, and for other situations that come up, often suddenly, in cooking.

Another butter tip: Aren't those butter wrappers annoying? Run the whole cube, paper and all, under warm water for a few seconds. Behold! The cover slides right off. Very useful when you have a lot of them to do.

AN APPLE CORER. Sure, you can use a knife. But it's such a pleasure to use one of these, even though it's just a few seconds per apple (or pear).

SCISSORS. For snipping parsley. (Personally, I prefer using a chef's knife.)

A PARING KNIFE. If you feel like it.

POULTRY SHEARS. Makes cutting up a chicken easier.

ANOTHER SMALL CHOPPING BOARD. For garlic and other strong-smelling substances. Most would say this is essential. It is, but it's not absolutely essential.

A SALAD DRYER. A cunning hand-operated device that is, yes, a gimmick — and is definitely worth getting.

A FOOD MILL. Mashes, purées things. Another clever object that becomes indispensable once you own one. (You can use *an electric blender* instead, but the texture of the blend isn't quite the same. But a blender is certainly nice to have.)

A MORTAR AND PESTLE. Many excellent cooks never use one. Others like to have two: one for garlic and one for other things, usually spices. Ceramic and marble are good choices.

A BASTING SYRINGE. Though I prefer basting with a spoon rather than a syringe, in certain oven situations you will be able to get down closer to the last good drop in the pan (for instance, in the corners) with one of these.

A LONGER SPATULA. For turning delicate things, like fish.

AN OVEN MITT. Safe and snug.

ANOTHER WHISK. A larger, longer one for beating egg whites.

CHEESECLOTH. For straining soups and stocks — and actually for making cheese (see page 236)!

LITTLE CHEESECLOTH BAGS. For certain dishes, to put herbs and spices in while cooking for easy removal afterward. These may seem a bit esoteric, but they cost little and can be stuffed anywhere.

A TIMER. Obviously very useful for sundry reasons. I still think if I got a timer that it would interfere with my timing, but that's just stupid, because it wouldn't. But I still don't have one and the one on my stove doesn't work.

### For Baking

A FLOUR SIFTER. This may be hard to swallow, but there have been, there are now, and there will be *trillions* of fabulous bakers (of bread, muffins, some cakes and pies) who have never possessed a flour sifter. But I still think you should have one. A 5-cup one is a good size.

ONE BAKING PAN, 9 BY 9 BY 2 INCHES. Pyrex is nice — easy to clean and you can see what's going on inside. But things bake faster in it. Shave 20° to 25° off the baking temperature when using Pyrex. Metal pans are fine, too. (Because they absorb more heat, Pyrex and dark metal pans will tend to give you crustier results.)

ONE OR TWO LOAF PANS, 9 BY 5 BY 3 INCHES. Metal or Pyrex. For baking bread and other things.

A ROUND TIN for pies and A MUFFIN TIN for muffins and popovers. Many excellent cooks favor nonstick utensils. I don't happen to, but a nonstick *muffin tin* is a real time-saver, and the coating will not wear off with normal use.

A BAKING SHEET. For cookies, biscuits, etc. Get a firm, thick-gauge one. The failure to communicate this to new bakers has probably caused more cookie-making problems than anything else.

TOOTHPICKS. For testing the doneness of cakes.

You may have noticed that there are *no measuring implements* on this list. Further, I recommend that you do not purchase a *meat thermometer* right away — not until after you've already learned how to tell by smelling, looking, and touching when the roast is done. If you've already got one, give it to somebody so they can hide it from you till you finish this book.

### Herbs

The worst things for herbs and spices are light, heat, and air. Take this seriously. Put your herbs and spices in a dark, cool place in airtight containers.

Use fresh herbs whenever you can. One portion of dried equals about *three* portions of fresh (the opposite of what you might think).

A good assortment to start with:
*Parsley.* Always try to get fresh.
*Basil*
*Thyme*
*Marjoram*
*Tarragon*
*Rosemary*
*Bay leaves* (dried)
*Chives.* Not an herb, but an onion — sold freeze-dried in herb sections. Or put a pot of fresh chives on your window-sill.
*Dill weed.* (It also comes in seed form.)

## Spices
*Celery seed*
*Caraway seeds*
*Paprika*
*Cayenne pepper*
The following are common baking spices, but used throughout cooking as well.
*Cinnamon*
*Nutmeg.* Use fresh and grate your own.
*Coriander.* Ground is okay; don't neglect this one.
*Ginger.* Use fresh if possible. Because fresh ginger is moist, the pieces get stuck in your grater when you try to fine-grind it. To remedy this, keep it in the freezer wrapped in freezer paper.
*Cloves,* whole and ground.
*Vanilla extract.* Use the real stuff, not an imitation.
*Pepper,* whole black peppercorns. Grind your own with a pepper mill, always.
*Salt.* Kosher or sea salt is best.

## Sauces
*Mustard.* Prepared (bottled) Dijon. Grey Poupon (made domestically) is good; there are many others.
*Soy sauce or Tamari sauce*
*Maggi.* In soups and stews and such, by the *drop.* A friend once wheedled the recipe of a salad dressing I liked from the chef in a hotel. All the ingredients were familiar except for one or two drops of Maggi.

**Other Herbs and Spices**
*Oregano*
*Summer savory*
*Sage*
*Fresh mint*
*Chervil*
*Allspice*
*Anise*
*Cardamom*
*Cumin*
*Curry powder.* If you really like curry, try mixing your own.
*Fennel seeds*
*Mace*
*Mustard (dried)*
*White peppercorns*
*Saffron.* The world's costliest spice, but very little is used in a given dish.
*Turmeric.* An exotic yellow spice that isn't as hot as it looks.
*Tabasco sauce.* Some cooks use this once every 250 years. Some use it every three days.
*Worcestershire sauce.* The same applies.

You will try always to keep fresh parsley, lemons, and garlic on hand (like having musicians to play during meals). But garlic *powder* is absolutely forbidden, and so are parsley flakes. Both are disgraces to food, especially when fresh garlic and parsley are so easy to get.

I must report, however, that many good cooks, especially of the old school, use garlic powder and even parsley flakes. Still, I won't retract. There's no telling where such practices may lead to in our kitchens (lettuce powder? duck flakes?).

If you really *can't* get fresh garlic or parsley, you can use garlic powder or parsley flakes.

### The Way It Is
I've remarked that basic principles are rarely spelled out in cookbooks. This book will probably contradict many instructions that *are* found in other cookbooks, not because I think these instructions are wrong, but because often they're just opinions disguised as facts.

Now if you suddenly have the uneasy feeling that you have mistakenly purchased an "upstart" or renegade cookbook or some kind of anti-cookbook cookbook, you should rest assured that anyone who writes a cookbook that is at least not half bad actually incorporates into his own cooking the very fundamentals I wish to convey to you.

In the quite modest kitchen setup just outlined, remember, there were *no* measuring implements. That may be scary, but I don't think anybody can cook decently unless they've been scared.

Look, here's a chance to be scared in real life and if you blow it, it's all right. How many opportunities do you have in your life to do this?

# 4
# Action

— Knock knock.
— Who's there?
— The Cooking Monster.
— Come on in, I'm just starting dinner.
— But I came to . . .
— Here, the spinach needs washing.

There's a lot of fear and inhibition bound up in words that stand just for modest Arm and Hand Movements — or, to be more correct, basic body movements — like *basting*. These words put the beginner off by suggesting that everything is more of a production than it actually is.

These various verbs of movement depict simple actions. The words themselves (mostly one-syllable) are expressive and accessible. A beginner whose blurry image of the activities in the kitchen may be filled with complicated, even chaotic, motions can begin to experience cooking as a vital world comprising a rich content of movements that are simple, dynamic, and satisfying to perform.

This is an unalphabetized list, for easy reading:

***Breaking Down, Combining With***
*Stir.* Means to stir.
*Beat.* Beat.
*Shake.* Always means to shake hard.
*Sift.* To pass through a sieve, used in reference to flour.

*To fold*

*To cut in*

*Mash.* Even a fork can do it.

*Purée.* To make a smooth, thickish mixture (called *purée*) by passing food, usually cooked, through a food mill or fine sieve or by blending it in a blender.

*Blend.* More intermingled than *combine* — but really, did I have to tell you?

*Fold* (used a lot in baking). To incorporate a food ingredient into a mixture along with the air trapped inside — for example, stiffly beaten egg whites or whipped cream — by repeated (gentle) overturnings without stirring or beating. You can use the flat of your hand or a rubber spatula.

*Cream.* To work butter or another fat to a creamy consistency — often along with sugar — by working it with a wooden spoon against a bowl until the fat becomes light, almost fluffy.

*Cut in* (used mainly in baking). Cutting, slicing, or breaking fat into flour; use two *butter* knives crosswise, a pastry blender, or your fingers.

*Knead.* A simple rhythmic body movement in which dough, in contact with the hands, is made more uniform and more elastic by stretching and folding in before being baked.

### Cutting Up
*Chop.* Chop.

*Slice.* Slice.

*Julienne.* To slice into long, thin strips. If it looks like a matchstick, it's julienned (*see next page*).

*Sliver.* To sliver — not as long but thinner than julienne.

*Tear.* Yes, sometimes tearing is an approved kitchen movement.

*Mince.* Usually means finely minced (*see next page*).

*Shred.* A good knife is all you need.

*Grate.* Graters are satisfying to use.

*Flake.* To separate food such as fish gently into pieces by inserting a fork or whatever into the natural cleavages.

### Putting On
*Baste.* To moisten at intervals with a liquid during the cooking process (for example, with melted butter, fat, or pan drip-

*To julienne*

*To mince*

pings). You can use a big spoon. It has nothing to do with thrashing or beating.

*Dribble.* You know what this means.

*Brush.* To spread a thin coating of something, like melted butter, over something else. A pastry brush can be used, or a crumpled butter wrapper.

*Dot.* To put big dots (dabs) of something like butter on top of something else, such as fish.

*Coat.* To cover lightly with, for example, flour, bread crumbs, crushed nuts, or sugar.

*Dredge.* The same as *to coat*, generally used for flour.

*Dust.* To coat very lightly.

*Bard.* To cover lean pieces of meat with something fatty like salt pork or bacon to keep the meat from drying out during cooking.

*Garnish.* To add decorative or appetizing touches to food.

*Dress.* Basically, to prepare, but it has many applications. To prepare a killed animal for market, to stuff with a dressing, to apply a sauce.

*Preheat.* To turn on the oven or broiler 10 or 15 minutes before putting in the food. Very important when broiling or baking. Applies to pans on top of the stove as well: Preheat before adding oil.

### Taking Off

*Skim.* Skim.

*Sieve.* To strain.

*Drain.* Often a colander is used.

*Blanch.* The basic meaning is to whiten, but it is used most often in cooking to refer to immersing food in boiling water either to remove the skin (for onions, almonds, or tomatoes) or to partially cook something ("parboil" it) before subjecting it to some other cooking process (or freezing).

*Shell.* To remove the shell.

*Peel.* Peel.

*Deglaze.* By the addition of some hot liquid, such as wine, and some scraping up of delectable particles, to remove (usually for use in sauce or gravy) all the good substances left in a pan that meat, poultry, or fish has been cooked in. If desired, it can be thickened or extended.

### Shaping Up

*Truss.* To bind the legs and wings of fowl in preparation for roasting. It can be done with one single piece of twine.

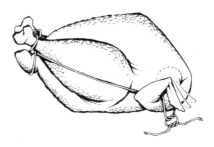

*Marinate.* To place meat, fish, or a vegetable to soak in a *marinade* — an acid sauce (lemon, vinegar, wine) or an acid and oil sauce similar to salad dressing — in order to improve the flavor and to tenderize it.

*Handle lightly.* Handle lightly. Especially important for pastry and biscuit dough. (Also *hamburgers.*)

# PART THREE

# BREAKFAST
## *A Good Way to Begin*

# 5
# *Lucifer Toast*

*Beat the Devil*
— Film title

Put the bread in the toaster and push it down. When it pops up, push it down. When it pops up, push it down again. When it pops up, it should be all burnt. If not, repeat.

If you don't have a toaster, use a skillet. Put some butter in the pan, enough so that when it melts it floods the entire surface. Put in the bread. When burnt on one side, turn over and burn the other side, which won't take as long as the first side because it's already a little cooked.

Put the result on a plate and look at it; then throw it away. It's a complete failure. You may never again produce such an utter failure as this incinerated object. If you think that something you cook from now on is a failure, just compare it with Lucifer Toast.

. . . . . . . . . . . . . . . . . . . . . . . . . . . . . . . , . . . . . . . . . . . . . . . .

GUIDE TO
**Lucifer Toast**

BREAD
Burn like Hell.

. . . . . . . . . . . . . . . . . . . . . . . . . . . . . . . . . . . . . . . . . . . . . . . . .

The next adventure is almost as foolproof a success as Lucifer Toast is a failure.

# 6
# Eggs Guinevere
# (and Toast Butterfield)

That is why . . . I have not always given exact and minute specifications regarding weights and proportions of ingredients. In the first place, few . . . work with scales when adding salt, pepper, butter, and so on. They work by rule-of-thumb methods, by tasting, by intuitive assessment, and these seem to me the right ways. It seems logical to me (but readers may scent a paradox) that the first effort at a new dish (whether from this book or any other) should not be strictly successful. [One] adapts and rectifies, consulting [one's] own and [one's] family's tastes and those of frequent guests.
— Robert J. Courtine, *Real French Cooking*

We begin with eggs because no food requires more sensitivity to timing or care in the management of the heat than a simple egg dish. If you can cook eggs, and if you've crossed the "glup barrier" (Chapter 18), you can cook just about anything.

I assume you know how to break an egg without breaking the yolk: one "springy" hit on the edge of the bowl or the skillet. In order not to damage the yolk, hold the egg close to the bottom of the bowl or pan when you release it from the shell so that it doesn't have far to fall. If you haven't learned to do this yet, it means that you've been afraid to fail the necessary couple of times in order to get it right. Remember Lucifer Toast and keep on going. (*Warning:* The sharper the edge, the "springier" should be the hit — to avoid breaking the yolk.) Should any pieces of shell break off into the egg (this happens to the best of us), don't fish them out with your finger or a spoon; "egg" them out with an eggshell. Surprisingly effective. Begin to heat the pan, moderately; *then put a glob\* of butter in.* Enough to flood the bottom of the pan and then some. But don't overdo it. Use the *smallest* possible pan that will accommodate whatever number of eggs you're making. Crack the eggs into a bowl, season them to your taste with salt and pepper, and put in a tiny pinch of thyme or marjoram for each egg (optional, but try it).

*Note:* Salt, as a rule, enhances more subtly when applied during the cooking process. (The properties of salt will be taken up as the occasion arises.)

When the butter sizzles, slide the eggs into the skillet. *Immediately cover the pan with a tight lid.* Wait 10 to 20 seconds; then turn the heat down to low. In a couple of minutes, you can peek. (After you've cooked Eggs Guinevere once or twice, you'll know when to peek.) When the whites are beautifully cooked, top and bottom, by the steam trapped in the pan, they are ready. The yolks will have a splendid, delicate coating — as if you had turned them over very gently. The total cooking time should be about 3 or 4 minutes. Lift the eggs onto warm plates. They are delicious.

You will never again have to turn your eggs over.

But in spite of my warning, suppose you cooked them too fast, or your pan's too big, or there's too much air space inside the skillet, or too much steam is escaping, or who knows why — maybe your pan's too flimsy. Still, if your eggs are not able to achieve their beautiful coating over the yolks even though the whites are cooked to perfection, then, in the midst of the

\*You really don't need a more specific indication, but since we're near the beginning:
1. Look at (or imagine) a stick of butter (which is ¼ pound).
2. Divide it up in fourths (with your fingertip or your mind).
3. Divide one of *those* parts in half and call it a *glob*. A glob is just the right amount for two or three eggs. (It is often referred to as a *tablespoon.*) After you've done this once — that's right, *once* — you'll never have to do it again. You'll know how much a glob of butter is (or sour cream or what-have-you). And you'll know no matter what kind of shape, or glob, it's in.

And while we're on this subject, take a tablespoon of flour or sugar or anything dry and *pitch* it into a bowl. From now on, you can call a tablespoon a *pitch* or something and not worry about it.

cooking, raise the heat quickly and add a dash of hot water to the skillet (cold will work too). Immediately clamp the lid back down and lower the heat. The steam from the water should make the coating appear.

Remember that any recipe, even though you "followed" it, may not work the first time. You might think it's your fault. But maybe it's the recipe's fault. Or it could be that nobody's to blame. Why? Because even though the more thorough cookbooks tell you about differences in kitchen equipment, they can never take them into account enough. And it's a good thing they don't, or they'd be there all day explaining this and that. And what about the ingredients? How big are the eggs? How old are they? Are they fertile? Are they at room temperature? (Nice if they are, but they don't *have* to be.) Crescent rolls (croissants) made in France taste differently from ones made elsewhere because French milk is different, French butter is different, etc. Variables can be especially significant in cooking more delicate and sensitive foods, like eggs.

But don't let all this hang you up. Just cook. At this stage it's helpful simply to know that these variables exist because, for one thing, they explain why you can't duplicate someone else's recipe. To some degree, regardless of what any cookbook may tell you, you will always produce your "own" food just as a potter does a pot or a carpenter, a table. These variations, which are often subtle, express themselves through the appearance, aroma, texture, and taste of the food. They are an important "ingredient" in cooking and in the experience of eating. By acquiring an interest in what creates these differences and becoming more aware of them and respecting them, eventually you will learn more about food and about cooking than a thousand books (including this one) can tell you.

Now maybe you saw your grandma *baste*\* her eggs. And maybe you're saying, "Now I'm not going to use any weird lid thing. I want to *baste* my eggs the way Grandma did. But when I try, it still doesn't work. I can't get a nice coating on the yolks by the time the whites are ready." To baste eggs well, try taking the pan *off the heat*. It's your pan. If you want to take it

---

\*Arm and Hand Body Movement, p. 33.

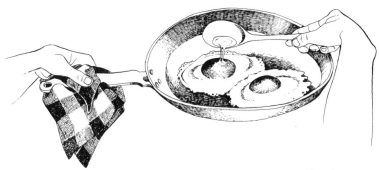

*Basting eggs*

off the heat, you can do it. If it's a heavy-bottomed pan, as it should be, it will hold the heat for quite a long time, much longer than you might think.

And of course bacon fat, instead of butter, can be used for frying eggs and has been so used since time immemorial.

So you see, you can do one thing in different ways. The important thing is to attend to what is happening on that stove.

Let's go back to the original recipe (page 41). Why do you suppose the instruction "then put a glob of butter in" is in italics? This is why: I could have asked you to crack the eggs into a bowl and to season them *before* putting the butter into the skillet. But this is one of the major differences between this book and some other book.

Once the butter's in your skillet, it's almost an emergency. *You've got to move,* and you don't have time to think about how to do it, or to fiddle around, or even to worry about the butter being out of your control. The first time you will probably forget to have the lid ready, or the pepper, or something else. But after you get a feel for it, you can relax and put the butter in whenever you want — and even clean up as you go!

Perhaps you wondered why I asked you to break the eggs into a bowl instead of directly into the pan, even though most cooks — and, I'll bet, most cookbook authors (including those whose books tell you to do it) — never use a bowl. Though now and then I've seen someone break eggs into a bowl before frying, you can make wonderful "sautéed" eggs without having to wash yet another bowl. In days of yore, though the quality of the average egg may have been better, you might have occasionally gotten a bad egg, and by breaking the eggs into a bowl first, it was easier to eliminate it without messing up the others. But this is not my reason, because today this rarely occurs.

If I'm hyperactive and dashing about wildly in the morning, putting the eggs into a bowl first tends to quiet me down. I don't know if it's the sound or the "feel" of the eggs cracking against the bowl (much different from on the edge of a skillet), or the way they slide gently into the bowl and cozily nestle there, or the way they ooze into the pan, or what.

On the contrary, if I'm sleepy in the morning, I need all the help I can get. Cracking the eggs right into the pan really perks me up.

Now who's going to put all this in a recipe?

"If you're sleepy, crack the eggs directly into a pan . . ."

You can't put something like that in a cookbook!

### Toast Butterfield

Most of us like our breakfast eggs with toast. Please note, however, that the electric toaster is a comparatively recent invention. I have a friend who thinks that such a device "irritates" bread into being toast. In any event, I am addicted to it like everybody else.* But the dryness of the toaster-toasted product makes it very susceptible to copious amounts of butter. However, instead of buttering the toast upon its removal from the toaster, you can muush it down (rhymes with "push it down") into either the same skillet you cooked the eggs in — after putting in a bit more butter and turning up the heat — or another skillet heated with some butter just melted in it, *not burnt.* Muush the toast around in the butter for about 5 to 10 seconds.

---

*Putting bread under the *warmed-up* broiler until golden brown on top, then turning it over for about half the time = NICE, DRY TOAST. Buttering it (*after* turning it over) will make it take *longer* and = VERY NICE TOAST. Missing it by more than a few seconds = LUCIFER TOAST.

Not only do you need about one third the amount of butter than when buttering the usual way, but the result has an intriguing nutty flavor. And if herbs were used in the skillet, so much the better. They'll add a nice subtle touch to the flavor. It's so good, you don't even have to use jam (but, of course, you can *always* use jam if you want!).

. . . . . . . . . . . . . . . . . . . . . . . . . . . . . . . . . . . . . . . . . . . . . . . . .

GUIDE TO
**Eggs Guinevere**

EGGS
BUTTER
SEASONING
Melt the butter over medium heat; add the eggs.
Cover the pan immediately after the eggs and seasoning go in.
Wait 10 or 20 seconds; then turn the heat down low for 3 to 4 minutes.
If necessary, add a dash of warm water halfway through.

. . . . . . . . . . . . . . . . . . . . . . . . . . . . . . . . . . . . . . . . . . . . . . . . .
. . . . . . . . . . . . . . . . . . . . . . . . . . . . . . . . . . . . . . . . . . . . . . . . .

GUIDE TO
**Toast Butterfield**

TOAST
NONBURNT BUTTER MELTED IN PAN
HERBS (optional)
Muush for a few seconds or until satisfied.

. . . . . . . . . . . . . . . . . . . . . . . . . . . . . . . . . . . . . . . . . . . . . . . . .

# 7
# Scrimbled, Scrambled, Scrumbled Eggs (Depending On How Fast You Cook Them)

> "I know who I *was* when I got up this morning, but I must have been changed several times since then."
> — Lewis Carroll, *Alice in Wonderland*

What to pay attention to? The beginning — and the end — of this exercise with eggs is to see what is going on, what is happening to them as we cook. Eggs go through a remarkable transformation, turning into food right before our eyes.

As we go on cooking, we discover what it means to be more and more attuned to these transformations, these little songs that somehow blend together, whose interplay of rhythms blend with our rhythms. These are not measured songs marked with conventional bar lines, but more like those you sing in the shower or hum while walking along.

A burnt piece of toast, a slopped-up egg, an occasional weird, inedible dish — these are but ephemeral (and in some cases purgative) dunkings on our voyage across a boundless and abundant sea.

You say you never get scrambled eggs right? Or sometimes you do and sometimes you don't? Most cookbooks can help you only if you like scrambled eggs their way, which is a certain kind of moist egg cooked over low heat or even, as some will command you, in a double boiler.

This is an acceptable way to cook scrambled eggs. (You think I'm crazy? Would I challenge Escoffier and company in this little book? Certainly not. But great cooks seldom tell the whole story. In fact, *most* men and women who can cook a mean scrambled egg or two have never even *heard* of their method of doing it. That's because they know the real secrets of scrambled egg cooking and are not stuck on just one of its savory renditions.)

### *In Search of a Scr(i)a(u)mbled Egg*

0. Before you begin cooking them, you can warm up your eggs to room temperature by taking them out of the refrigerator well ahead of time — up to an hour, depending where you put them. Or, before cracking them, set them in a bowl of warm water for a minute or two, or put them under warm running water for a while. Taking the chill off the eggs will give you a more delicate result.

1. You can cook scrambled eggs over any kind of heat. The heat (and to some extent the pan) determine whether you're cooking Scrumbled Eggs (low heat), Scrambled Eggs (moderate heat), or Scrimbled Eggs (high heat). Each of these has a different texture and a different taste. Contrary to what you may read, most people seem to prefer moderate heat. But how will you find out what *you* like unless you try?

2. If you're making a lot of eggs at once in a relatively small pan, the heat will have to be raised a little from what the directions say, and then lowered near the end.

3. You have to know when to begin stirring — or *scrambling* — the eggs and how rapidly to do it. (Use your friendly wooden spoon.)

4. The "cooking curve" for eggs rises very steeply. This means that no matter what heat you are using, eggs cook faster and faster as they approach "doneness," and must be removed from the heat *before* this point because they'll still be cooking on the plates, especially if the plates are warm. (As far as we know, no one has ever been cast into Hell for having cold

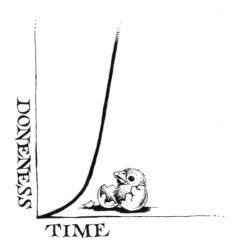

plates, but warm them for a few minutes in the oven if you can manage it.) You'll get the best results if you do the last 5 or 10 seconds of scrambling with the pan *off the heat entirely.* (I don't mean turn the heat off; I mean *lift the pan from the heat.*)

But *when* do you lift the pan off the heat?

Okay. There's a certain moment when all the egg in the pan begins to coagulate into one jelly-like mass, and that's when to remove it from the heat.

5. The Number One Thing in cooking Scr(i)a(u)mbled Eggs is to *pay attention to what is happening in the skillet.*

Begin to heat the pan on low or medium heat. Break the eggs into a bowl; season to taste with salt and pepper. If you like your eggs lighter, thinner, add a little water. If you like them creamier, heavier, add half a swallow of milk. The more you add, the creamier, the more like custard, they get. I happen to like mine sometimes with a little water — and sometimes without adding *anything.* They're eggier and thicker this way.

Beat until the yolks and whites are thoroughly mixed. I prefer to do this gently, more like rapid stirring, in order not to froth the eggs — at least not too much. Really vigorous frothing, which is inimical to certain omelets, is all right for scrambled eggs, but it gives a somewhat different texture than a creamy blend.

After beating, drop your lump of butter — for two or three eggs, a glob* — and swirl it around to cover the bottom and a little on the sides if you find it necessary.

### Scrimbled Eggs
I don't like my eggs like this, but some people do. When the butter has sizzled but has not yet turned brown, the pan will be hot. Keep the heat on medium or a little higher and spill the eggs into the skillet. When you're *scrimbling* the eggs (high heat), you must begin to scrimble as soon as the eggs make contact with the pan, and you must be quick about how you do it. Nothing must stay on the bottom or against the sides of the pan for very long. Keep stirring and *watch* the eggs cook. If you like them a bit moist, then be sure to lift the pan off the heat well before they're done to your liking. Scrimble off the heat a bit longer, then, with love, dish them out. They should be lumpy, and the lumps should be firm.

### Scrambled Eggs
I like my eggs like this.

The butter is just beginning to sizzle; if it's already sizzled, lift the pan off the heat. Pour the egg mixture in, and put the skillet back on the burner. Keep the heat medium to low. You'll begin stirring when the eggs are just beginning to set a little on the bottom. This doesn't take very long after they go into the pan. Adjust the rhythm of your stirring to the way the eggs seem to be congealing. If you scramble *too* rapidly, the eggs will probably be too smooth. Slow down a bit for nice, tender, lumpy eggs.

Finish the same as above, removing them — for God's sake, remove them — before they're actually done because they'll keep on cooking as they're going onto the plates. If you're using an implement you feel comfortable with (I like a wooden spoon), it somehow makes it easy to adjust the rhythm of your stirring to the cooking process.

*If you really *have* to, see page 41 for *glob.*

### Scrumbled Eggs

I like them this way, too.

Here you can even put the eggs into a fairly *cold pan*, just after the butter has melted (over medium or low heat). The heat should be *low* during the cooking. Wait a good while for the eggs to start to set on the bottom, then begin stirring fairly slowly, breaking up the eggs. But as you approach the sharp point of the "cooking curve" (page 48), you have to be just as alert as with scrimbled or scrambled eggs.

If you're scrumbling eggs, don't skimp on the butter, because slow-cooked Scrumbled Eggs will absorb a lot of it. To make sure, *use a little extra.* Your pan will like it, too. And don't forget to coat the *sides* of the skillet just a little.

### Keep Your Eye on the Eggs

Perhaps you'll end up making your own "scroombled" eggs. This is okay as long as you attend to the eggs lovingly and, when required, you are firm, thorough, and quick.

### Legendary Refinement for Sundays, Holidays, and Company

Swirl a lump of butter (or a little cream) into the eggs after you remove them from the heat to stop the cooking — and to add a luscious quality to the dish.

. . . . . . . . . . . . . . . . . . . . . . . . . . . . . . . . . . . . . . . . . . . . . . .

GUIDE TO
**Scr(i)a(u)mbled Eggs**

EGGS, blended (with milk or water optional)
BUTTER, a glob — or a little more
SEASONING
Cook over medium to low heat.
Start scr(i)a(u)mbling when eggs begin to set on bottom.
Finish scr(i)a(u)mbling with the pan off the heat.
Eggs are always done just *before* you think they are.

. . . . . . . . . . . . . . . . . . . . . . . . . . . . . . . . . . . . . . . . . . . . . . .

## Nonlinear Eggs

Perhaps you think we've more or less covered the scrambling of eggs, that any other possible scramble should reside somewhere on our "scrambling spectrum." But somewhere, somehow, eggs will always ooze out of our tidy classification.

*Nonlinear Eggs.* Nothing could be simpler or more pleasing.

Put the skillet on medium heat and melt the butter — a goodly amount, as in other kinds of scrambled eggs. Prepare the eggs as before, taking the chill off them (if you remember to do it), cracking them into a bowl, and adding salt and pepper to taste. Herbs take beautifully to this dish.

Stir thoroughly, but do not beat the eggs vigorously and add no other liquid. When the butter has melted and before it sizzles, pour the eggs into the pan and turn the heat down to fairly low. (If the butter is sizzling or foaming, cool the pan off the heat before putting the eggs in.) Immediately, with your shortest wooden spoon held *vertically*, begin stirring rapidly in little whirlpools all over the pan, as though you're a human eggbeater. (Children like to do this.) Whirl in either direction; in fact, change directions frequently as the spirit moves you. *Keep it moving.*

After a few minutes — don't stop stirring — the nonlinear wonder before you will begin to form. When the eggs are just a little softer than you want them, dish them out onto warm plates, where they will complete their cooking.*

There is nothing quite like these eggs. Are they scrambled, a custard, an omelet, or what?

And you don't have to reserve them just for holidays. You can have them tomorrow morning.

In addition to the texture and taste of this egg dish, it is an excellent way to prepare a *single* satisfying scrambled egg.

Another remarkable feature: Suppose in the midst of cooking these wonderful eggs, the toast pops up to be buttered or the phone starts ringing or something else happens that you have to attend to. You can **turn off the heat,** let the eggs rest or

---

*As pointed out in the last chapter, if you are making a lot of eggs in too small a pan, the heat can be turned up a little during cooking. But if they seem to be setting up too fast, reduce it again.

play cards, do what you have to, **and then come back and pick up where you left off.**

### If It's Christmas, a Decorative Touch

It's Christmas morning. How about a thin ribbon of grape jam (or some other) flowing across the eggs? To produce this, you could use a pastry tube, but that's not necessary. Just take some freezer paper and roll it into a cone with a small hole at the funnel end. Put the jam in the cone and squeeze it out.

· · · · · · · · · · · · · · · · · · · · · · · · · · · · · · · · · · · · · · · · · · · · · · · · · · · · · · · · ·

GUIDE TO
**Nonlinear Eggs**

EGGS (preferably dechilled). Whites and yolks thoroughly blended.

BUTTER

SEASONING (herbs if you like)

Use medium heat to melt the butter. Turn down to low (or medium low) before the eggs go in.

Whirl the eggs throughout cooking with a vertically held wooden spoon — changing directions, if desired.

Just before they're done, they're done.

· · · · · · · · · · · · · · · · · · · · · · · · · · · · · · · · · · · · · · · · · · · · · · · · · · · · · · · · ·

# 8
# *The Omelet Myth*

An omelet expands to fill the skillet.
— Parkinson's Last Law

The directions are given below for two basic kinds of omelets: Thin Ones and Thick Ones. Contrary to anything you might have heard or read, omelets are easy to make.

### Thin Ones
Use a heavy pan that retains heat; cast iron or enameled cast iron is fine. You don't have to have a fancy pan with sloping sides. I produced wonderful omelets for years with a straight-sided skillet. If you happen to own a cast iron skillet with sloping sides, that's nice. By all means use it for your omelets. It may be that it's a little more fun to manipulate, but once you understand omelets, you can cook one on a washboard.

These particular omelets are made one egg at a time, but you can use two eggs or more if you like. One of the features of this recipe is that you can make a fairly substantial omelet with only *one* egg — and without adding liquid.

Omelets are mostly a matter of heat adjustment. Here's how:

For a single egg, use about a 7- or 8-inch skillet. The size is important because it is on this that the thickness — or, rather, the thinness — of an omelet depends. Heat it up, slowly. (Pans prefer to heat slowly.) The pan for omelets must be *hot* — but for a single egg, not *too* hot. Put in about half a glob of butter over medium-high heat.

After the butter melts and just before it starts to sizzle, put the egg in. If the butter sizzles, cool the pan off the heat for a few moments before slipping the egg in.

For two eggs, you can use the same size pan even though the omelet will come out a little thicker. In this case the pan should be hotter. Put in a whole glob of butter over medium-high heat. Wait for the butter to foam up and then settle down. Just *before* it starts turning brown it releases a nutlike fragrance. *That's* when to put the eggs in. *(Don't let the butter turn brown. If it does, dump it and start again.)*

Another tried and true method for determining when to put the butter in: Heat the pan slowly. It's ready for butter when you fling a drop of water in it and the drop doesn't just sit there — and it doesn't disappear straight off. It *dances around.* (Really.) For a single-egg omelet the pan shouldn't be quite so hot; the drop should *just sit and fizzle where it is.*

You've got your warm plates ready. But first you have to know: The entire cooking process is going to take 20 to 30 seconds — 40, at the outside.

A beautiful, circular, oval, or seven-sided shape has nothing whatever to do with the making of omelets. One thing that can hang you up here is the Fear of Sloppiness. *Let it be.* Did you ever see a perfectly round apple? A perfectly square slice of bread? No, you haven't. Once this delectable omelet gets onto the plate, it looks wonderfully appetizing, like a delicacy passed down in secret from your great-grandfather.

Okay. The plates are warm, the pan is getting ready. The eggs have been sitting around for an hour somewhere getting their icebox chill removed. Or, you can run each one under warm (not hot) water for a minute or so (or let them sit in a bowl of the same) before cracking them. Omelets can be made without bringing the eggs to room temperature before cooking them, but the results won't be quite as succulent.

Break an egg into the bowl. Season to taste with salt, pepper, and chives. Add either basil *or* tarragon to all of this and fresh minced parsley as well. Use a pinch of each (but just a pinch, crushed either between thumb and forefinger or the heel and palm). If you happen to have some chervil, put in a *big* pinch of it. The herbs will blend into a bouquet, so don't blanch when in this case I tell you to use two, three or even *four* herbs. Of course, if you want, you can use just one or two.

THEN, flip a good pinch of white all-purpose flour right into the bowl — no more than you can balance easily on the end of a small pointed knife, like a paring knife. (The flour lowers the temperature at which the egg coagulates, making it a little more delicate.) You can try the omelet without this addition to experience the difference; the touch of flour does something subtly ethereal to the dish.

Water, milk, or cream are unnecessary. Indeed, many cooks believe that adding milk or cream makes omelets tend to stick to the pan. But try a few different ways for yourself.

Stir rapidly, with a gentle touch; do not beat the eggs furiously. There's nothing wrong with wildly frothy, beaten eggs — for example, in a Yorkshire pudding — but the best omelets don't result from this kind of treatment. If you care to experiment, you can see for yourself the different effects that stirring rapidly and beating vigorously have on the texture of eggs. Be sure, however, that you stir enough to blend the yolk completely with the white.*

Lift the pan off the heat while you spill the egg mixture into it; keeping the heat up, immediately put the skillet back on the burner and begin shaking it gently back and forth. (Voilà! A chef!) Shake it the whole time. No fancy movements. It's easy. In your other hand you are holding your spatula. Lift up any edge you like with the spatula and let some other part of the egg have a chance to run underneath and cook on the bottom of the pan. If necessary, tilt the pan a little. If things look terribly messy at this stage, you're probably doing it right. Altogether you'll lift up the edge about three times during the cooking.

When the egg is still a little runny and creamy on top (it will be runnier and creamier than you will want it to be, but remember that it will still be cooking during the next operation), simply tilt the skillet, letting the omelet slop — excuse me,

---

*Of course, you can stir together all the eggs at once with the flour and the seasoning, then simply "eyeball" an egg's worth into the skillet for each *omelet*. If you do it this way for Fast Production when you have a lot to make, keep all the butter you'll need out at room temperature for fast melting. Do not melt the butter in advance; it gets icky.

*roll* — pleasingly onto the plate, folding over only once, in half, as it curls out of the skillet. No fancy folds needed. (But suit yourself. Tucked in thirds is very nice: One "tuck" happens in the pan; the other as it rolls onto the plate.) A spatula is not required for this, and you don't need to grasp the skillet in some special, contorted way. You have only to lift it up and tilt it with a simple rolling motion. Shaking the pan all the time assures that it won't get stuck on the bottom. But if it does, don't stand on ceremony. Bang the handle with your other hand. Or use the spatula. Serve immediately.

The first time you try this omelet, it won't work.

Why? It's the *Omelet Law*. With one exception (the next recipe), omelets never work the first time you try them.

The most crucial variable — as it usually is in egg cooking — is managing the heat. You may find that after, say, the first lifting-of-the-edge-of-the-burgeoning-omelet, you wish to lower (or maybe even raise) the heat slightly. To lower, you *can* lift the pan off the burner, but then it might be more difficult to keep shaking it. After you make the first one — which really will taste quite good — you'll know the direction toward improvement. Generally, I find that when making a lot of omelets, I have to adjust the heat *up* for the next few, and then down a bit for the ones after that. If omelets take too long to cook, they get a bit leathery; if too short, they're too tough on the bottoms. Heat up, down, or constant — this depends a good deal on your skillet and on your stove. So in the beginning, to get to know how your own equipment responds — or someone else's unfamiliar utensils — *use the water-drop method (page 54) between omelets to determine how hot the pan really is.*

Again, the omelets go onto the plates before they look finished since they'll finish cooking by their own heat. Folding or rolling them over helps.

If you like, before you send them out on their own, turn up the heat even higher to brown the bottom. (Why not try it both ways to see which you like?)

Another classic touch is to sprinkle chives over the finished omelet, whether or not you used them in the herbal bouquet.

But there are many other things you can put over it as well. Find out. Some suggestions are given in the next chapter.

Eggs are phenomenal. What other substance can be transformed into such a delectable dish in so short a time?

The delicacy of this omelet means you will take more bites per egg. Perhaps this is one of the reasons that this one-egg dish is more substantial than it looks.

There's no law, by the way, against making a two-, three-, or even a three-hundred-and-three-egg omelet — provided you've got a big enough skillet. A three-hundred-and-three-egg omelet requires a 10-foot skillet.

. . . . . . . . . . . . . . . . . . . . . . . . . . . . . . . . . . . . . . . . . . . . . . .

GUIDE TO
## Omelets, Thin

EGG or EGGS (dechilled). Whites and yolks blended.

BUTTER

SEASONING (include HERBS: TARRAGON or BASIL, FRESH PARS-LEY, CHIVES — CHERVIL, too, if you have it; use extra chervil).

KNIFEPOINT OF FLOUR

Use a pretty hot pan and shake it all the time. (For a single egg, it should not be quite so hot in the beginning.)

Pour the egg in while the pan is off the heat. Keep the heat up around medium high.

Lift up the edge of the omelet with a spatula every so often to let liquid egg run underneath.

Let it cook for 20, 30 seconds or so and roll it out, or fold it in thirds or at least in half.

. . . . . . . . . . . . . . . . . . . . . . . . . . . . . . . . . . . . . . . . . . . . . . .

### Thick Ones

Delicious, thick, foolproof omelets. This is essentially an exercise in basic heat management, one of the fundamental lessons in cooking. At first you may find yourself anxiously poised over the pan, but after a few omelets you'll see it's not necessary.

Break eggs into a bowl — two or three per person. They're at their best at room temperature, but it's not absolutely essential (see comment on page 47). Season to taste with salt and pepper,* if you like salt and pepper. Add herbs if you want, but this one is fine without. Stir the eggs quickly but gently, making sure the whites and yolks are thoroughly mixed.

Put a modest amount of butter in the pan, one glob per serving, waiting for it to foam up and relax as before — or until a droplet of water dances around in the pan, but no hotter. Then turn the heat down to low. Put the egg mixture in and immediately *cover the skillet* **AND DO NOTHING FOR 1 MINUTE.** You can go by a timer or a watch, but this is a good situation in which to practice "guessing" because the "1 minute" isn't that critical. After this ambiguous minute, hold the handle of the pan with one hand and the lid with the other, and shake the whole kaboodle back and forth. After a while look inside.

When the omelet is just a little runny and creamy or almost all set on top (depending on how you prefer it; I happen to like mine quite moist, but many people prefer theirs fairly dry), turn it out with one fold, in half, onto the plate. Or in thirds if you like.

If the omelet is taking so long to cook that the bottom is getting dry while the top is still not ready to be folded, use a spatula to allow some of the top egg to seep down along the sides to the bottom.

Don't forget that the omelet will keep on cooking with its own internal heat after you have removed it from the pan. If you like the bottom browned, turn the heat up high for a few moments before dishing it out.

I don't see how you can miss even on the first try with this one, but you can have some sour cream or some basil handy — or any number of things — in case the Omelet Law prevails.

---

*Some say salting an omelet before cooking, especially one that gets cooked longer, tends to toughen its texture. My own experiments show that the slight changes are more than offset by not overcooking the eggs. If you tend to use a relatively large amount of salt, you may want to salt afterward; see if it makes a noticeable difference. Also, if you're going to stuff the omelet with something salty, use less salt during the cooking.

GUIDE TO
## Omelets, Thick

EGGS (2 or 3), dechilled, blended
BUTTER
SEASONING
Use a pretty hot pan when the eggs go in, then turn the heat down low.

Cover the pan immediately.

After about a minute, start shaking the whole business (still covered).

After a while, take a look. If necessary, use a spatula to allow the top egg to seep down around the sides to the bottom.

Roll it out just before it looks ready.

# 9
# Lists Are as Odious as Comparisons (And a Detour into Hors d'Oeuvres)

Lists spring eternal from the human mind.

Now we can get into all sorts of variations. The herbs I suggested for the omelet can be changed. For instance, use marjoram or oregano instead of basil or tarragon. Or something else. (Herbs are treated in Chapter 17.)

Accompaniments and fillings of infinite variety can be tried, but here, and throughout this book, I am going to refrain from listing more than two or three. Why? Two reasons.

First, I didn't promise you a *recipe* book but a *cooking* book.

Second, one difficulty with many cookbooks is that they give you either no variations (rare) or too many variations.

If you're not one of those for whom such lists are overwhelming, then don't take my remarks personally. But many of us need to begin with a less confusing panorama. Until the cook feels free to select from somebody else's personal assortment, a list often has the effect OPPOSITE to what was intended. A list can not only cramp the cook's own imagination, but it can also be discouraging, and produce the feeling of "I can't try all these things, and which ones will I choose?" Endless . . . confusing . . . stifling . . . Since we can't take it all in, we may end up pitching it all out.

These proliferous offerings also deprive the cook of that "kick" or little energy boost that comes when you discover for yourself that such-and-such works with such-and-such. These are the experiences that get the cook *cooking* and attending more to what the food *is* — and the people who are going to eat it — rather than to someone else's printed page. Sure, a list can sometimes help get you going — and can remind you of some possibilities you forgot. (No law against keeping your own lists, either!) The number one reason people open up cookbooks at all is just to get suggestions for what to cook for the next meal. But lists can also make you lazy and prevent you from exercising your imagination.

"Imagination? But I don't have any imagination."

That's ridiculous.

"No, I don't."

Look, as far as I'm concerned, imagination is like filling a gap — between what you've got to work with and what you'd like to end up with.

"But I've never been very creative or anything like that."

Horse pucky. You're on a desert island, or lost in the woods or something, and you have to survive. Are you going to just sit there? Look, it's because no one ever got you to try. I mean, for *real*. Say you've got to make some hors d'oeuvres. What will you do?

"I don't know. What?"

Well, you can think of some food, some ingredients that would taste good — right? Go ahead — think of, say, three different things.

"Okay, I did."

Now you can STUFF them into something or stuff something in *them*, depending on what kinds of things they are. What was one of the foods you thought of?

"Brussels sprouts."

Brussels sprouts! Well, if you insist. Cook them and then chill them. Then, let's see. You can cut them in half the short way and scoop each half out a bit in the middle. Stuff them with something. Sour cream. You can sort of "taste" that the two textures will blend together pleasingly. (You have a "mind's eye," right? And a "mind's ear"? Well, you've got a "mind's taste," too, so use it.) Also, you can put some dill on the sour cream because dill always tastes good with sour cream, especially in vegetables or salads. (This Brussels sprout thing turns out to be a sensational hors d'oeuvre.)

You know about ingredients. You can WRAP things (like bacon, noodles, or whatever). Or MINCE things. Stuff, poke, or spread things, and so on. Now, try to think not of thousands of food things, but of just one thing that goes in the middle and one thing that goes on the outside. It's like that.

"You mean that's what imagination is?"

It's a good start, isn't it?

"When you put the whole thing this way, I see that I *can* come up with these things. But it seems hard just to do this much. I never noticed this before, but it's like pushing big rocks around."

Sounds like you just started to do it. What's missing is more of a sense of how it's going to turn out and we'll talk about this more in Chapter 29. It isn't as impossible as you think if you just try to imagine (!) how it's going to taste before you do it.

### The Omelet Is Waiting

Almost everybody knows that you can put sautéed mushrooms in (or on) an omelet, at the end. And grated cheese, near the beginning — after the eggs have set on the bottom — since the cheese needs time to melt.

With mushrooms, you can also sauté them in butter for 3 or 4 minutes, then pour the egg mixture into the same pan, using a wooden spoon to turn them. Be careful not to cook them too much, because they'll still be cooking while the omelet is forming. (Just before spilling the egg mixture into the pan, *add more butter.*)

Pieces of bacon or ham. Seedless GRAPES!

Other cooked, hot things (such as buttered vegetables) should be cooked and hot before being added at the folding or rolling-out stage.

GUIDE TO
## Variations

OMELETS
Put Stuff in them (cooked beforehand if necessary).

# 10
# French Toast

In the course of your work you will need to bisect a line.
I must point out that the usual method, that of inter-
secting arcs, entails no fewer than four possibilities of
error. I fear your teacher will be further shocked by my
suggestion of another method. With the compass point
at one end of the line intersect it where you *suppose* the
middle to be. If you have a good eye you may be right at
the first attempt, but test your guess by repeating the
intersection from the other end of the line. Most probably the space between the two cuts is so small that you
can mark the halfway point with confidence.
— Allen W. Seaby, *Pattern Without Pain*

The French, of course, do not make French Toast. (But what do
*they* know?) This is one very good way to use old bread that's
not too soft. If you don't have any old bread, then leave some
slices out overnight. (If the bread is too soft and fresh, it may
disintegrate on its way to the pan.) Good white bread can be
counted on to make delicious French Toast. You'll have to
experiment when it comes to other kinds of bread, some of
which you may ordinarily prefer to white bread but that may
not be as successful in becoming French Toast (or they may be
even better).

For every two or three pieces of bread, break one egg into a
bowl and add enough milk to make the blended mixture about
the consistency of half-and-half — a little thinner is okay, but
no thicker. Put in a decent splotch of salt to your own taste and
a couple dashes of cinnamon and some vanilla.

Practically everybody I know who makes good French Toast puts some vanilla in it. Not just a few drops, but a little more, enough to know you felt it go in. Guess at it. That's the quickest way to learn. A little too much or not quite enough vanilla in French Toast never bothered anybody. And once you try it on your own, you'll do it better next time. (Of course you don't really *have* to use vanilla if you don't have any.)

Now why aren't I telling you ¼ cup or ⅔ cup or whatever of milk for every one, two, or three eggs? Because I've got this fetish not to have you measure anything? No, that's not it. My recipe is actually more precise than you'll find in any cookbook. How big are your eggs? How fresh? How big, how thick, is your bread? How much milk do you have left in the icebox? Also, how do you like your French Toast? If you like the egg mixture to goo up on top, make the batter thicker. If you like it to soak in more, make it thinner.

Take any five cookbooks of your choice and look at their French Toast recipes. *They're all different.* The point is, *nobody who cooks,* including the authors of cookbooks, measures the amount of milk or vanilla or cinnamon or anything else they put into the bowl.* Or, you can say that in a sense we're always measuring — but with our tastes, our noses, our eyes, our arms, our bodies, ourselves, and who knows what else. Like when you used to put sugar on cereal. Did you have to measure how much sugar to put on?

After you've got this stuff in the bowl all mixed up, then soak the bread slices, one at a time, until each one is *soaked.* The more you soak, the better. Ideally, the bread should be a little puffed up from having absorbed the batter before you put it in the pan. In fact, this is one way to make non-white-bread French Toast very tasty.

You've got the biggest skillet you own heated up with butter in it. Or, if you've got a lot to make, use all the skillets around. If you've got a griddle, you're frying high.

Put the slices in a hot pan with the heat lowered and cook

*To avoid lawsuits, and only to avoid lawsuits, I hereby qualify this statement. There may be somebody who cooks — and who even writes cookbooks — who measures such things. In a world of human beings, almost any crazy behavior is possible.

until golden brown on one side. Then turn once and finish on the other, which will take less time. The back side never looks as nice as the front (but it tastes just as good!). Yes, the front side gets all the glory, but from the toast's viewpoint, it's rather ephemeral, isn't it?

In my opinion, the best thing to serve with French Toast is real, honest-to-goodness, 100% pure maple syrup. A little extra cinnamon, or cinnamon and sugar combined, is nice over the top of the finished toast. Or honey, preserves, applesauce — do what you like!

. . . . . . . . . . . . . . . . . . . . . . . . . . . . . . . . . . . . . . . . . . . . . . . . . .

GUIDE TO
**French Toast**

OLDISH BREAD
BUTTER
EGG(S)
MILK
CINNAMON
VANILLA
PINCH SALT

Submerge the bread in a batter (like thin cream; not too thick) made by combining the last five ingredients. Preferably, soak it until the bread "expands" ("puffs" a little).

Cook in a skillet or on a griddle until golden brown. Turn and finish.

. . . . . . . . . . . . . . . . . . . . . . . . . . . . . . . . . . . . . . . . . . . . . . . . . .

# 11
# Making More Than
# Adequate Coffee

According to an old tradition, coffee was discovered by
a goat-herd who perceived a strange restlessness and
hilarity in his flock whenever they had browsed on cof-
fee-berries.

— Brillat-Savarin, *The Physiology of Taste*

If you are stiffening your hackles because some know-it-all is
about to tell you — the same you who makes the world's most
superb pot of coffee — just which method, which type coffee
pot, which kind and grind of coffee you ought to employ in
your quasi-sacred ritual, please calm down.

I intend only to point out those details that, after undertak-
ing an informal but extensive survey, I find to be either
unknown by many or else waved aside as unnecessary
refinements. The following refers primarily to *drip* methods,
which I believe produce the most superior brew. I have aimed
some suggestions specifically toward those methods using
cones that require disposable filter paper only because of the
popularity of this method (see page 22).

*One: The Freshness Spectrum.* (1) Roast your own beans (a
bit much). (2) Buy beans (store them in the refrigerator or,
better yet, in the freezer in a moistureproof container) and
grind *just* before use. (3) Buy beans freshly ground (store in
refrigerator or freezer). But since places that grind beans for you
also sell whole beans, why not get a little coffee grinder and

take 10 or 15 seconds to grind your own? Well, I'm lazy. (4) Buy coffee in a can (a kind that you like). Experiment, remembering that cost is not always a reliable guide to quality. But no matter what form you buy coffee in, *the fresher it is, the better it is.*

*Two: Water Temperature Control.* This is an easy sub-routine to insert into your present coffee-making system and will noticeably improve your coffee. Experts on coffee will tell you that the water that comes into contact with the grounds should not be at the boiling temperature, but 5 to 10 degrees *lower.* They are right. (Water for tea — noticeably better if poured *over* the leaves or teabag — should be *at* the boil.) After the coffee water boils, it takes anywhere from half a minute to 5 minutes for the temperature to drop after you remove it from the heat, depending on the material and size of your pot. But don't be overly fussy about it. If you want quicker service, *pour the water into another, unheated, container, which will help lower the temperature to just the right amount.*

While the water is still boiling, pour or splash some of it into the coffee pot; then pitch it out. Especially try this if your coffee tends to get cold too fast. It really helps.

*Three: The Daily Grind.* There's a great myth, doubtless perpetrated by the manufacturers of paper filters, that the finer the grind, the better the coffee. But it's more complex than that. Too fine a grind — for example, *one that is too fine for the brewing method you are using* — can produce a bitter and klutzy cup of coffee.

If you buy your coffee already ground and it tastes too bitter, even though the people who sold it to you "know" what grind you should use, let your *own* taste experience be your guide, not theirs. Try a slightly coarser grind. And if you grind your own, subtract a few seconds grinding time and experience the difference.

*Four: A Very Helpful Step.* Many persons do not follow the well-known suggestion that when making coffee by any of the various drip methods, one should pour a little of the hot water over the grounds in the beginning and let it soak in for 20 seconds or so before the actual drenching begins. Some say that this releases certain undesirable, volatile oils in the coffee; others, that it causes the grounds to expand, permitting the liquid to pass through more freely, and thus avoids "overbrewing" the coffee. Whatever the reason, it is advice you should heed.

*Five: Total Contact.* One of the commonest oversights of those who use the filter paper method is not to permit all of the water to make contact with all of the grounds. How often do you see filters with grinds clinging up the sides and the maker carefully pouring the water into the center of the filter so as not to disturb the "already used up" grinds? If this has already happened, then pour water down the sides. Get those grinds back down there!

But the better way is to avoid this situation entirely by pouring the water more or less continuously into the cone and not letting the level sink below that of the grounds. It requires a little more patience and care than the former method, but it's the best way.

*Six: The Water.* The better the water, the better the coffee. (Coffee is almost 100% water.) I'm not going to urge you to obtain better water unless you can afford to, but you can help free up some of the hydrogen and oxygen — and desirable minerals — that drinking water is supposed to have by boiling it for *at least* a couple of minutes (when you have the time).

*Seven: The Filter Paper.* Experiment with different brands of filter paper. Some leave a perceptible chemical taste (even if they tell you they don't). In South America (*they* should know) and in certain East Coast coffee klatches, little bags of pure flannel are used. These are prepared by immersion in boiling water for 10 or 15 minutes. I confess that I've never made it this way.

*Eight: Grounds for Separation.* The used grounds should be gotten rid of at once. (*Unlike tea leaves,* coffee grounds may be dumped fearlessly down the drain.) Their presence around freshly brewed coffee will eventually give it a stale taste.

*Nine: How to Dilute Coffee Properly.* If you wish to make a weaker brew, first make it your usual way; then dilute it with hot water. This may strike you as being cruder than using more water or less coffee in the brewing, but the latter methods only disrupt a process that has been rather carefully worked out.

\*

Now, who's going to remember all these things? And, in truth, they're all unnecessary because coffee can be made without following any of them. However, since most of them are simple to incorporate into your routine, why not begin by picking just one or two to test?

I know you make the world's most satisfying cup of coffee. But why stop there?

# PART FOUR

# COOKING
# ON BOTH SIDES

# 12
# Tales of Kitchen Terror
# (or, How to Cook
# Chicken Rustique)

"But nothing promised that is not performed."
— Robert Graves, *To Juan at the Winter Solstice*

There I was again in the market with this idea of wanting to cook. I was getting hungry but wasn't sure what I wanted to eat. In the poultry area I saw things wrapped up in packages that looked like chicken pieces.

The thought of cooking chicken always put me off. I was *afraid* to cook chicken. Why? Chicken is too complicated. It has a weird shape — you know, it's not flat, it's got bones sticking out, and so forth.

"But this is ridiculous," I said to myself. "I'm a human being. If millions, *billions* of humans from time out of mind have cooked chicken, then I can cook chicken."

I took the first package I picked up — some breasts. When I got home I started mechanically thumbing through my one cookbook, and as usual, even before I got to the page in question — in this case, the one with the chickens on it — I shoved it back up on the shelf. I took a deep breath and quietly said to myself, "What the hell, I'm *hungry*. I'm going to cook this damned chicken."

At the market I also picked up a package of rice and some

fresh sweet peas. I had some clean lettuce, mushrooms, garlic, and onion slices from the night before.

Now, putting the chicken inside the oven frightened me even more than the fact of having a chicken to cook. Why? Because I couldn't imagine cooking anything as complicated as chicken without being able to see and hear what was happening to it. So I put a big cast iron skillet down on the burner. (Later on, I learned that you can hear informative sputterings from inside the oven.)

*Knock, knock* at the door. Uh-oh, what was that? A friend I hadn't seen in over a year, just passing through. On his way south . . . has a couple of hours . . . wants to exchange current life stories . . . he got married . . . has three dogs . . . go out for dinner? Well, I'm cooking up chicken, you want some? There's plenty for both of us. Poured us some decent dry red wine left from last night.

To the skillet. I started heating it up. I added some olive oil, enough to cover the bottom of the pan plus a little more. I could have used butter too, but I didn't. Then I put in the onion slices and four pieces of rinsed-under-the-faucet chicken, skin side down, filling the pan. Tarragon goes well with chicken. I rubbed some over each piece — a fair amount because when you use fresh herbs you have to use about *three* times as much as dried. I knew about that, perhaps from a book. Of course, my hands got all oily because I should have done it before, so I'm not recommending this sequence. I'm just telling you a story.

I sprinkled some salt and about half as much freshly grated pepper over the chicken. Then I covered it all with a big glass lid and, except for adding a few things and turning the chicken, I kept the lid on throughout. The chicken began to sizzle.

After a few minutes I wanted to put some liquid in there. The wine bottle: nice dry wine. A few glugs into the skillet, plus another. The next day another friend said that was a big mistake. I should have waited until the cooking was further along before putting in the cool wine. Well, maybe next time.

After about 10 minutes the liquid was getting low, so I poured in some water along with more wine — and even a little more oil. Later more water went in, until the liquid was a third to halfway up the chicken. I could have put all kinds of other things in if I'd had them — celery, carrots, you name it — but the aroma that was beginning to come out was wonderful. I did have some mushrooms that I sliced lengthwise and started to put in — well, really, a few did go in — but I remembered that mushrooms are delicate, so I waited till about 5 minutes or so from the end. A crushed clove of garlic went in, too.

How long to cook the chicken? Well, *I* like chicken when it's falling off the bone. If you cook it in the oven or any way at all *without* liquid and it overcooks, it becomes stringy and tough. But if you're cooking chicken in liquid, as I was, you *can't* overcook it. Why? Because it will just turn into *chicken soup.* Now I'm not suggesting that you serve yourself and your friends chicken soup when you're all expecting chicken non-soup. It's just that you don't have to be afraid of overcooking it, and this is one of the reasons that cooking chicken like this is a piece of cake. *It's easy.*

But in my opinion, chicken is even worse when it's under-cooked. If a cookbook tells you to poach chicken for 30 or 40 minutes, ignore that advice. (Maybe the author has some bizarre equipment or something.)

Moving right along, we shall turn our attention to the rice. Into a slightly smaller, but not too small, skillet goes oil and a little butter — or it could have been either. When the butter melts, put in the rice and a dash or two of the wine — not too much! (*A dry white is best for this,* but I had red and that's what I used.)

Stir it all around with the heat medium high. Hey! It's like flying a plane. You can't just stop and say, "Well, I'm going to the store now" or "I'm going out to jog" or whatever.

You're *there.* In the kitchen. You've got skillets!

The rice was on the left side of the stove, my counter on the right with the oil and the wine, the salt and the pepper, and whatever else that needs to be handy while cooking (like wooden spoons). That's why this is called Rice à Gauche, which is Rice on the Left. It was being stirred with the left hand. But how much rice?

The usual answer is that rice, when cooked, expands to three

times its dry volume. In my opinion this is not the method that cooks use; that is, picturing how much rice is wanted for each serving, dividing it mentally by three, then multiplying that times the number of people eating.
Forget it. Even *measuring* is better than that. The way most cooks do it is much simpler. After you cook rice *the first time*, for however many, you get a sense of what a "one-serving heap" of dry rice looks like or what the weight of it *feels* like when you shake it out of the package — if you just *try* it. That's all there is to it. And the remarkable thing is that you can remember it even if you don't cook rice again for a year.

Scatter a few mushrooms into the rice and keep stirring; don't let the rice hang out in one spot, especially on the bottom of the pan, where it can burn easily. Add a small pinch of celery seed (too much and it will overpower the dish, as I once found out). Wait! I'm obviously going to need some hot liquid in this. Like boiling water — and pretty soon. (In other words, I forgot to heat up the water.)

A quick, graceful (?) but probably fairly nervous movement — clutching the teakettle from the stove, over to the sink, cold water (a lot), back to the stove, and onto the hot flame. Then to the rice — stirring. (I lowered the heat because I now had to wait for the water to boil.) Checking the chicken. It looks like it's almost ready to turn. (I can't believe it. I'm in a kitchen — cooking chicken!)

I resist the temptation to add something else — except a little hot water. I didn't want to overdo it with wine — but what if I had? It would have been just fine. But this *was* taking longer than I thought. (Will the tarragon hold on? I did add more tarragon.) I turned the chicken; the water for the rice was boiling. I would have liked to use one of the classical 9463 ways of measuring water for rice. A knuckle's depth of liquid from the top of the rice up. (When using this method — which happens to be number 3502 — I use the knuckle closest to the tip of my index finger.) However, the rice had been cooking a while in the pan before water was added, so a bit less water would be needed. In addition, the water was *boiling*, so do you think I'm crazy? Therefore, I *estimated* the amount. You will find out what happened. Then I remembered that I was cooking chicken and that I had some chicken bouillon cubes. I tossed a cube into the rice water, which I could have done even if I hadn't been cooking chicken, and also a glob of butter, which helps separate the grains and adds to the flavor. (You just plunk it in. It will melt and suffuse throughout.) Some salt. You know how much salt you want; don't overdo it. About half as much freshly grated pepper. I put a lid on the skillet.

Then, much more calmly than you would have ever supposed, I shelled enough peas for two. How many did I shell? Enough for two.

I put a raw pea in my mouth (yum) and removed the caps of four or five herbal candidates. (I didn't have any more fresh herbs.) I sniffed the bottles and tasted the pea. Tonight, how about marjoram? I knew enough about herbs to know that the time for sprinkling this one over had not yet come. Marjoram is delicate, though not weak, and generally goes in near the end or at the end.

I put the sweet little green pealets into a pot of salted (or unsalted) boiling water that just came over the top of them.

Now, a word about **the integrity of peas** (and other delicate vegetables). Peas have integrity when they are (1) raw peas, (2) slightly undercooked peas, (3) cooked *à point*, to perfection, peas, (4) slightly overcooked peas, and (5) pea soup.

When peas come out somewhere in between any of these categories, they are ambiguous, pathetic, or *wrong*.

No matter what anybody tells you, there's really a **very short** time span for *perfect peas*, and perfect peas are modest, magnificent, tasty, and loving. If you personally cook peas, or someone you can see actually doing it cooks peas, then you can taste *perfect peas*.

Otherwise, can you be sure?

In my refrigerator I had about half a head of washed butter lettuce from the day before. Out it came. Why not make the salad clean and simple? Not even a mushroom. I tore the lettuce, without malice,* into bite-sized pieces and tossed them into the salad bowl, then put it in the icebox to get cool and crisp.

In a couple of minutes I made the salad dressing, but there's so much going on here that I'm going to put the dressing (which is actually a sauce) in the Salad chapter. For now, you can pour some pure olive oil into a screw-top glass jar (an almost indispensable kitchen accessory) — about half a coffee cup's worth (this is about right for four people). Then add red wine vinegar (or the more delicate white, or lemon juice), eyeballing a little less than *one third* of the amount of oil in the jar. Put in a peeled, well-bruised or split clove of garlic, some salt, about half as much pepper (or less), and (this is optional) either two pinches of dry mustard or a couple of small dabs of prepared Dijon. Screw down the top and shake vigorously. Taste. It will possibly need more salt and maybe a bit more vinegar — or mustard. (Prepared mustard also contains some vinegar.) A single fresh herb is a joyous ingredient in a salad. But the dressing will sing without it, too.

Don't dress the salad until the last moment.

There are many special and opinionated things to say about salad dressing, like, for example, the misfortune of conditioning your palate to crave too much vinegar in a dressing. In my opinion, this is a culinary disaster. Aside from ruining any wine you are mistakenly trying to drink with it (wine and the vinegar or lemon juice in salad dressing are not especially compatible), it simply overwhelms the delicacy of gentle greens. With harsher, more pungent greens, a more vinegary dressing can be tried. But don't immediately believe some person or some book that tells you to make salad dressing using half as much vinegar as oil. If you try it, and if you prefer that to the more mild and subtle one described here, that's fine. But give your palate a chance to be reconditioned.

*Though this is common practice in the United States, I know at least one fine cook (she is French) who would writhe in distress if, in her presence, you tore the lettuce. She would then explain that you should, if possible, leave lettuce leaves whole. After she left, I went back to tearing my lettuce (tenderly).

The chicken (the jar of salad dressing stayed out on a counter) was going great. Almost done! The rice had used up all the liquid. I could *hear* it sort of sputtering and popping, but it didn't taste quite tender enough for me. Too bad! So in went more liquid (a glug or two) and I let it cook for 4 or 5 minutes more. Sure, I took the cover off to add more water, and maybe you shouldn't do that. But I did.

Then I quickly set the table — easy enough under these circumstances — and opened up another bottle of red wine. My friend was quite relaxed all the while and continued to narrate a series of quasi-interconnected anecdotes about contemporary life.

Me? I was humming.

I turned off the heat under the rice and left the lid ajar to allow steam to escape. I like rice and other grains to rest at least 5 or 10 minutes after being cooked. You can test this yourself with rice (especially brown rice). Then do what you like. Remember that a heavy skillet will hold the heat for a long time.

I turned the heat off from under the chicken. It had been cooking for at least 1 hour. Maybe an hour and 15 or 25 minutes. How should I know? But the meat was just barely falling off the bone.

The salad. I shook the dressing up again and removed the garlic clove. Or instead of putting it into the dressing I could have rubbed the salad bowl with a cut clove of garlic. (The inside of the bowl. Cooking isn't *that* subtle.) Or I could have minced the garlic and left it in for a more garlicky flavor.

I poured the dressing over the greens *sparingly* (less than you think) and tossed the leaves around gently with my hands to get them coated. (Do not leave a puddle in the bottom of the bowl. Get it all on the leaves. If a puddle forms, transfer the salad to another bowl. Yes, I'm serious.)

I sprinkled a few drops of lemon over the rice, tossed the rice around delicately with a fork and tasted it; then put some on the plates, with the chicken. (Poured a little lemon over the chicken, too.)

A few minutes before the end, I had crushed some marjoram with the heel of one hand rubbed back and forth across the palm of the other. I dashed it on the peas. It was a new bottle and the aroma of the herb was very strong, so I was extra cautious.

When the peas were ready — just tender, not mushy, at all — I turned them into a colander to drain briefly, then spooned them onto the plates and let my friend salt and pepper his own.

"Hey, wow, where'd you get this recipe?"

Oh, it was just a little of this, of that, of these, of those . . .

And it was true. I could hardly believe it myself. But the experience in its own right was so challenging and rewarding that even if it had all turned out just so-so (whatever that means), it would have been a most agreeable and memorable experience.

There was just that indefinable dash — like a trace of nutmeg in a stew — that somehow was the equivalent of making it to the other shore after a long swim while carrying a small child on your back.

Exhilarating!

. . . . . . . . . . . . . . . . . . . . . . . . . . . . . . . . . . . . . . . . . . . . .

GUIDE TO
**Chicken Rustique**

CHICKEN

OIL, BUTTER

RED WINE, a lot

Rub with TARRAGON. Add some more midway through.

Minced or crushed GARLIC is optional (or maybe not optional!). Add after it's been cooking awhile.

WATER. The liquid should come from a third to halfway up chicken segments.

SALT, PEPPER

ONIONS? MUSHROOMS? (Add these 5 or 10 minutes from the end.) What else?

Keep covered.

Simmer till done, turning at least one to three times. It's

done when *you* like it (you should at least be able to wiggle the joints a lot).

The pan juices will be good. Add a bit of lemon juice at the end.

. . . . . . . . . . . . . . . . . . . . . . . . . . . . . . . . . . . . . . . . . . . . . . .
. . . . . . . . . . . . . . . . . . . . . . . . . . . . . . . . . . . . . . . . . . . . . . .

GUIDE TO
## (The Complete) Rice à Gauche

BUTTER, OIL

ONIONS, if you like them, sliced or diced up. An optional clove of GARLIC which, if you remember, you can remove later.

RICE: Sauté for a few minutes over medium-high heat. Keep stirring around. Don't let anything scorch or burn.

Add a *small* glug of DRY WHITE WINE (or a dash or two) for 2 people (though I used red because I didn't have any white).

Put in some WHOLE CELERY SEED, which will reinforce a particular zone of the grain's flavor spectrum. Use whole celery seed sparingly — just a wee pinch per serving — and it will noticeably enhance without becoming prominent.

SALT, PEPPER. But don't forget that the stock (or bouillon cube) may be salty.

Certain seasonings like THYME or MARJORAM will bring forth fragrant, earthy flavors in the rice. Put *one* of these in (especially if you're not pouring a lot of seasoned liquid over the rice when served).

Sliced MUSHROOMS are good, but not essential.

Put in a glob of BUTTER — and a CHICKEN BOUILLON CUBE — just before you:

Pour in BOILING WATER (of course you can use diluted chicken broth or stock instead of the bouillon cube), estimating about a knuckle's depth above the top layer of rice — or a little more than twice as much liquid as rice.

*Cover the skillet.* Adjust the heat to low and simmer till done. White rice takes about 15 to 20 minutes; brown rice, about three times as long.

Taste. If not done, and if liquid has been absorbed, then add more boiling water.

When done, let sit for at least 5 minutes — partially covered or covered.

Mix in fresh minced PARSLEY, if you like, with a fork or two (so as not to bruise the rice).

Dash some drops of LEMON JUICE over everything.

Toss (fluff up) carefully with fork. Taste again. Serve.

*General note on wine and seasonings:* When serving four, don't *double* the amount for two. Put in a little *less* than double. As you make larger (and larger) quantities, you may have to taper off some of the additions. Taste will tell.

. . . . . . . . . . . . . . . . . . . . . . . . . . . . . . . . . . . . . . . . . . . . . . . . . .
. . . . . . . . . . . . . . . . . . . . . . . . . . . . . . . . . . . . . . . . . . . . . . . . .

GUIDE TO
## Perfect Peas

Add PEAS to BOILING WATER that just covers them.

SALT and maybe PEPPER

Some pinches of THYME or MARJORAM are optional. Be careful! Peas are precious.

A little FRESH MINT is nice.

Or HERB BUTTER.

Or BUTTER itself.

*No matter what cookbooks tell you,* young, tender fresh peas are twice as good as frozen peas. But frozen peas are good too — in fact, they are the best of the frozen vegetables (along with spinach when used in stuffings). Actually, good frozen peas are even *better* than old, big, tough fresh ones.

. . . . . . . . . . . . . . . . . . . . . . . . . . . . . . . . . . . . . . . . . . . . . . . . . .
. . . . . . . . . . . . . . . . . . . . . . . . . . . . . . . . . . . . . . . . . . . . . . . . .

GUIDE TO
## Vinaigrette or Basic French Dressing

A quantity of pure, good quality OLIVE OIL in a glass screw-top jar

WINE VINEGAR, a third as much as the oil (estimate)

SALT, and about half as much PEPPER, or less, or none

Add a peeled, bruised GARLIC CLOVE; or mince up in the dressing; or rub the inside of the salad bowl with a cut clove.

(Optional) A pinch DRY MUSTARD for one serving, a good pinch for two, etc. Or use a dab or two of prepared DIJON MUSTARD.

Screw the top down and shake with vigor. Taste. If it wants something, try first to correct with salt, mustard, vinegar, or oil.

At the last moment, remove the garlic clove. Shake again and pour over salad.

Toss gently with your hands or two long utensils (I prefer wooden ones). Because you have not used too much dressing (your hands will give you up-to-the-second reports) and because you have tossed sufficiently, you did not leave a puddle on the bottom of the bowl. Good.

. . . . . . . . . . . . . . . . . . . . . . . . . . . . . . . . . . . . . . . . . . . . . . .

# 13
# *What Makes Cooking Go*

Oil [n.] fr. L *oleum* olive oil, fr. Gk *elaion*, fr. *elaia* olive.
Any of numerous unctuous combustible substances
that are liquid or at least easily liquefiable on warming,
are soluble in ether but not in water, and leave a greasy
stain on paper or cloth.
— *Webster's New Collegiate Dictionary*

A closer look at my first chicken dinner, including comments
on some of the major factors in cooking: butter, oil, wine,
garlic, onions . . .

## *Butter and Oil*
When do you use oil? When butter? When both?

Butter tastes "rounder," "butterier," "closer" than oil. You
knew that, but that's one reason for deciding on which one or
on what combination to use. Simple, direct.

There's a lot of latitude here. You can heat oil to a higher
temperature than butter before it burns, so if you're using butter and you're afraid it's going to burn — not only in a skillet,
but, say, when you're basting under a hot broiler — then add
some oil.

*Sweet (unsalted) butter* is always recommended. Why? First
of all, it burns at a higher temperature than salted butter, so it's
safer and easier to use. Second, when it gets rancid you know
it, whereas salted butter can actually disguise rancidity and off-
flavors, but go on to affect adversely the taste of your food and
the condition of your stomach. Once you've got the sweet but-

ter taste habit, and this is the third reason, salted butter will just seem weird. Keep sweet butter in the freezer until you are ready for it. (But if you're out of sweet butter, certainly use salted butter.)

As for oil in cooking, I sometimes use pure olive oil because I like its deep, soft, "olive fruit" flavor (imagine the olive as a fruit, which it is). I also use, especially when cooking something delicate, any of a number of other mixed and pure vegetable oils including peanut, safflower, and corn, none of which has as strong a flavor as that of olive oil when used in cooking (though peanut and corn oil are more noticeable than many cookbooks would have you believe). You should try different oils and find out which you prefer. You can also mix them.

An almost equal combination of butter and oil with a slight bit more butter — or the opposite! — is an especially pleasing one for sautéing.

### Processes

Since you will often come across terms like *sautéing* or *roasting* in the world of cooking, it will help to be clear about what they stand for.

The richness of life embodied in each of the following processes is one of the secret things that cooking is all about. It may seem odd to you that a cook can have as much of a rapport with a particular process like baking as with a particular substance like wheat or onions. But it's true.

To **sauté** means to cook or brown food, usually quickly, in an open pan with a small amount of hot fat. Sautéing often implies that the food is moved about either by shaking the pan, tossing the contents with a flip of the wrist, or using a wooden spoon or other utensil to keep things going. (*Sauter* is French for "jump.")

To **fry** means somewhat different things to different people — even experts. Some say that it is distinguished from sautéing by the use of a large amount of fat. Others, that the food must be totally immersed in the fat (the term *deep-fat frying* always means this); still others, that while in sautéing the food may get tossed about, in frying it does not.

What we did with Chicken Rustique was to **simmer** or **poach** it.

Browning the chicken first and then simmering it in liquid would have been to **braise** it.

To **stew** it would have meant having the simmering (not boiling) liquid covering the chicken instead of coming partway up.

To **boil** means to boil.

To **steam** means to boil some liquid and cook something in the steam that results. To prevent the steam from escaping, the food is covered.

To **bake** means to cook with dry heat, like in the oven. To **roast** means exactly the same thing except that it includes cooking over an open fire.

To **broil** is an extension of roasting in that the food is brought right next to, or actually into, the fire itself.

One advantage of knowing names is that it's a convenient way to recall different ways of doing things. If you find, for example, that you're always sautéing some particular food, then just by recalling the name of some other process it may help you to try something else — even something that might not occur to you otherwise. Usually, it works. For instance, you can bake eggs. (They're good.) Or boil bread. (Not so good!)*

A drawback of relying on names is that our conceptions of what are acceptable cooking operations can jell into fixed categories, or into our limited versions of them. This may blo⌐k new possibilities, such as a combination of processes or what may take place "in between" one process and another — that is, the flow of it all.

### Chicken

I am not a health food faddist. But I do feel that you owe it to yourself or to your family to try at least one kosher chicken or turkey. Or a good organic one. Don't do it for health reasons if that turns you off. Don't do it for moral reasons if that also turns you off (because of how chickens are raised on most chicken farms). Do it for reasons of taste. If it turns out that you don't like these birds —· or that it doesn't make any difference to you — fine. You tried and found out.

Any decent cook will tell you never to buy separate chicken parts, like breasts, thighs, and so on, but to get a whole chicken and take the few moments to cut it up. And they are right. But suppose you don't know these things, or someone gives you thighs or wings for a present? Just make do.

On washing chicken: Mary's Hungarian mother washes it, but some say you can just rub lemon or even vinegar all over it. (This will also tenderize it a little if it needs that.) The idea is to do something to it before you cook it. Whole or part, I always rinse it off under the faucet. (*Note:* Wash poultry and fish. But don't wash meat; just wipe it off.)

Since cooking my first chicken, I doubt if I've *ever* cooked it

---

*But just to demonstrate that there are ways to do almost anything to almost everything if you know how, *bagels* are made in part by boiling bread dough.

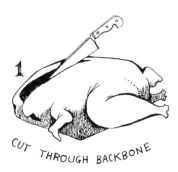

CUT THROUGH BACKBONE

CUT OFF LEGS

CUT DRUMSTICK FROM THIGH

CUT OFF WINGS

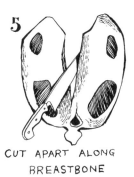

CUT APART ALONG BREASTBONE

*How to cut up a chicken*

exactly the same way twice. Sometimes I turn the chicken once, sometimes two or three times. Sometimes I brown both sides first in oil, putting the liquid in later. As far as what it cooks in, it depends on what's around or what I feel like. And sometimes it depends on what I think someone else would like even if it's not just what I would have cooked for myself. This often produces the finest results.

You want a shortcut to cooking? Invite people over for dinner and ask them what they'd like to have. When they respond with something you *never* would have attempted, that's what to cook up.

As far as poaching chicken goes, how can you miss if you just know when to stop. (In this case, *not too soon.*)

### Wine, etc.

Of course a dry, white wine would also have worked for Chicken Rustique. But I didn't have any. And you don't have to have white wine with chicken or even with fish. Or red wine with heavier meats, either. It depends on the wine, on the fish — and on you. (I take it back about red wine and fish. That's going overboard.) For cooking, I usually use a dry white or red. For poaching chicken, I prefer red; for cooking rice, white. Some prefer a rich, somewhat fruity red. The main thing to realize is that the taste of the wine will go into the taste of the food. Therefore it makes sense that the wine with which you cook a dish should be one that you could enjoy with the dish. This means that if you use a crummy-tasting wine — I didn't say inexpensive, I said crummy — just to have the food cooked in wine, it's better not to use any. For example, any wine labeled "cooking wine," which ipso facto means you can't drink it, should never be used for cooking.

One other point: Wine must always be cooked when used with food. If it's going into something that's already been cooked, then the wine has to be *reduced* — that is, cooked down — by boiling it in a pot or something. Though the word *boil* grates a little on the ear when coupled with something as rich and subtle as wine, nevertheless, boiling is more common than simmering for this kind of reduction. (When heat-sensitive substances like flour or egg yolks are involved, slow simmering and careful watching are required, and I shall take this up in a later chapter.)

As far as wine goes, you do need to know that it can be used more liberally — say, by the half glass — than something like Madeira or other fortified wines — which you would use by the half *liqueur* glass or even by the tablespoon. (Too much Madeira can really "oog" up a dish.) But let's don't go on and on about wine. You just put it into the cooking liquid. Or, if the cooking time is short, reduce it first — at least by a third.

By the way, to the cooking liquid, which most often has a water or "stock" base,* various other spirits and flavorings may be judiciously added — brandies, whiskeys, beer (when it's *flat*), vinegar, soy sauce, coffees (!) — even Anita's sour cream–apricot juice blend, which can be dribbled over the top of the chicken as it cooks. I am not enumerating these as a catalogue of things to try lest the Fear of Lists paralyzes you. I'm simply reminding you that you've got more usable things in your kitchen than you realize. It doesn't mean to begin — or to derange — your cooking practice with the production of weird and bizarre dishes. The reason I included sour cream–apricot juice is that it really is *not* a weird basting substance for chicken. After the chapters to come on Inventing Food, and a few others, you will move sensibly — even lip-smackingly — through what now might appear to be a maze of confusing possibilities.

### Garlic

There are many ways to put garlic into things. Its effect depends on (1) *the form in which it goes into the cooking process;* i.e., pulverized a lot, pulverized, slivered, cut up, broken, half crushed, whole peeled clove, or whole *unpeeled* clove, and (2) *how long it's going to be cooked.*

Garlic, a member of the onion family, is an unsurpassed

---

*Stock, the definition of which I'm going to toss off here as though it's sort of by the way, is one of the most important factors in cooking. Stock is the liquid in which meat, poultry, fish, or vegetables have been simmered or otherwise cooked. It can be used as the base for soups, sauces, gravies, or stews. But it is also perpetuated by being used as the liquid that something *else* begins cooking in, which then adds *its* juices to the stock. (Stock is taken up in Chapter 30.)

"binder" for other flavors and seasonings. It even absorbs weird flavors you don't want. Garlic, of course, can be overpowering, and even if you're a complete garlic nut, it's better — **in my opinion** — to reserve the use of gargantuan quantities to isolated situations. But generally after 20 minutes or so of cooking, the flavor of a single clove of garlic practically vanishes, leaving only a subtle trace. This is why you can put twenty or thirty whole (absolutely unbruised and even unpeeled) cloves into a dish that's being cooked for a while (for example, chicken), and they'll end up permeating the food with something subtly pleasing that's not at all like raw garlic.

By the way, never burn garlic; it's a disaster. So if you're putting garlic in a pan to brown along with, say, some onions, you'll want to put the onions in first because they take some minutes to brown; garlic has to be put in later and watched carefully. Many cookbooks say never even to *brown* garlic. But this is only so if the garlic is to be eaten, not if you remove the garlic from the dish after it has browned. (For easy removal, you can stick the clove with a toothpick before putting it in, but I never do this myself.)

These two factors — how crushed and when put in — are the "controls" for garlic.

Why does garlic have such a special appeal? (I think one of the most interesting answers is that garlic has a "meaty" taste, yet it isn't meat.)

I'm surprised that few people seem to know that the cure for too much garlic or onion on the breath, or in the stomach — well, at least a partial cure — is none other than *parsley.* Parsley has other neutralizing capabilities in cooking — it's a "universal rescuer" — and we'll look into it in Chapter 17.

Now, a trick. One of the commonest ways to put garlic into something is to mince it. Here's a simple way to do this. First, put the clove down on the cutting board and slice off the hard, flat end. Then, with the *handle* of your chef's knife, holding it by the flat of the blade, give the clove a sharp rap or two. The skin easily parts and comes off.

With the clove (or many cloves) on the cutting board, put a piece of waxed paper over it and, still holding the chef's knife by the blade end, rap the clove *hard* once or twice with the hefty handle. You now have instant usable garlic smithereens. If you like, you may do a bit more quick mincing with the blade, which will now be much easier than if you had started from the whole clove. If you try this quick method just once, you may never go back to the old way.

On garlic presses: Never use one. A press holds back some of the finest, subtlest juices and releases all of the coarsest oils. In any case, it's obvious that you don't get *all* of the garlic, right? This device was invented by someone who didn't know (or didn't like) the above method of mincing garlic. What do the experts (I mean the *real* experts) say about garlic presses? I'll save you some legwork: They are divided. But it's a lopsided division, and most of them are on my side.*

Look, if you like your garlic press, use it. And don't forget to wash it each time. (Washing a garlic press is almost as irritating as washing a strainer.)

We have allotted much space to garlic because it is so important. Now, a word of caution.

A judicious use of garlic helps the cooking of so many different foods that there's a tendency to use it excessively. There's nothing wrong with this for someone starting out. Anything that helps keep a person interested or confident enough to go on past the initial drop in the well-known "learning curve" ( ⌣ ) is fine with me. But eventually one needs to explore other realms. If you start your cooking life deep in a bed of garlic, eventually you need to accommodate other intimate, lifelong companions in your food world. But of course you absolutely have to ignore anybody who tells you how "risky" garlic is and how there are all these *other* people who are supposed to detest it who may even have been eating it all their lives, in food cooked all over the place, in which it has been modestly used.

### Onion Notes

Let's say something about onions in general. I do not intend to go into the almost ubiquitous place that onions occupy in

---

*I realize that this line of reasoning is dangerous, but I'll go to great lengths to get you at least to consider giving up such a dumb gadget.

cooking — in much of the world's cuisine — for not only are they delicious in their own right, but they also have the remarkable power to entice the flavors in other foods to come forth. One reason that cooks, when beginning to sauté, like to toss sliced (or diced) onions into the pan is because of their favorable influence on the meat or the other vegetables, which generally go in later.

Cook onions *gently*, "watching" them with a wooden spoon, so that at first they appear to shimmer and become translucent. If you continue cooking them they will turn golden, and eventually they will brown. But do this slowly. It should take at least 10 to 20 minutes to brown onions properly. This leads us to:

### The Onion Paradox

One might think that the longer you cook something, the milder, the weaker, the flavor. This is true in many cases, but not with onions.

If you cook peas for a long time, they're all washed up. If you boil a radish, for example, after some minutes its sharp "tang" disappears, and it tastes like a weak turnip. (You can purée it and put it in a sauce.)

With onions, it's the opposite. Sautéed (or steamed) for a certain time, to the translucent stage, they are mild. But the longer you cook them the stronger the flavor becomes. So how they come out depends on the cooking time.

The same holds true for many vegetables of the notorious mustard family, except radishes. Broccoli, Brussels sprouts, cauliflower, cabbage (which, however, loses its "tang" in the process) — all get "smelly" when cooked too long. (But onions, when *boiled*, will tend to become mellow, and finally very weak in flavor.)

I was going to say something about the different kinds of onions, but isn't it much better to discover each one for yourself?

To peel an onion painlessly, especially *many* onions, simply drop into boiling water for a minute and guess what? The skins slide right off. (The same goes for tomatoes, almonds, and other skinned foods.)

### Rice — and a Note on Bulgur Wheat

I prefer brown rice as a main dish, but white rice may be more suitable as a neutral background for other foods, though the vitamin content is impaired by the milling process. (Isn't that obvious when one *tastes* the two kinds? Brown rice obviously has more "guts." So instead of trying to get people to eat brown rice primarily because it has more vitamins, how about encouraging people to appreciate its richer flavor?) Actually, sautéing the white rice a little first, as we did here, gives it a somewhat nuttier and less neutral flavor. I hope you find, as I do, that simple, easily obtainable long-grain rice is far superior to "minute" or "converted" rice. Cheaper, too.

White rice cooks faster, about one-third the time it takes for brown rice.

Bulgur wheat, which is partially cooked cracked wheat, can be cooked the *same way* as white rice — for example, Bulgur à Gauche — and is a favorite of many (including myself). But we always forget about it. Don't. It makes pilaf, tabbouleh, and a minimum of eleven thousand other things. It is wonderful.

One of the things that made the rice especially good was the little bouillon cube that was thrown in at the same time that the boiling water went in. This works in bulgur wheat as well. Adding this cube to the cooking rice makes for a quick and surprisingly useful substitute for broth, which in turn is a quick substitute for *stock*. Later we'll propose some ways of "beefing up" or "chickening up" these quasi-ersatz items. Stock is so profound and potent a medium for transforming foodstuff into food that even a substitute of a substitute can work wonders.

We'll get into at least two of the trillion other ways (I lied when I said there were only 9463 ways) of cooking rice. Some of the other methods may seem comfortably less arbitrary to you than the "knuckle" method, which has, after all, only been used for at least twenty-five hundred years.

But what's behind a "method" like this?

Once you know your pots and the people you usually cook for, you develop your own personal scale of measurement. You know, for instance, that in a pot more or less this size with about this much rice, the water's going to come up to this wrinkle here on my finger. After a while, you know even more directly — by the weight of the water you dumped into the pot or by some other way of your own.

I divide all rice-making methods into two types. In one, you use just enough liquid for the rice to absorb *all* of it. When cooking rice this way — by far the method most commonly described in cookbooks and written up on rice packages — if you have trouble getting consistently good results, try using a wider pot, one with a lot of surface area on the bottom; the grains may separate more easily.

The other method is one in which you use a *lot* of water, boiling the rice in a big pot. We'll cook some like this later in the book.

Like eggs or potatoes or tofu, rice is a great *receiver*. A receiver accepts and is compatible with a remarkable range of foods and seems to act as a medium in which these other foods can develop their flavors.* You can even try a little white rice, warm or cold, with lettuce in a salad. Here it becomes as much a *texture* as a taste.

### Salt

There may be a question about the ability of some foods, such as certain vegetables, to absorb salt from the cooking water; but there is no argument about this when it comes to cooking starches. If you want some salt to get into rice (or cereal or pasta), you should salt the cooking water because the starch will absorb it while cooking and this is a more subtle way to salt. This method is "kinder" to the food than putting it all on afterward. However, too much salt is hard to correct later.

You know how to salt. You've been doing it all your life. Do not let the Fear of Bland Exteriors make you oversalt everything. There may be more flavor there than you think if you

---

*Once I put a little strawberry jam into rice that was going as an accompaniment to game. When I tried it again (I think it was with chicken), I used raspberry jam. It still worked, though I'm not suggesting that you fiddle around with something as silly as this. But if you do, the idea is to put in little enough so that it affects the flavor slightly but not enough for anyone except you to know what it is. It was less than a teaspoon for four people.

just give your palate a chance to savor it. Some salt alternatives (rather than "substitute" which is a somewhat demeaning term) will be given in Chapter 17.

**Lettuce**
Leaving the leaves whole, cracking them into middling shapes, reducing them to bite-sized pieces, or shredding them — each gives a quite different salad. (A person who has never eaten salad might not understand this.)

Lettuce should always be dry — otherwise the dressing won't adhere properly — and preferably crisped up in the refrigerator (not the freezer) before using. Of all the various activities during the production of a meal, drying the lettuce (and the parsley) is one of the most annoying for many cooks. You shake it, but that only does part of the job. You use ever more and more of your paper towels to roll the leaves and then you find you've put the towels down on an (oops!) wet counter or something. Or you've got one of those French lettuce basket things that you swing over and around your head in great arcs that splatter little, irritating water drops all over everything and everybody — and some will still say that it's not dry enough.

Well, believe it or not, you can *wring* the lettuce, but very delicately, and this helps to rid it of a good bit of the unwanted water, making the paper towel procedure work better; and you can let the lettuce drain in a colander or on a straw basket while you do something else. But regardless of whether or not you wring the lettuce (I know many cooks who, understandably, cringe at the thought), try shaking the leaves out over the sink, wrapping the whole collection in just a couple of paper towels, and leaving it in the colander in the refrigerator for 15 or 20 minutes.

Or use a salad dryer. This is an amazing invention — and I tend to resist new gimmicks — into which you put the lettuce, parsley, or whatever and then cover with the lid. Turning a little handle on the top (or pulling a string on the bottom), you rotate the basket inside at a pretty decent speed. In 10 to 15 seconds, your lettuce, parsley, or whatever is dry. DRY. (But you may not want the parsley that dry. So back up . . .)

### Dressing

Always, always, always make your own salad dressing! Does someone else dress *you* in the morning? A dressing is something you can always get right because you can modify it at any moment. There is simply not the faintest comparison between a dressing you can make and one you find in a store. Anything they can do, you can do better.

The adventurous world of salad and salad dressings, which includes the intriguing and all-important operation of "balancing the dressing," deserves its own space. It is reserved for Chapter 23.

### Peas

The peas were delicious — because peas *are* delicious — if possibly a touch overspiced. Maybe not. I took note for next time.

But why do you need to put an herb on the peas? What's wrong with the clean taste of *fresh peas*? Maybe with a glob of butter melting down over them?

Mmmm. You're right. But suppose you have some fresh mint around from somewhere. Mint is so good dashed on peas that it's worth getting some peas just for that.

Fine. But don't forget that really tender, young peas are wonderful — or maybe with a glob of butter melting down over them.

Agreed. But you should know that the next time I added marjoram to the peas instead of crushing the herb over them. I melted some butter in a skillet, added a little lemon juice, and put the crushed marjoram (or whatever you're using, or nothing at all) into the butter and poured *that* over the peas. This is one version of *herb butter*.

Now, reread the last paragraph. Does it sound like a big deal just because someone *named* it? It is the simplest thing. It's even easier (and a lot more satisfying) to *do* it than it is to read how to do it. And remembering proportions isn't a problem. There's nothing to measure, only to taste.

# 14
# The Cornstarch Adventure

"Wwww!"

Get some pure *cornstarch* at any market.

Take a shallow baking dish or pan — 9 by 9 by 2 inches is fine — or whatever's handy. Pour ½ cup or so of this fine, clean, white powder into the dish. Slish it around a little. Very fine, very elegant.

Now add about the same amount of coolish water, and with your fingers stir it into the cornstarch until the whole thing's a fairly thin liquid. Very soft, kind of like gentle soap.

Pour more cornstarch into the liquid, about a spoonful's worth at a time, mixing thoroughly as you go. Very soon the liquid begins to thicken in a most extraordinary way. Keep mixing it around (at first it's very sticky), and soon you'll have a substance that if you don't reveal what it really is, someone who has never experienced it will probably think that you just exchanged gifts with an extraterrestrial.

First, push your finger to the bottom of the pan and meander through it. The stuff *follows* you. (You have to experience this to understand what I'm saying.)

Add a bit more cornstarch so that it thickens a little more. Pick up a big glob in your hands and roll it around between your palms. As long as it's moving, it feels like a solid, but the *moment* you stop it turns into a liquid right before your hands and eyes. (Have you ever felt you were actually *holding* a liquid?) Quickly, you begin rolling it again and it turns back into a solid. And your hands are wet — or are they dry?

Add a little more cornstarch. Play with it. Eventually it will suddenly thicken into lumpy solids, which are also intriguing. Then add more water, and so on.

Even those who can explain the mechanics of what happens during "the cornstarch event" can still experience the wonder of it.

Put down this book and go get some *cornstarch.*

# 15
# *The Other Side of Things*

"They don't keep this room so tidy as the other."
— Lewis Carroll, *Through the Looking Glass*
*(And What Alice Found There)*

**Glup**

You know why some of you don't do any cooking? Because
the stuff you have to cook up is covered with goop and is all
bumpy and uneven, and how do you know what to *do* with
objects like that? I mean, here's a whole duck, say, and it's cold
and guppy and slimy, with pieces of skin flopping around.
Here's some broccoli, for instance, with no discernible geome-
try. Where do you start chopping, and what do you do with all
those asymmetrical pieces?

In other words, you are not yet an experienced "organic material handler." Nothing anybody can say will help. Doing it is
the only way to discover that it's natural and enjoyable. (Did
you enjoy your cornstarch adventure?)

This organic material — it never comes exactly round or
precisely square or triangular, or anything you can pin down
exactly; it's always slanted or twisted or wrinkled, or squushy,
or gooey or crumbly or something.

"But I'm a flute player," "a writer," "a computer pro-
grammer," or "a banker," and I just don't get into organic material handling — at least not when it's goopy or crumbly.

First we have to acknowledge that there wouldn't be any
flutes or pens or computers or dollar bills (or five-dollar bills
and up) or anything else unless *somebody handles organic material*. (For example, we have to eat.) And all these spherical,

rectangular, uniform objects that are fabricated start out their careers as non-uniform, earthy "stuff."

Furthermore, we have to realize eventually that *handling organic material is normal and necessary* for human beings and that in most cases it is inherently pleasurable. If we find organic material unpleasant, if we shy away from it or resist it in some way, we shouldn't blame the material (unless, of course, it really is foul or fetid), but put the cause simply on our own inexperience in working with these kinds of real substances. There's nothing to bemoan; your experience just happens to be in other areas. For some, handling organic materials means a whole new set of adventures, whole new domains to explore: bread dough, meat loaf, duck — even cornstarch.

Organic material handling is approved by God, and therefore by all of our ancestors as well as all wise beings on other planets and in other galaxies. Whether you will or no, you are part of the vast and profound body called the universe, and there is nothing real to stop you from, and eventually you are going to plunge into, *the handling of organic material.*

Why not get started? Duck is a good way to begin. Get a duck, and do what it says in the guide below. (One of the purposes of the guides is to help make novice organic material handlers feel at home.)

"Duck? Isn't that hard to cook?"

No, it is not hard to cook. Is anything hard to cook? Of all those things that practically every human being has learned to do, is there anything harder to learn than to walk? We learn walking first; after that, learning to skip, run, roller skate, and ride a bike is child's play — or should we say "duck soup"?

. . . . . . . . . . . . . . . . . . . . . . . . . . . . . . . . . . . . . . . . . . . . . . . . . . .

GUIDE TO
**Beginner's Duck with Rosemary, Apples, and Crème Fraîche\***

It is to demonstrate that, having become at least a working partner to "glup," you can go right ahead and produce an ele-

\*A "deviation" from a recipe in *La Cuisine* by Raymond Oliver.

gant dish such as this, even from a book. (I see no reason to encourage the Fear of Books.)

1 5-pound (approximately) DUCK; SALT and FRESHLY GRATED PEPPER; ¾ stick BUTTER; 4 APPLES, peeled, cored and quartered; 1½ cups (about) CRÈME FRAÎCHE (see next Guide); 1 cup MUSCADET; ¼ cup CALVADOS (an apple-based brandy); some FRESH ROSEMARY SPRIGS. For the cavity of the duck: another APPLE (peeled and cored), an ONION, a CELERY STALK (optional).

Rinse and pat the duck dry. Rub it with a little rosemary. Rub the salt and pepper in the cavity and put in the apple, onion, and celery. Truss up the legs and wings with a single piece of twine, as though you're tying a package. (There are fancier ways, but this will work.) Nothing difficult. Prick the lower breast and thighs thoroughly with a fork to allow grease to escape (there will be a lot of it). Put into a preheated 350° oven on a rack with a sprig of rosemary under and on top of the duck. Put a pan under the rack to catch the drippings. With a basting syringe (or a big spoon), remove some of the excess fat now and then. Roast for 1½ hours, or until the juices run clear (you can prick the area between the leg and body with a knife or fork). Put the cooked duck on a hot platter and keep warm. How simple.

Pour off all the remaining fat from the roasting pan, then add the Muscadet to what's left. Bring to the boiling point and cook for a few minutes until the wine has evaporated. Stir in the Calvados, then the *crème fraîche* (or heavy cream, if you must), bringing it to the boiling point again, *stirring constantly*, and cook gently until the sauce is thick and smooth. (If it should curdle, it will taste just as good.) Remove from the heat and stir in 2 globs of room-temperature butter. Do not reheat the sauce. In a skillet, quickly sauté the apple pieces in the rest of the butter until they are golden but not too soft.

Carve the duck by cutting through the skin of a leg with a sharp knife to see where to sever the joint. Sever it, and do the same with the other leg. Then the wings. Putting a fork into the upper part of one side of the breast, slice off portions as needed. Put the duck into a somewhat deep serving dish and coat with the sauce. Surround the dish with the sautéed apples.

Raymond Oliver notes that "the flavor of this dish depends

on the Muscadet and the Calvados. It is not advisable to make substitutions for these ingredients. Both . . . are available at good wine stores." I agree.

. . . . . . . . . . . . . . . . . . . . . . . . . . . . . . . . . . . . . . . . . . . . .
. . . . . . . . . . . . . . . . . . . . . . . . . . . . . . . . . . . . . . . . . . . . .

GUIDE TO
## Crème Fraîche

Stir 1 teaspoon BUTTERMILK into 1 cup HEAVY CREAM (I try to avoid the "ultra-pasteurized" kind, but they all work). Heat slowly (it doesn't take long!) to lukewarm and let stand in a glass container, covered, at room temperature or a little warmer. (I usually do it on top of my stove on a towel.) When thickened — from 8 to 24 hours, depending on the temperature — stir gently and refrigerate. It keeps a week.

. . . . . . . . . . . . . . . . . . . . . . . . . . . . . . . . . . . . . . . . . . . . .

# 16
## Grendel's Law of Mess

"What a mess!"
— Everybody from time to time

I'll bet that nine out of ten cookbook authors have, at least once, cooked a sizable meal and left the kitchen in chaos. It's desirable to clean as you go — when it's possible. But if you're cooking a lot of dishes, you have to pay attention. You can't always walk off and leave pots on fires in order to rinse some object unless you especially need it for something.

Real cooks, like most authors of cookbooks, know that the atmosphere around serving and eating, as well as around cooking, is part of the process. But generally they don't seem to be interested in pointing out that cleaning up is also part of cooking, and that means you have to include it, and *that* means the atmosphere surrounding "the mess" influences everything, including the cooking.

Most of the time we don't want to clean up. Most of the time we don't even want to think about cleaning up, especially while we're cleaning up. So cleaning up becomes a "big chore" that we try to get past in order to go on to the next non-chore. Naturally authors tell you that after you've come with us on all these wonderful cooking journeys and eaten this exquisite food, it's best not to lower the aesthetic level by talking about the — ugh! — mess! What better way around this than to tell you to rinse or clean as you go. And when possible, this is indeed desirable, for cleaning up as you go not only helps in the obvious way by clearing the decks — and your head — for the next steps, but continual cleaning gives you the useful illusion that you are in charge, that you know what's going on.

Certainly one of the best ways to begin to have more of a relationship with cooking is not by just standing there in a daze surrounded by spinachy pots, goopy bowls and forks, and slopped-up cutting boards, but by working at cleaning them up. After all, the fire gods are working, the salt, the butter, oil, and margarine gods, and so on, are all toiling and moiling for *your* dinner.

Now, what do you notice when you start trying to clean up as you cook? A rhythm that not only helps you cook, but also helps you develop the all-important sense of the timing of the entire meal.

But what about those of us who are temperamentally unable to lift a finger to clean anything up while cooking? What can we do? What can help?

Grendel's Law of Mess, that's what can help.

Most everyone is familiar with Murphy's Law: "If anything can go wrong, it will."

But maybe you're not acquainted with Hofstaeder's Law, developed originally as a variation on Murphy's: "Everything takes longer than you expect, even if you take Hofstaeder's Law into account."*

Grendel's Law states: "No matter how many pots or how many utensils or how many saucepans or plates or cups there are to be washed, *there are more*, even if you take Grendel's Law into account."

How does this help?

Look, while you're washing up, suddenly here comes that big spoon with the blue handle. "Hey, I forgot about you! I'll be darned, and there's that little saucepan I made the herb butter in, and the lid on the casserole! And the fork we mushed the bread crumbs with. Where do all these forks come from — I don't even *have* that many forks. And the grater — damnit, I *never* remember there's a grater to wash, and where did I get this grater, anyway?" It just comes at you and comes at you.

*Omni*, May 1979.

And just when you think you're done, the colander is recovered from behind the toaster. ("Who put it *there*?")

We need to acknowledge *mess* in our cooking and not pretend it isn't there. And beware. If you pretend it isn't there, the God of Mess is not going to like it *at all*. And it's not *his* fault. He's the Mess God and he has to watch over all this. Somebody has to do it. So let him into the kitchen, and he'll help you. Otherwise, he smashes wineglasses when nobody's looking, destroys cups, drops spoons down the garbage disposal — all because he wants your attention!

Mess is cheerful! Be that way too, and you're practically a cook already.

# 17
# How to Invent Food:
# Herb Lore

> Thyme tells mysterious, old tales; marjoram moderates
> and sings; basil rounds the sharp edges with delight;
> oregano has a lusty . . .

Who came up with all our food, anyway? How did they know
what to put with what? We're now going to find out how it's
done, and if you really try what these chapters on Inventing
Food suggest — even if you only try half as much — you will
soon be doing it yourself.

### Fear of Herbs and Spices
This is not really a big Fear. Why? Because herbs and spices
are tiny bits of stuff in bottles and tins. Except for one or two,
it's hard for many people to remember which herb is which.

But if you employ the Secret Method of Seasoning, you will
quickly acquire a working repertoire of herbs and spices.

In order to put this method into practice, you have to get
some seasonings. If you're wondering what to go out and buy
first, then along with some *fresh parsley* (which you should
immediately wash, shake or spin almost dry — just as we did
the lettuce on page 97 — and store in a plastic bag in the
vegetable compartment of your icebox),* I suggest you get

---

*The vegetable compartment is the *warmest* place in your refrigerator. If
vegetables get too cold, they freeze.

some *leaf-dried* (not powdered) *basil* and *thyme*. With basil, thyme, and parsley (and salt and pepper), you can, in a pinch, pleasingly season almost anything.

### The Secret Method of Seasoning

The Secret Method is based on the following: You can visualize any color in your mind's eye. Right now, for example, you can conjure up red or blue. It's actually quite marvelous.

Similarly, any familiar sound can be heard in your mind's ear. How about a car horn? Or the sound of rain?

You have a mind's nose (the scent of a rose) and a mind's palate (salt!). For brevity, we'll call the conjunction of these two mental senses your *mind's taste.* You can recall, for example, the taste of roast chicken or of a crunchy, red apple.

The method, then, is simple. Take any herb — thyme, basil, marjoram, summer savory, whatever — one you feel you don't "know."

First, you have to experience the herb. Smell it in the bottle or tin. Better yet, try it in something fairly bland — a "receiver" — such as eggs, potatoes, butter, rice, or mild cheese, which doesn't force its own flavor to the foreground and therefore is ideal as a medium for experiencing the particular effect of an herb in a simple, unambiguous way.

After you have savored the herb in question, *immediately,* right then and there, recall it to your mind's taste. Sniff it again to be sure. Then two or three times during the day, while you're away from the kitchen, simply recall the herb to your inner taste. As you "learn" each new herb, it helps to review the previous ones in your mind's taste. It takes only *seconds.*

As you get to know what these herbs are like, you apply this knowledge to "pretasting."

Pretasting has been practiced for as long as people have cooked. Cooks who have never heard of it, and who don't even believe in it, do it. It simply means that you "taste" a particular combination before you put it together in reality. It's one of the basic procedures in cooking. It applies, not only to flavorings and foods that go into a dish, but also to the selection of foods that are combined in the same meal.

For example, you're cooking pork chops. Which do you want,

thyme or rosemary? You can actually experience *how it would be.* (The sweeter rosemary, for me.)

"You mean it's . . . it's just *that? That's* the secret method?"

Yep.

"But it's so obvious."

Right. In addition, I suggest that as you learn each of these herbs, you "overuse" it for a while in order to get to know it well. (I don't mean that you should put too much into a particular dish, but simply to use the herb *more often* than you normally would.)

After you're on somewhat familiar terms with parsley, thyme, and basil, then try tarragon (first in your salad or on your eggs) and part of a bay leaf (which you can slip into a stew or a white sauce). These could be followed by rosemary, oregano, and savory. (You can always sprinkle chives over your eggs or potatoes.) For spices, you can begin with paprika, nutmeg, ginger, and cayenne pepper, followed by celery seed, cloves, cinnamon, mustard, and caraway.

### Parsley Power

Parsley is usually minced or chopped, and though used alone, it is often added to other herbs to give not so much a unique taste as a freshness or slight sharpness to the dish. Parsley is undoubtedly one of the most frequently used herbs in American and European cooking. There is hardly a (non-dessert) dish in which it can't be used.

Fresh parsley is often put in things or scattered over them at the last moment, as are slivers of fresh chives. Why? This is a seasoning trick. Including even one fresh herb like parsley, whenever other dried herbs are used, helps create the impression that the other herbs are also fresh. This even works to some extent when a fresh herb is added to a canned soup. (Even your own dried herbs will seem fresh in comparison to the soup's long-dormant seasoning.)

"Can you say something about a few of the other herbs and spices?"

Not too much. I mean, you have to get your own direct impressions.

"Come on. Just a couple of suggestions for each one. You

don't have to include everything. Just something to start with."

A list, you mean?

"Yes."

**Herbs**

The following herbs, some of which may be used in heartier soups and heavier meats, are all used frequently on lighter foods, such as eggs, salads, vegetables, fowl, fish, and cheese. (See also "The Relative Strength of Herbs," page 118.)

*Thyme.* If I were to envision a map of all the herbs, thyme would be closest to the center — perhaps slightly below. Neither sweet nor bitter, neither high up (like tarragon) nor especially deep down (like oregano), neither overpowering (sage) nor very delicate (chervil), thyme is complex, subtle, with a "stern" taste, and blends easily with other herbs. It has been used in stocks, soups, and stews for thousands of years. Clam chowder and thyme are almost inseparable, and it's good with lighter meats: lamb, chicken, fish.

*Sweet marjoram* is a close relative. It's not as subtle or complex as thyme, but more "up front," and a little sweeter. In many recipes that call for thyme, you can substitute the less severe marjoram — or use a little of each — for a somewhat sweeter result. (Try it with lamb chops.)

*Sweet basil* is a warm and friendly herb and, especially when fresh, has a very aromatic undertone. Though its special affinity with the tomato can hardly be exaggerated, basil is really one of the most widely used herbs, alone or in combination with others. Basil and thyme — and, of course, parsley — are almost sure bets when you're starting out and you haven't the faintest idea of what to try.

*Tarragon.* Aromatic, somewhat tangy with a hint of licorice, tarragon is often considered the aristocrat of herbs. It is frequently used alone or with parsley, for if its distinctive flavor is submerged, it doesn't seem to help the dish. If used with another herb or spice, it may be best to complement its flavor so that you taste both the tarragon and, for example, the ginger. Try using *with basil on chicken.* Tarragon is one of the most cherished salad herbs and is superb with egg dishes.

*Chive* is not strictly an herb but a member of the onion family. As such, it imparts a mild trace of that illustrious bulb to any dish. It is always used either fresh or freeze-dried, and is scattered on the soup or on other innumerable dishes just before serving. Its use with potatoes (baked or in a salad) is legendary.

*Fines herbes.* This group includes parsley, chives, chervil (a very tender herb reminiscent of anise and celery, considered somewhat exotic in this country though very common in France), and, depending on which authority you believe, tarragon (most agree on this), basil, thyme, and a few others. Three or four of these herbs are minced finely and combined for use in omelets and other delicate dishes.

By and large, the above herbs are put into a dish in the middle or toward the end of cooking. No rigid rules, though. Parsley and thyme can go into soups and stocks early on. In a long-cooked tomato sauce, basil can go in halfway along (though some would put it in at the beginning). But in correcting seasoning, more might be added near the end.

*Rosemary* is a sweet, resinous herb that can be overpowering if used with a heavy hand. It's excellent with lamb and with meat dishes generally; surprisingly delicious (unless you "pre-taste" — then it's not surprising) with the "red" fishes: salmon and red snapper. The needle-like leaves are not pleasant to find in your food, but they can be easily crushed by rubbing them through a fine strainer.

*Summer savory* is a grassy herb worth getting to know (use the secret method), not just because of its well-known use as an accompaniment to all sorts of beans (it's sometimes called the bean herb) or the freshness it can bring to scrambled eggs, but because of the part it plays in herbal blends, especially in meat and poultry gravies and stuffings. Summer savory, basil, and either thyme, marjoram, or rosemary is an excellent combination. (More on this later.)

*Oregano* is actually wild marjoram, but its taste is quite different and much more pungent. It is frequently found in tomato sauces or with chicken, often teamed up with basil. Earthy vegetables like zucchini or Brussels sprouts welcome a sprinkling of oregano. So do lentils and dried beans. (Can't get much earthier than beans.) Oregano is sometimes called the pizza herb.

*Dill weed,* a distinctive herb often used alone, is excellent with lighter foods, especially fish, and in salads for something different. It's justly famous with cucumbers and beets, superb with cottage cheese. In rice or bulgur it's sometimes used with one or two other seasonings.

*Fennel,* mildly licorice-flavored, is an intriguing accompaniment to fish. Or wherever you might want such an aroma. (Carrots, maybe?) A treat in salads.

*Sage.* Yes, the stuffing. But try something else next time. Sage is used a good deal with pork (and in pork sausages). Sage can really take over, but parsley tones it down.

*Bay leaf.* Almost indispensable in stock, it's used in hearty soups, stews, and sauces and often finds its way into liquid in which seafood is cooking. Like garlic and onions, which have the ability (in an "oniony" way) to absorb "off" flavors, bay leaves perform a similar task, but in an "herbal" way. This distinction will prove very useful in our discussion of herbal blends. Bay, especially California bay, must be used sparingly: about ⅓ leaf for two servings, ½ leaf for four.

*Fresh mint* is used occasionally in salads (also on chicken), and almost everyone knows about mint tea. (But did you know about *sage* tea? Or *rosemary* tea? Try them — as long as the herbs haven't turned into the ultimate end of all herbs, tan straw. Brew just like regular tea, but for a few minutes longer.) Mint is classical on peas. You'll undoubtedly get other sudden inspirations, but be subtle with it.

*Cilantro.* The *leaves* of the coriander plant are sometimes referred to as Chinese parsley. They have a unique pungency, are very distinctive — not everyone likes them at first — and must *always* be used fresh. They're excellent in chicken salad. Float some whole leaves in a thin beef soup or consommé. Ah! Yes!

### Spices

Spices come from the seeds, the bark, or other harder portions of plants and are generally much stronger than herbs, which come from the leafier portions. Spices can be used whole — in the case of caraway or celery seed, and sometimes cloves or peppercorns or cinnamon sticks — but function more often in powdered form. For freshness and superior flavor, it is much better (and cheaper) to grate your own. This is especially desirable, and always possible, for pepper and nutmeg. When fresh ginger and horseradish are obtainable, do the same. (See also "The Relative Strength of Spices," page 119.)

*Celery seed.* I put this first because, although being a seed it is technically a spice, to me it "feels" like an herb. It has a celery flavor but does not come from the same plant as the familiar green stalks. I find celery seed a very useful seasoning, not only in rice, but in meat loaf and stews of all kinds, even occasionally in salad dressing. But use *very* sparingly, in small pinches. Too much and it will overpower everything. You should not be able to taste the celery per se.

*Caraway.* Get to know caraway; it's not just for good old rye bread. All members of the cabbage family can be cooked with it, moderating their sometimes oppressive cooking flavors, as well as cheese dishes, some soups, coleslaw, and potato salad. *Don't cook it more than 30 or 40 minutes.* It gets bitter, which may be why some people think they don't like it.

*Paprika.* This is almost the "parsley" of the spices because it can be used almost everywhere (for example, on poultry). But of course you will use it tastefully.

The following spices, from nutmeg to vanilla, are all widely used in baking and desserts. Most of the suggestions, however, apply to other parts of the meal.

*Nutmeg,* one of the great cooking aids. We all know how much it participates in baked desserts (and eggnogs). But nutmeg is a finishing touch to many soups — creamed dishes, generally — stews, meats, and vegetables. Use FRESH NUTMEG. It looks expensive, but one nutmeg goes a very long way because you use but a *grating* or so at a time.

A secret that all cooks know is that nutmeg seems to have an affinity for many (not all) white and off-white foods. Now that sounds utterly bizarre. I don't have even a fake explanation for this, but look: It works with cheese dishes, rice, rice pudding, apples (inside, they're off-white), white sauce, custards, *cauliflower,* cream soups (cream of cauliflower soup with a scrape of nutmeg is served in Heaven), and other creamed dishes. Paprika also shares this feature.

*Mace* comes from the same plant as nutmeg and is not as finely concentrated in flavor. Mace has long been immortalized in pound cake — and, yes, it is the doughnut spice! Here is an interesting experiment to try with either nutmeg or mace. Sniff one of them and think *spinach* (which they both enhance). Can you not actually detect the aromatic flavor element that seems common to both the vegetable and the spice? Discovering correspondences like this one is one way new combinations in cooking are found.

*Ginger,* though different in flavor, can also be used as a finishing touch to perk up almost anything (including white and off-white foods). Curiously, many recipes that call for mustard, like sauces or dressings, will accept ginger as a substitute. Ginger is one of the basic spices in Chinese cooking. Store fresh ginger tightly wrapped in the freezer. (Perks up soups at the end — and try it on fish!)

*Cloves,* which many people only think of as going with sweet fruit dishes or ham, have other important culinary uses. A few whole cloves, often stuck in an onion, can be put in the stock pot or the stew pot or the court bouillon (broth for cooking fish in) or the bean pot. Their (careful! strong!) flavor seems to call forth flavors hidden in the very marrow of things.

*Cinnamon (ground),* the favorite spice of children, can also be used as an occasional alternative for cloves in stews and meat dishes (for example, lamb). Cinnamon goes into many fruit desserts — especially apple. *Stick cinnamon* is commonly used in ciders and mulled wines, occasionally in stew. It's very strong. And cinnamon in apple desserts — forever.

*Allspice* tastes like a combination of cinnamon, nutmeg, and cloves, with a touch of juniper (the gin spice). As you might guess, it can be used in meat stews, especially beef.

*Coriander* is fascinating. It is an essential ingredient in curry powder. But you can start out using it on fruit: apples, peaches, and pears. It can be put into breads. In India, coriander seeds are frequently roasted briefly over a burner or in the oven. This makes them nuttier and sweeter, and in this form they can be put into a heated mixture of half water, half milk, with *real* raw sugar (you can use brown sugar) for a delicious children's bedtime drink. If you come across some whole seeds, roast a few for a few minutes, sniff them, and try to imagine what other foods they might go with (crushed or whole). Cheese? Carrots, maybe? Stew?

*Cardamom* is a favorite Swedish baking spice. Put some in your coffee for a special treat. A little ground in the meat loaf is an intriguing experience.

*Vanilla.* Get pure vanilla extract, not imitation. I have always believed that most baking recipes are too timid when it comes to vanilla. I discovered the real truth about this in a "gourmet" market — at no extra cost — when I found a better brand of vanilla (Dittman's; and there are others in health food stores) than one of the popular kinds. Though in this case the popular brand is very good, the better ones are much more densely flavorful and "vanilla-like," probably more like the way vanilla was in bygone days when the bread that we bought was real bread, chickens were real chickens, cucumbers didn't have preposterous wax all over them, **and tomatoes were real tomatoes.** It's just that most of the recipes didn't adapt to the "new" vanilla. Remember what I said earlier about recipes? Watch your step.

*Mustard.* One of the world's most important spices, mustard is used in dressings, sauces, and with beef and ham, not to mention in ten thousand sandwiches. Use dry or prepared; if the latter, be sure it's something good like Dijon. Do not use bright yellow "ball park" mustard in cooking.

*Horseradish.* Another well-known beef condiment, it's a nice, pungent addition to salad dressing too. Get it fresh and grate your own. A sprinkle of lemon juice will keep it from discoloring. Store in a jar of *white vinegar,* and use with discretion unless you have acquired "immunity."

*Turmeric.* Yellowish and exotic, it looks horribly hot, but it's not. It's used in curry powder. Try it on chicken.

*Cumin.* A touch (in the beans?) — and Mexico! Curry powder wouldn't seem like curry powder without it. A dash in the spaghetti sauce? For a (radical) change, put a tiny pinch in your scrambled eggs. Use with caution.

*Saffron,* the world's most expensive spice. You need only a tiny thread to infuse your rice with a saffron glow. Crush or pound it and steep in a little of the hot cooking liquid for about 5 minutes, until a rich yellow-orange color appears; then mix back into the rice. Once in a while, it's really worth it.

*Cayenne pepper.* This is the most "lethal" of all the spices we commonly use, but it's one of the world's most popular. Use a pinch, a dash, a smidgeon. If you work with it this way, it can really perk up liquid dishes like soups and stews, and also cooked mushrooms and many cream and cheese sauces. If you overdose a dish that you served someone, you'll not only be sorry, you may get beaten up.

### Pepper

*Pepper* in its various forms, which include cayenne and paprika, is unquestionably the world's most popular spice. Black pepper should come into your kitchen in the form of whole peppercorns, not ground. Ground pepper is like the *notion* of pepper.

*White pepper,* which doesn't have quite the guts of black pepper, is often used in white sauces to disguise the presence of pepper (as if someone would faint if they saw little black specks in the white sauce). On the other hand, I think it's a nifty idea to disguise something as intriguing as pepper. It may just be for appearance; but appearance is not only interesting, it's important.

### Grinding, Crushing, Heating

How do you grind seeds, such as peppercorns, cloves, fennel, etc.?

For peppercorns, use your pepper mill.

But even these can be crushed along with the others by . . . how do you suppose? *With something heavy.* A knife. A plate. Anything. Just go c-r-u-n-c-h.

With dried herbs, in order to help release the volatile oils in which their flavor is concentrated, crush them between your thumb and forefinger or the heel and palm of your hand.

The three enemies of herbs are heat, light, and air. This means that those cute little spice racks over the stove are okay — if you are a spice and herb supplier, or if you don't mind many of them more quickly turning into that common condition of all tired-out, unusable herbs: beat-up straw. If an herb looks like that, it's finished.

### The Relative Strength of Herbs

If you should peruse various cookbooks on this subject, what do you encounter? A maze of contradictions. One tells you to be careful about using marjoram, as it will overpower your dish; another says that thyme is much more to be feared, or savory. You can even find those who warn you about basil saturating your sauce. Why are these good people telling you different things?

First off, it must be said that though there are times when the seasoning is actually one of the major ingredients, like the basil in Pasta al Pesto, in general, seasoning should be a subtle enhancement or complement to the food. Therefore, one should not be reckless in the use of any spice or herb. (But this judgment must be tempered by the author's experience with various types of beginners. For those who tend toward the extravagant — and there are many born cooks as well as future cooks in this category — a nagging restraint may serve only to prolong the period of indulgence.)

Many factors affect the strength of a particular herb. How old is it? Dried dill fades fast. So do oregano and marjoram. Some herbs are gone after six months; after a year, most of them have turned to the inevitable brownish fodder and need to be pitched out. (Even if you have half the bottle left.)

Sage and rosemary are unequivocally strong; too much will easily overpower the dish. In a blend where you wish no one herb to stand out, you should use less of these. The relative strength of thyme and marjoram is interesting. Though marjoram is more "up front" than thyme, the latter seems to have a more pervasive nature, and if too much is used, it tends to smother the dish. Generally speaking, go easy with thyme, and you can trust it to become one of your most appreciated seasonings. There is so much going on in those little leaves that they have a "response" and a word of encouragement for many different foods. Marjoram, especially when recently dried, is quite strong. *Use your nose.*

Another ambiguous situation comes up with the use of summer savory in the various blends. When savory is more in the background, participating quietly, its more subtle qualities come out to support the other herbs. When used with other herbs in equal amounts, it may detract from their flavor.

Here is a little chart you can use as a rough guide — but only until you have your own experiences which may (and probably will) be different from mine.

Strongest: Sage, Rosemary
   Next: Thyme, Oregano, Marjoram, Savory (in blends)
   Next: Most others. Chervil goes at the bottom — use about two or three times as much chervil to blend with other herbs.

I'm not going to tell you anything about parsley. You already know about it. You will use it fresh, and it's very flexible.

Note on bay: since bay is used as a whole leaf — or a recognizable fraction thereof — it can't be gauged in the same way as other herbs. Bay is strongly aromatic.

### The Relative Strength of Spices
People wonder about the relative strength of the most common (grated or powdered) baking spices. Roughly, cinnamon and nutmeg are twice as strong as ginger. Ginger is twice as strong as allspice, which is twice as strong as clove. This means, for example, if you use an equal blend of ginger and nutmeg, it will taste more nutmeggy than gingery.

I think I've said enough. After all, it's just to get you started!

### Blends
In many dishes, especially those which are blends themselves (such as soups and stews), a blend of herbs can provide a savory finish to the preparation. Basil (which can well stand alone), thyme (which often prefers companions), and marjoram can all be blended, or any two. The addition of savory with one or two of these gives a nice blend for meats, fowl, gravies, and many other dishes. Rosemary can be substituted for the thyme or marjoram, which will give a gingery sweetness to the blend.

Or oregano, for a more pungent, earthy addition. Parsley can always go in. We can call this the *herbal* approach.

Another approach, distinctly different (so as not to confuse you at the outset), could be called the *oniony* approach. Here the herbs and spices are excluded and the seasoning is chosen exclusively from onions, leeks, shallots, garlic, and chives (and maybe celery, which somehow seems to fit in). Again, parsley can always be added.

For the *spicy* approach, try selecting from mustard, paprika, nutmeg, cloves, cinnamon, coriander, and cumin. Go easy here. You could be playing with fire.

As a general rule, when you're first getting acquainted with spices, be careful about mixing them with herbs. Celery seed and caraway — which to me are more herbal than spicy — and the peppers, including paprika, are probably the easiest to add without undesirable results. A few cloves stuck into an onion sometimes goes into stocks, soups, stews, or beans along with other herbs.

Finally, none of these "rules" are rules. If you try something that works, then it works.

### Bouquet Garni
A third of a bay leaf, a couple sprigs of parsley, a few pinches or a sprig of fresh thyme. Sometimes a little marjoram is also added. There are, in fact, many variations. They can all be put into a cheesecloth bag — or, if all the ingredients are fresh, tied inside a celery stalk — for easy removal from the soup, stock, braised dish, or stew they are seasoning.

Bay, parsley, and thyme (in or not in a bag), with the addition of a few cloves stuck into an onion and a dash of nutmeg, is a very common combination — a sort of "grand" bouquet garni.

### Other Seasonings
Back to the list. All of the following, though not herbs or spices, are most certainly significant — in some cases, fundamental — in the world of seasoning.

*Onions, carrots,* and *celery* — the great trinity of aromatic vegetables. *Garlic* (immortal) and *shallots.* Shallots, which are more commonly found in Europe than in the United States, are mild onions with a slight garlic flavor and are an outstanding seasoning, one of the most used in French cooking. Their compatibility with most anything sautéed in butter and wine is a culinary legend. Shallots are diced like onions; that is, sliced in each dimension. The white portion of the *scallion* can be used as a substitute for shallots. *Leeks* (wonderful in soups), *parsnips* (use sparingly in soups and stews), *mushrooms, capers* (drain the liquid they're put up in, then use in salads, sauces, on fish), *mashed anchovies* or *anchovy paste* (no cook should fail to try this in a sauce, in gravy!, or with other fish), *pickles* (in dressings and sauces), *Tabasco* (that is, hot red pepper) *sauce, Worcestershire sauce,* and *lemon juice.* And, oh yes, *salt!*

I've mentioned before (but it bears repeating) that you should use *kosher* or *sea salt* in cooking. Try it and you'll see why. On the other hand, most of us probably use too much salt, reaching for it to cover up anything that tastes bland at first bite. This is an interesting subject because, for example, soups are often undersalted, causing the diner to salt it a lot after it has been served, which does not give as subtle and pleasing a result as salting during cooking. But it's always better to undersalt than oversalt.

Those who have restricted their salt intake for dietary reasons have discovered that a good use of herbs and spices reduces the craving for salt. Lemon juice, and other citrus in some situations, is an excellent alternative to salt. Strange but true. Celery seed, paprika, and many other spices may take the place of salt.

Of course there are more seasonings. But you know what? If you have only onions, garlic, parsley, and lemon, I'm not worried about you. Everything will be delicious.

# 18
# Sauce Making

Let not the sauce be better than the fish.
— Old French proverb

The following is aimed at two categories of cooks: the beginner, and the cook who cooks pleasingly and well without much benefit of cookbooks — except when it comes to making sauces.

Somehow, the apparent necessity to consult a book is, well (as a good cook once confided to me), *humiliating* when it happens in the midst of cooking the meal. It can then be an actual hindrance to the activity of cooking. According to my friend Jenny, the difficulty of preparing a meal generally depends not on the number of ingredients or courses it contains, but on how many different pages of a cookbook she has to consult *plus* the number of paper scraps that mark various other pages that fall to the kitchen floor during the process.

This seems absurd to you? It's true, anyway; ask a few cooks.

Sauce making, to be sure, does have special features of its own — just like baking does or the preparation of salad dressing (which is itself a sauce) — but it isn't separate from food preparation in general, subject to different laws and different standards. Practically no other domain of cooking produces more arrogant, opinionated methods of how something should be done than that of the making of sauces. Many modern cookbooks delight in commanding their readers to adhere rigidly to some particular method without letting them know that it is but one of a dozen usable ones. For example, in preparing a basic white sauce, there isn't just one sure-fire method of preventing the notorious lumps. There are many ways to add liquid to the flour and butter mixture.

Of course, having a definite procedure that an author persuasively swears by may be the only way that some people feel secure enough even to try.

You may think that I am exaggerating the resistance to sauce making, but the fact is that there are multitudes of good cooks who are intimidated by sauces, as if there were an alien "sauce-making world" that is somehow different from the "food-cooking world," where spoons and stoves plot how to burn, curdle, lump, or otherwise ruin one's concoction from the very first step.

### The Fear of Sauces

This almost merits a spot among the Big Fears. Now this fear actually has a real basis: It is *the mystery of thickening.* There is something strange about cooking because there is something strange about life — of which cooking is an essential part.

So when we come to sauce making, we are immediately confronted with an *obvious* mystery: thickening.

Starch, for example, can thicken things. I'm not going to explain how this happens (the starch expands on being heated). So can egg yolks.

We're a little afraid because something's really *happening* in this pan and maybe it will get out of control.

You should really begin to make sauces and you'll see it's just like the rest of cooking. Things happen, they take on color, they thicken, they "cook." Get past the Fear of Sauces because sauces are wonderful. They have a savory* quality that seduces the dullest of palates. But this doesn't mean that they make bad food good. (Actually, let's face it. When you goof up some dish, *sometimes* you can improve it with a good sauce. But that's not what sauces were invented for.) Sauces can produce a variety of harmonies and countertastes, like tang on bland or

*Originally, *savory* meant "agreeable to the taste or smell," not necessarily pungent or piquant. The original meaning is the one intended here.

mellow on coarse, or they can merge their texture and flavor right into the dish, heightening certain subtle qualities to create deeply satisfying taste experiences.

The idea is to know about the primordial sauce-making ingredients and a few of their simple (though as yet mysterious) properties along with the Three Essentials for making warm sauces. Knowing this, you can prepare a sauce for any occasion without a recipe.

In cookbooks, sauces usually arrange themselves, more or less, in dictionary order, alphabetized, as it were, by *how the sauce is put together.* This is quite sensible. But there are many (very many) for whom this constitutes a map of alien worlds and, faltering and stumbling before this kind of list, they wind up knowing how to make, say, one sauce for company and one or two for everyone — and on everything — else.

This chapter takes the "complement" approach, employing simple categories that correspond more to the question: What kind of sauce do I want for *this* dish tonight? The simplified arrangement that's suggested here has helped many a beginner, and nonbeginner, get something more substantial from the prodigious compendia of sauces found in some other cookbooks. (Except for baking, more cooks seem to require recipes for sauces than for any other category of food preparation.) With this method, it not only becomes much easier to remember how to make a particular kind of sauce — without necessarily having a recipe — but also you discover *that you actually know more about making sauces than you supposed,* but in order to find this out, *someone has to take the recipes away.* One of the rewards is that afterward, one can open up the sauce section of a cookbook and not only appreciate the author's store of knowledge, but really benefit from it.

In this approach the sauces are grouped by *texture,* which is often the feature first envisioned by most cooks when faced with the question "What kind of sauce?" Furthermore, it is the texture of the sauce, by and large, that determines its general makeup.

Let's look at it simply. A sauce is not a crumbly or chopped-up thing; it's a kind of liquid. This means that in order to produce a sauce, you have to produce a liquid. It may be as thin as the pan juices from a roast, or it may be as thick as bottled mustard. In the latter case, something has to be incorporated into the liquid to make it thick. If it needs additional seasoning, that has to go in. And that's a sauce.

### The Three Essentials
Knowing these essentials for making *heated sauces* will clarify the procedure.
(1) *Heat management.* As I've said, this is one of the most basic cooking principles, so it's not surprising that it would be a major factor in sauce preparation. Especially since some substances commonly used in sauces, like eggs, will curdle if boiled. (2) *"Watching" the sauce* with a wooden spoon or a whisk. This may mean either occasional stirring, constant stirring, or vigorous, nonstop beating. (3) *Anticipating the time required* for preparing the sauce. This is also a reminder that sauce making often takes place during a critical period of the cooking of other dishes — near the end — so the cook must rise to the occasion in order to reduce the chances of a disastrous lapse or all-round panic.

Did I tell you that it's always best to make sauces in a heavy, thick-bottomed pan? Aluminum and plain cast iron will discolor the sauce if wine or egg yolks are used. A small enameled cast iron pan is one good choice.

And almost all sauces become more elegant and rich if a pat of butter is swirled in at the end, after the sauce is removed from the heat.

### The Categories
In the *natural* category are vegetable stock and simple purées such as tomato sauce, composed essentially of tomatoes, butter or olive oil, and salt and pepper (though I can't imagine it without onions that have been sautéed for a few minutes until transparent and/or garlic minced into it). Season with, say, basil and *maybe* some oregano, or, perhaps better, marjoram or thyme. You can add part of a bay leaf. (Wine or Worcestershire

sauce — just a little — can be a nice touch.) If you want a somewhat thicker sauce and more color, add a small amount of tomato paste.

In any case, I would simmer the whole thing for at least 45 minutes or an hour. But you can get away with 20 minutes if you have to. If you're not absolutely delighted with the tomatoes you find in the store (I am usually not delighted with them at all), you may find that it's better to use *canned Italian plum tomatoes.*

Of course, all sorts of other things can go into the sauce, like mushrooms, green peppers, and ground beef. Some people even put a touch of sugar in the sauce.

A vegetable purée is simply a cooked vegetable that has been put through a food mill or into a blender and, well, *puréed.*

The *natural* category also includes sauces or gravies made with the pan juices from cooked meats and extended, if necessary, with stock, wine, or other spirits — or, if you must, with water. Also, when meat has been cooked, there is usually some "good stuff" in the glaze that clings to parts of the pan. The term *deglazing* means getting it all out and into the gravy or sauce. When you brown meat to be used in, say, a stew and the water used in deglazing joins the stewing water, then it's not a big issue if you deglaze the pan with water. But for a sauce, water will serve only to dilute whatever delicious flavor you're starting with. If you have sautéed something, then add some wine or some stock, or both, and scrape around the pan to loosen up all those particles. Bring to a boil to reduce the wine, and serve.

If you have roasted something, first skim off the fat with a spoon and add, say, some wine, or if you need to extend the quantity further, add stock and bring to a boil. It's ready, just like that.

A bit of the water vegetables have cooked in can make a nice addition to the gravy for lighter foods such as chicken or turkey. Books will tell you to be careful of the water in which stronger vegetables were cooked — like those of the cabbage family — but in my opinion this may depend on how long you cooked them, how you seasoned the food, and how much water you used.

Once I boiled some Brussels sprouts for a big turkey dinner (but I did *not* overcook them), seasoning them with oregano, caraway, salt, and pepper. As an experiment, I passed a glass of the cooking water around before the meal. (People were standing around in the kitchen. I guess they were hoping to steal little tastes of everything in advance.) No one had any idea that the rather tasty liquid that they were sampling was the dreaded *Brussels sprouts water.* (Sounds grim, doesn't it? But it went into the gravy — with some of the water the *potatoes* were cooked in. If you just look around, there are all kinds of opportunities for using almost everything.)

Any of the *natural* sauces can become a sauce in the *dairy* category by the addition of a *dairy* ingredient: butter, milk, cream, sour cream, yogurt, buttermilk, *crème fraîche,* egg yolks. Once a cook has tried, for example, adding half-and-half or heavy cream to the pan juices while reducing them and using, say, a particular liquor or wine, it's a simple matter to vary the flavoring ingredients to produce a somewhat different-tasting sauce. But why call it a "new" recipe?

... there are far too many recipes in the world ... A cream sole à la *This* becomes a creamed sole à la *That* simply by virtue of the addition of a pinch of saffron; and the suppression of a nothing-at-all-of-nutmeg converts it into a creamed sole à la *Those.* The woman (for example) cooking for her family scorns such niceties. Her interest is to acquire a sound knowledge of how to cream soles; the trivial difference between one and another will be dictated by her mood, her means (saffron, nutmeg, or anything else) and the occasion. I think most readers will agree [Robert J. Courtine, *Real French Cooking*].

Basically, after you have put in the wine or other spirit, brought it all to a boil, and let it reduce to about half, you then add the cream, at the same time lowering the heat so the cream doesn't boil. It's best to add the wine first because putting the acid into the cream may cause it to separate. (This kind of sauce is delicious on veal.) The Guide to Beginner's Duck (page 102) gives another example of a dairy ingredient (*crème fraîche*) added to the pan juices.

### Curdling

Sour (acidic) dairy ingredients like sour cream, yogurt, and even cream (if it is not very fresh) will curdle if brought to a boil. This will affect only the appearance, not the flavor; so if it happens, just make up a story. Reasonably fresh *cream*, however, may be boiled fearlessly, but only if there are no acidic ingredients such as tomatoes, vinegar, or wine in the sauce; otherwise, if boiled, the cream will most surely curdle. Egg yolks will "scramble" at around 150°. When yolks are present in the sauce, special care must be taken. Using these ingredients at room temperature will help.

### Butter

Now let's back up. One of the most triumphant and all-knowing sauces (admittedly, on the expensive side) is simply *butter*, plain or seasoned. Almost any dish that you might think could be served with a lump of butter melting over the top, can be — and often is. This includes steaks, chops, vegetables, grains, pastas, and fish.

Herb butter is almost as obvious as it sounds, but it is best to use sweet (unsalted) butter because the herbs will "take" better. As a guide, estimate one part fresh, minced herbs to three or four parts butter. Or whatever suits you. Any herb such as basil, thyme, dill, tarragon, marjoram, or parsley is suitable. If you're using dried herbs, estimate about a teaspoon for each half-stick of butter — or whatever you like. Don't be fussy about it.

To blend the herbs, *cream* the butter with a few drops of *lemon juice* (real lemon only). To cream, use the back of a wooden spoon, working it back and forth against the side of a bowl. Then add the herbs and cream them all together. If you're using dried herbs, it's nice to include some fresh, finely minced parsley just before serving to give the impression of fresh herbs and to bring out the flavor of the dried ones.

But that's misleading. That's dried tarragon, and you're pretending it's fresh.

Did you ever wonder about clothing? Is clothing misleading? What about stage sets? Movies?

### Other Basic Butter Sauces

Brown butter — or in French, *beurre noir* — is easy. Heat some sweet butter slowly until it browns, add a dash of vinegar, and serve on broccoli or artichokes — or even asparagus sometimes. Add some (bottled; drained) capers and serve over fish. How about some minced parsley? Or a touch of mustard? Or some . . . ? Well, you can decide.

Another bit of magic is to add some finely chopped (drained) anchovies to the butter, or use anchovy *paste*. Proportions: about three or four parts butter to one part anchovy.

Incidentally, a hint of anchovy sneaked into almost any sauce makes people sit up and take pleasurable notice — but they can't tell what it is.

### A Note on Crème Fraîche

*Crème fraîche* is actually a fresh cream virtually unobtainable in the United States. But even though the Guide given on page 104 does not duplicate precisely the flavor of that esteemed French dairy product, it is such a superior substance in its own right that it doesn't matter at all to me if it is or isn't exactly like some other food. When used with the sauce for duck (page 103), to top baked fruit, or on any number of other things you can experiment with, it causes all diners to go "ahh," "ohh," etc. In anthropomorphic heaven, winged beings dine on it. It is an expensive sauce because it uses only cream and a touch of buttermilk. But a little goes a long way.

### Egg Yolks and the "Aises"

Egg yolks can thicken things. For example, gravy. Many who have cooked for years have never tried it. One egg yolk thickens ½ cup of liquid. The primordial method with almost *all* yolk sauces is to beat the yolk, then beat some of the juices *into the egg* to "prepare" it — estimate ¼ cup per yolk. Then pour *that* mixture back into the rest of the juices, taking care not to get it too hot. Test it with your finger. As soon as you go "ouch!" it's probably time to remove it from the heat. (Grandma did it that way.) An even safer way to work with yolk-thickened sauces is to beat a little cream into the yolk (some add drops of lemon juice). Then do as above.

Just look at what egg yolks do: with cream they make custards; with chicken broth and lemon they make egg-lemon soup; with heavy cream they make a nice sauce; with butter they make hollandaise sauce (and with a few other things like tarragon, shallots, and wine vinegar, they make béarnaise sauce); with oil they make mayonnaise. Eggs are in a class by themselves.

Hollandaise sauce is sometimes considered difficult. It isn't. The secrets to success are brisk, nonstop beating, adding the butter slowly enough, and adjusting the proportion of egg yolks to the amount of butter according to how you are managing the heat.

The first secret is obvious. Beat, beat, beat.

The second secret is: the gentler the heat, the longer it takes to make the sauce. Making it in a double boiler over hot water is an example of gentle heat. Making it over direct heat (managed by lifting the pan off the heat when it's in danger of heating up too much) is an example of more rapid heat. Obviously, it takes a bit of practice to do it with higher heat. The main thing to remember is that for the rapid heat methods, you need to beat constantly and vigorously. Until you have acquired the knack, use an extra egg yolk. That is, use three yolks with each stick of butter. One of the main reasons hollandaise sauce curdles is because the oil (butter) is being added too fast.

The rest of what you need to know is given in the guide at the end of the chapter.

Mayonnaise is one of the most useful sauces both by itself and as a natural base for additional sauces.

In my opinion, you should make your own mayonnaise (at least twice). Then, knowing how good it is, you will continue to make it as long as you cook. It's not that homemade is superior (which it is); it tastes like a different substance than the commercially made product. I certainly don't suggest that you feel guilty about buying mayonnaise. You'll do it anyway, and it can be used very effectively with or without additions, but it won't have the grace or subtlety of a home blend. A guide to making mayonnaise is given at the end of the chapter, including a way to elevate the bought kind.

### Flour (etc.)-thickened Sauces

This category comprises those sauces thickened with solids such as flour, cornstarch, and so on. Gravies or other sauces can be thickened with flour alone, including flour browned on a cookie sheet (it loses half of its thickening power, but intensifies the color of the sauce), or flour that has been shaken vigorously with cold water (use a screw-top jar). But most commonly, flour is used after having been cooked with butter to form what is called a *roux*.

There are many opinions about how to blend the *roux* with the liquid, which for the most basic warm sauce in American-European cooking, *the white sauce*, is usually *milk*. As usual, different methods work best for different people, depending on their cooking equipment, their cooking tempos, and who knows what else. One good method is given at the end of the chapter.

The idea of the white sauce (known as a *mother sauce*) is that by changing the liquid or the seasoning, or by adding this and that, you get other, intriguing sauces. I have given a *short* list of some of these.

Thickeners such as cornstarch, potato flour, and others, along with the more familiar white all-purpose flour, are well treated in many cookbooks, but whole wheat flour, though heavier textured, can also serve as a matrix for very palatable sauces.

In fact, there are hundreds of possible melds and crossings, many of which fall into the spaces between customary designations. The point is to understand the rudiments of making any flour-thickened sauce: to attend to the heat, to the general order that ingredients go into one another — and to recognize that cooking is not any one person's patented method.

The basic key to sauce making is a relationship to the ingredients. After you've made a sauce using egg yolks — or even just *eaten* such a sauce — you know something about the velvety texture they can bring to a sauce. An egg yolk can thicken about ½ cup of liquid; therefore, any white sauce or one of its derivations can accept an egg yolk. Now, as you will see when you come to the Guide to White Sauce, a tablespoon (a pitch) of flour thickens ½ cup of liquid. (For a thin sauce, it will thicken a cup.) That's right. This means you can substitute an egg yolk for about half the flour in a cup of white sauce. Unfortunately, it sounds much more complicated in words than it is in practice.

### Legendary Enrichment

Almost all sauces become more elegant and rich if a pat of sweet butter is swirled in at the end, after the sauce is removed from the heat. (Remember Scr(i)a(u)mbled Eggs?)

### Reprise

Remembering the three categories — *natural, dairy,* and *flour* — makes it possible for the cook to remember and sort out the various sauces; to know how to make a particular one; and most important, to decide *what* sauce to make. The cook first imagines the *texture.* Then, by recalling the categories, he will know what the fundamental components of the sauce will be. As for the various shadings and nuances — which are vital to the sauce's appropriateness to the given dish — the cook is free to choose. Naturally, traditional combinations are proven ones, but there are many delectable possibilities that will never find their way into anyone's list of suggestions, no matter whose it is. A whole cooking world can open up, and, as noted previously, we can discover that we know *much more* about making sauces than we thought. After all, how were recipes invented? By cooks, cooking.

### The Invisible Sauce

Finally, you must be given the usual caution about not overdoing it with sauces. I would like to make an impassioned plea that you make constant use of the *invisible sauce.* The *invisible sauce* looks like *no sauce.* When the cook puts something in the serving dish, he or she merely smiles over it.

What I mean is that at some time or other, every different kind of food should be prepared with the meagerest of complements so that the pure taste of that particular food can be experienced — just butter (sometimes), maybe a little salt, not even pepper (well, maybe pepper).

What is important is to cook with goodness. If you can remove a splinter from a child's finger (or a thistle from a dog's ear), you can learn to cook this way and make the simplest dish delicious.

The evidence of the true cook.

. . . . . . . . . . . . . . . . . . . . . . . . . . . . . . . . . . . . . . . . . . . . . . . .

GUIDE TO
**Separating Eggs**

Crack the EGG sharply on the edge of a bowl, or use a knife. Pass the yolk from one half of the shell to the other, allowing the white to fall (into a bowl or something) below. A more organic way is to put the egg in *your hand* and pass it from one hand to the other, letting the egg white slip (and goo) through your fingers. (Eggs separate more easily when they are cold.) When beating egg whites, even a little yolk in the whites will make it a bit more difficult (a *tiny* bit doesn't really seem to matter *that* much, but try to remove it with part of the shell).

It's best to whisk EGG WHITES at room temperature. Whisk just before using.

I could give very complex instructions on how to hold the eggshells and so on, but in this case it's not necessary. All that's necessary is that you do it at least twice. The very first time you won't take into account how quick and elusive this organic material really is.

. . . . . . . . . . . . . . . . . . . . . . . . . . . . . . . . . . . . . . . . . . . . . . . .
. . . . . . . . . . . . . . . . . . . . . . . . . . . . . . . . . . . . . . . . . . . . . . . .

GUIDE TO
**White Sauce (and a *Few* Variations)**

The average MEDIUM WHITE SAUCE, also called BECHAMEL SAUCE, requires 2 tablespoons (pitches) of FLOUR and 2 tablespoons (globs) of BUTTER for each cup of, in this case, MILK. Melt the butter in a heavy-bottomed saucepan — not aluminum or uncoated cast iron. Stir in the flour with a wooden spoon, and cook for a couple of minutes until things bubble, in fact, a bit longer (to remove the raw taste of flour) — but don't let it brown. Stir constantly all over the pan. (Some figure-eight motions are helpful.) This is the *roux*. Add the milk to it, gradually, continuing to stir all the while as the sauce thickens. Here, the most variable instructions are given concerning the ⌐mperature of the milk. I am going to clear this up. It's easiᵤot if you add the milk hot (lifting the pan off the heat to prevent things from thickening too fast; if this happens to you, let the roux cool a little more before adding the hot liquid), but who wants to mess up another pan? So you can add the milk cold, but you should add it more slowly so that it gets a chance to heat up in the sauce itself.

At any rate, bring the sauce to a boil and add SALT and PEPPER (some add WHITE PEPPER for disguise) and a touch of NUTMEG. Simmer over reduced heat for about 4 minutes minimum. You can go on much longer if you wish, but it's now ready to use.

For a THIN WHITE SAUCE (useful for cream soups, for example), the proportions of the flour and butter are halved: one tablespoon each for a cup of liquid. For a THICK SAUCE, 3 tablespoons each.

The idea is that so many different things can now be done. Just imagine: you can sauté ONIONS, SHALLOTS, or other things in butter — thicken it into a roux with flour. Then add some kind of liquid. You can enrich the sauce by beating egg yolks in a bowl with a little HEAVY CREAM (or LEMON JUICE),* pouring some of the sauce — which might have been made with CHICKEN BROTH — into the yolks, whisking, and then pouring the entire mixture back into the main sauce. This is a major technique for using egg yolks: *the big into small into big technique.*

These few variations give you an inkling of the enormous range of possibilities. Most of these additions and substitutions have different names — even though almost everyone has a slightly different version of what precisely goes into them, or at least how they should be seasoned. Well, why not?

*All right,* I'll give you one name — Sauce Mornay, excellent with eggs, pasta, fish, and many vegetables. It's a CHEESE addition to a White Sauce. Into the finished sauce, stir GRATED

---

*Cream and lemon juice will also help prevent the yolks from curdling in the warm sauce.

GRUYÈRE and GRATED PARMESAN CHEESE (or PARMESAN, alone) — a total of ½ cup to ¾ cup. Simmer for about 5 minutes. Extra BUTTER can be added as well. Season with a pinch of CAYENNE instead of NUTMEG.

In most of these sauces, if there are larger food items — such as big pieces of onion — they are usually strained out or puréed through a food mill.

*Help with flour-thickened sauces:* If the sauce is too thick, thin it with whatever liquid you're using in the sauce. If it's too thin, the easiest way to thicken it is with *beurre manié*: flour and soft butter in equal amounts that are worked with your fingers into little balls. They can be used right away or stored for a couple of weeks in your icebox and brought out instantly, to be added one at a time while you notice how much each one contributes to the thickening process. You have to wait a little for the flour to be cooked in the sauce before it expands and starts helping you. Don't overdo it.

If your sauce lumps? Put it through a sieve.

. . . . . . . . . . . . . . . . . . . . . . . . . . . . . . . . . . . . . . . . . . . . . . . . .
. . . . . . . . . . . . . . . . . . . . . . . . . . . . . . . . . . . . . . . . . . . . . . . . .

GUIDE TO
## Brown Sauce

A BROWN SAUCE is formed from a roux just like a White Sauce with BEEF STOCK or BEEF BOUILLON in place of milk or chicken stock. Almost always, the roux will have been seasoned by an onion cooking slowly in it, often a BAY LEAF, and a great variety of other accompaniments depending on whose concept it is.

In this case, cook the roux until the flour is thoroughly *browned.* The stock is then added while being stirred and allowed to boil for a minute before being reduced to a simmer for at least 15 to 20 minutes.

Can you figure out how to turn a Brown Sauce into a Mushroom Sauce?

. . . . . . . . . . . . . . . . . . . . . . . . . . . . . . . . . . . . . . . . . . . . . . . . .

· · · · · · · · · · · · · · · · · · · · · · · · · · · · · · · · · · · · · · · · · · · · · · · ·

GUIDE TO
## Improving Canned Broth

Brands differ in flavor and quantity of salt. Some good brands are College Inn, Monarch, Swanson's, and Campbell's.

Simmer CANNED BEEF or CHICKEN BROTH with a BOUQUET GARNI, some RED WINE (for beef) or WHITE (for chicken). You can also add the AROMATIC TRIO (ONIONS, CARROTS, CELERY).

Thirty minutes is enough. FRESH PARSLEY (or any other FRESH herb) is a great help in the soup or sauce to give the impression of freshness.

· · · · · · · · · · · · · · · · · · · · · · · · · · · · · · · · · · · · · · · · · · · · · · · ·
· · · · · · · · · · · · · · · · · · · · · · · · · · · · · · · · · · · · · · · · · · · · · · · ·

GUIDE TO
## Hollandaise

Maybe I'm just lucky, but this simple method works fine for me.

Put 3 EGG YOLKS, 1 tablespoon LEMON JUICE, 1 tablespoon COLD WATER, a pinch CAYENNE, and ⅓ stick BUTTER in a *heavy* pot sitting on top of hot — not boiling — water. Stir all these things together with a wooden spoon; continue stirring constantly until they are thoroughly blended. Add another ⅓ stick of butter and do the same. Then the last ⅓ stick and stir constantly until sauce is as thick as you want it. Nothing could be simpler, really. Stir briskly. Eventually, go down to 2 EGG YOLKS, and you can even eliminate the cold water. Incidentally, I found out that I could make it just as easily in the same heavy-bottomed pot *directly on the stove* over low heat. Now there must be some secret that I didn't tell you. Yes! The butter should be very cold. (If things are getting too hot, you can just pick up the pot.)

Another method is to use melted butter; add a little at a time and whisk like absolute mad, removing the pot from the heat whenever you think it's getting too hot.

If for some reason your sauce starts curdling, put an ICE CUBE in it. One of my favorite odd cooking facts is that you can also put in a little BOILING WATER. (I've never tried it myself. It's just too crazy: ice — boiling water!) Another rescue method is to beat another yolk in a bowl with a tablespoon of cold water and add the curdled sauce, whisking. A curdled sauce does not taste bad; it just looks bad. Figure out a story.

. . . . . . . . . . . . . . . . . . . . . . . . . . . . . . . . . . . . . . . . . . . . . . . . . .
. . . . . . . . . . . . . . . . . . . . . . . . . . . . . . . . . . . . . . . . . . . . . . . . . .

GUIDE TO
## Homemade Mayonnaise

Take an EGG YOLK, ½ teaspoon DRY MUSTARD, ½ teaspoon SALT, and a pinch of CAYENNE, and whisk them in a bowl until blended. (A towel underneath the bowl keeps it from sliding around.)

Here is the heart of the process: beat in a mixture of OLIVE OIL and GOOD VEGETABLE OIL (just olive oil may prove a bit strong for most tastes) DROP BY DROP. I repeat: *drop by drop.* Of course, as the sauce begins to thicken, at a certain point you can start to increase the flow and gradually it will be a steady stream. Enjoy doing it. The result is a nice, thick MAYONNAISE. Store in a warmer part of the refrigerator (it will keep for a week), alongside the door, for example. But since it thickens more on standing and may separate if it gets too thick, you can add a little hot water if you plan to store it.

The most common way of rescuing a curdled mayonnaise is to use the extra egg yolk method, beating it in a bowl and adding the curdled mayonnaise to it, and whisking.

To raise commercial mayonnaise to another level, add an egg yolk and a pitch of olive oil to a cup. Surprise!

A fascinating fact is that during a *thunderstorm* it is very difficult to make mayonnaise. Who would have idly thought that mayonnaise and thunderstorms were mutually exclusive?

. . . . . . . . . . . . . . . . . . . . . . . . . . . . . . . . . . . . . . . . . . . . . . . . . .

· · · · · · · · · · · · · · · · · · · · · · · · · · · · · · · · · · · · · · · · · · ·

GUIDE TO
## Gravy (Thickened)

The basic idea is simple. You want to make a roux of FLOUR and FAT. If the meat has fat, pour off all but what you need — say, about 2 or 3 tablespoons. Or use that amount of the drippings in the roasting pan. Put a couple tablespoons of flour in a jar with ¼ to ½ cup cold water and shake *hard* until blended. Stir into the drippings (constantly) over low heat until blended. Add about 1½ cups (no measuring) pan drippings and stock — slowly. Let simmer for about 5 minutes. If you don't have enough stock, you can use canned bouillon or a bouillon cube. *Not water.* (This is the famous shaking-flour-in-cold-water-in-a-jar method that everyone thinks is a secret.)

Of course you can make up a roux from anywhere and stir it into stock and you've got gravy. Once you understand the principle, you're flexible.

Seasoning is important. Some suggestions: for BEEF — ROSEMARY, SAVORY, MARJORAM; for CHICKEN — THYME, MARJORAM, BASIL, MUSHROOMS; for LAMB, VEAL, and PORK — ROSEMARY, THYME, and for PORK, also, SAGE (sparingly). PARSLEY, anytime.

For VEAL, CHICKEN STOCK can be used with MARSALA added (reduce it, some). Also, SOUR CREAM, and CREAM itself, mixed in (and MUSHROOMS).

An excellent way to give color to a gravy is to use BROWNED FLOUR. Brown the flour in a moderate oven, about 10 minutes, shaking frequently, or in a dry skillet on top of the range. Stir occasionally. It can be stored in a jar in the refrigerator. You do need to use about twice as much flour since, being drier, it obviously won't absorb as much liquid. Bonus: no lumps! You can also slip a little BLACK COFFEE into the gravy for color. It's not supposed to add any perceptible flavor, though some cooks swear it improves it.

For an even quicker result, CORNSTARCH can be used; the gravy will tend to be clear, not opaque. Use half as much cornstarch as you would flour — one pitch thickens 2 cups (or a little less) — and use the shake-it-up-with-cold-water-in-a-jar method before blending it with the drippings. To prevent separation, *don't cook more than 2 or 3 minutes.*

. . . . . . . . . . . . . . . . . . . . . . . . . . . . . . . . . . . . . . . . . . . . . . . . . .
. . . . . . . . . . . . . . . . . . . . . . . . . . . . . . . . . . . . . . . . . . . . . . . . . .

GUIDE TO
**Emergency Sour Cream/Mustard Sauce**

That's what it is. SOUR CREAM and PREPARED MUSTARD blended together (much more sour cream than mustard). Add the mustard a little at a time and taste.

To this can be added LEMON JUICE, to taste, and WHITE PEPPER.

It's really much too good to be called an emergency sauce. So use it even if it's not an emergency.

Also, dip things into it, like artichoke.

. . . . . . . . . . . . . . . . . . . . . . . . . . . . . . . . . . . . . . . . . . . . . . . . . .

# 19
# Trout with Clout

> The fish is overcooked.
> — Murphy's Law of Fish
>
> The fish is undercooked.
> — Murphy's Other Law of Fish

I promised to cook a fish dinner for a friend and another couple. Before I went to the market, which had fresh-caught trout (fresh-frozen is an acceptable substitute), I quietly "pretasted" some vodka mixed with some baby-food applesauce (left by guests) and with a couple of other things described later, all going onto the trout.

Trout with Clout. It stood the test; it "played."

Now except for chicken, nothing is easier to cook than fish. (Actually, most things are simple to cook, provided you're willing to enjoy cooking them.)

The main thing, as is so often the case, is to recognize when to stop the cooking. Since fish is even more delicate than chicken, it cooks even faster.

I turned on the oven to preheat at 350°, your basic medium oven heat. (When in doubt as to oven temperature, remember 350°. You can, because nothing else is 350 anything.) Fish may even be better when baked at 500° (though not all cooks agree) — brown and crisp outside and moist within. But I had garlic bread going in at 350°. No one disputes that fish should be eaten immediately after cooking, and at higher temperatures, fish is in more danger of drying out because it will continue to cook outside the oven. Therefore, serve immediately.

You can *estimate* cooking time for fish at 10 minutes per inch of thickness, but it's only approximate because it depends on the temperature. A dense stuffing or a heavy basting sauce may increase the cooking time.

How something is timed can actually be of more concern than the ingredients that go into it. Ordinarily, not "What?" but "When?" is the newcomer's most earnest question. One of the big reasons food gets mistreated is the overdoing of everything, especially the overcooking of delicate foods like eggs, fish, and vegetables. Why does this happen so often to the inexperienced — and sometimes not-so-inexperienced — cook?

Because when food goes into a pan, once it "settles down," it usually looks as if it's just sitting there and nothing important is happening to it. And you get impatient, or worried, and you want to speed things up. But cooking is not a linear process; the food doesn't get the same amount of cooking in the first half-minute that it does in the last half-minute. The cooking curve for eggs — though eggs are an extreme case — applies in a milder form to the cooking of most things. The more delicate and sensitive the food and the higher the heat, the faster it suddenly gets done.

In much of cooking there's no absolute formula — so many minutes of this and that — that always cooks the food to what the French call *à point,* which means cooked "just up to the point" of optimum edibility. In some cases, as with the more delicate egg dishes, it might be a matter of seconds; in others, as with onions or potatoes, it might be minutes.

You need to have a general idea of the cooking time, but this usually presents no problem if you use the method of IRIFOY (which rhymes with *Iroquois*).

Irifoy stands for *"it's right in front of you."* You just look at whatever you're going to cook. Irifoy means: You've been around; you're not dumb. You know what different "stuff" is — its size, its toughness, and so on. You can tell for yourself, and nine out of ten times you'll be right. Thus an obvious, simple way to regulate the cooking times of a variety of different vegetables is to cut them into different sizes according to how fast you want them to cook. (Larger pieces take longer. And remember that beans and other legumes — including not-so-young green beans and peas — are exceptions, taking longer to cook than they look.)

Irifoy is so important that we'll go into it again in Chapter 21, on vegetables. But Irifoy turns up everywhere in cooking. For example, how do you know the fish you're buying is acceptable? Irifoy. Does it smell okay? Are the eyes bright? Is the flesh firm and moist? I mean basically, is it looking good?

As for the cooking itself, it's best to attend to it as if you were quietly watching for a sunrise. If you should miss it by a little, it's not a disaster.

A certain devil-may-care attitude can help, too. It can keep you from torturously hovering over the food. For example, you can sing. That's right, sing. If you're needlessly fussing over everything, sing. The worse your voice, the better it works.

After a time, all these considerations become irrelevant. Each dish just "signals" you when it's had enough cooking, or it wafts something or other at you when you're supposed to do something to it — things like that. Let philosophers, chemists, and physiologists decide what's really happening and just go on cooking.

**And what do you do when your timing is off and you're just staggering around?** You rely on hunger, on memory, on Irifoy.

Later, we'll talk about timing the meal as a whole.

My fish, at 350°, looked like at least a "10-minute trout." Therefore, some other things had to be started first.

### Potatoes

I put enough salted water in a pot to cover some little "new" potatoes, with thin, reddish skins. While the water was heating up, I scrubbed but didn't peel them. (The skins of new potatoes are not only colorful, they're tasty.) Larger potatoes should be cut up before boiling (try quarters).

"But about those regular large potatoes and medium-sized potatoes — don't we peel off those ugly, gnarled skins?"

You bet we do.

"Is that for appearance? Is it because we're conditioned to believe that ugly, gnarled skins are, well, ugly?"

Right. They're ugly.

"But if we got conditioned to believe that ugly, gnarled skins were not only ugly but were the best way to serve potatoes, then if someone peeled them off and the potato that came out was all white, wouldn't we say that's an unacceptable way to prepare delicious, gnarled, ugly potatoes?"

That's probably so. But it will never happen.

"Why not?"

Because ugly, gnarled potato skins are — *ugly!*

"They sure taste good."

It's not necessary to peel the beautiful, delicious, and nutrient-rich potato skins unless the diners are afflicted with the Fear of Potato Reality. Potato skins are not only superior, tasty food, they also prevent other vitamins from escaping into the cooking water. (But sometimes nicely peeled, boiled potatoes with parsley and butter are just right.)

The water was boiling. I put in the potatoes and put a lid on the pot, turning the heat down for a less turbulent boil. (In Chapter 21, we'll talk about covering and not covering pots.)

### Onions

I peeled some little white or "pearl" boiling onions and started cooking them the same way as the potatoes, covering the pot. If you don't already know that these are among the earth's sweetest, most succulent, and satisfying foods, then if you never do anything else in a kitchen for your whole life, you should at once cook *little white boiling onions.* When you buy them they should be dry and crisp. Cut the ends off and peel away the outer skin. (You can avoid crying by holding the onions under cold running water.)

Remembering your basic Irifoy, you know that little onions — and small potatoes — are going to cook faster than regular, large onions and big potatoes. Fifteen, 20 minutes?

### Garlic Bread

Next I took a loaf of fresh, sweet French bread and cut the hard end off one peeled clove of garlic so that the juice would flow more easily when I rubbed and rubbed and *rubbed* the outside of the loaf all over with said clove. I rubbed so that I could feel (and smell!) the juice working its way into the crevices of the bread. I rubbed until the garlic clove *disappeared*. (A small loaf will take one clove; a larger one, two.) **But I didn't put any garlic or anything else inside the loaf except, later on, some (nongarlic) herb butter.** I have a number of theories about why this is such a tasty way to make garlic bread, but do it yourself and invent your own theories. But when making garlic bread, wherever you put the garlic, put *a lot of it*. Everyone knows the major cause of inferior garlic bread. It never has enough garlic.

Depending on its freshness, size, and shape, the bread takes 10 to 15 minutes to heat up in a 350° oven. I placed the loaf inside. (One of the reasons I was baking the trout at 350° instead of at a higher temperature was that I didn't want to burn the garlic bread.)

On top of the stove I still had two unused burners that I would need for making the clout sauce and the special butter for the garlic bread.

### Broccoli

So where was I going to cook the broccoli? I didn't tell you about the broccoli. I had a bunch washed and sitting in a plastic bag in my refrigerator.

I had originally intended to cook them whole, slashing through the thick stems criss-cross fashion, which "thins" them out and allows them to cook as fast as the buds on top. I was going to boil them in a separate pot, dress* them with lemon butter, and serve them with the onions. But I had miscalculated how many burners I was going to need. This was not a big crisis. There were many ways to proceed, and the one I happened on has become a regular emergency cooking method.

I decided to cook only the buds, separating them from the main stems (which went into my edible scrap heap to become part of Tomorrow Soup, page 269). I could have cut the stems into small pieces that would have cooked at the same rate as

---

*Arm and Hand Body Movement.

the buds, but this didn't seem to be an attractive combination with the onions because my plan now was to mingle the broccoli buds, somewhat sliced up, with the onions.

I put the broccoli into my steamer (remember page 22?). I had chopped the buds into 1- or 2-inch-long budlets, whatever bulk I thought would steam in about 10 to 12 minutes. As I've said, after you've been cooking for a while, you don't think exactly in terms of minutes. If you don't believe me, ask different cooks. They'll say (not *all* of them, of course), "Well, I know more or less how long it takes" — some never even say that — "but I just sort of feel the thing I'm going to cook with my hands, or look at it or something, and I just know that if I put it in now it'll be ready in a little while, about when the spaghetti or the rice is done." Irifoy. That's how most of us *learned*.

After poking slivers of garlic here and there in the broccoli, I took the lid off the onions and put the steamer right on top of them! I clamped the lid back down on the whole affair, then turned to the trout.

So far, I'd only been in the kitchen 10 or 15 minutes. And already the potatoes, the onions, and the garlic bread were going, and the broccoli was steaming away. For a moment, quiet descended.

### Timing

Now you don't think I just went into the kitchen without any idea of what I was going to do, or what I was going to cook first, do you? You're right. You have to take a certain amount of time — maybe not much, but quality time — to consider what you're going to do, especially with regard to *the timing of the whole meal*. It's a symphonic process.

The timing of the meal is a major factor in cooking. And this is another reason why you shouldn't use flimsy, dinky pots. The finishing up of a meal, which is a fascinating study in itself, is rife with activity. Aside from sauces, gravies, etc., that are often made at this time, certain things have to be drained, skimmed, removed from and put back into various containers, judiciously positioned for heat containment, readied for garnishing, or whatever. (Oh! the simmering, the steaming, the aromas, the colors, the hunger, the meal!) Good heavy-gauge pots, which keep food warm for a fairly long time, will be appreciated over and over again, not only in the cooking, but also in the prevention of much needless pressure just before serving time.

Any meal that comes together rhythmically at the end is most pleasing to the one who manages it. Being attentive to this aspect of cooking is a time-honored way of acquiring that *je ne sais quoi*\* in the kitchen.

### Clout Sauce
To make the sauce, I put a small stainless steel skillet (that turned up in my kitchen one day) on the burner and slowly melted a cube of sweet butter in it; I added a good bit of lemon juice (from an actual lemon that I personally saw) and thus it became lemon butter. Turning the heat down very low just to keep the butter warm, on the one remaining burner I started to heat up the contents of the last remaining jar of baby-food applesauce. I turned the heat up fairly high and added two glugs of vodka. I tasted, remembering that this was all going into the lemon butter. A touch more vodka. I let the applesauce and the vodka boil for a few minutes in the open pan (like wine).

Some people will insist that because vodka is very volatile, or some such thing, cooking it down will eliminate its effect in the sauce. Not true. The vodka *does* lend something of its essence to the sauce, and in turn to the trout, in spite of having had its alcohols evaporated. But why believe *me*?

I poured the vodka-applesauce mixture fairly slowly into the lemon butter and tasted. A little more apple-vodka. Suddenly, ah! *I could no longer distinguish the flavors without especially trying.* A basic principle in cooking.

I smeared a little butter all over the bottom of the aluminum foil with the curled-up edges, where the trout was going to be cooked. And then I did something else.

---

\*If you don't happen to know what this means, then you know what it means.

### Parsley

To appreciate the following, you have to know that if you cook irregularly, or for a small number of people, the one thing you almost always have too much of (along with celery) is parsley. The need for fresh parsley practically goes without saying. (Would you buy canned lettuce because somebody was strange enough to produce it?) But what *do* you do with all those leftover clumps? Many cooks scatter them everywhere as a garnish (they *are* attractive), but very few seem to recognize it as a viable food, which parsley is — very much so. However, eating too many of these raw bunches at one time can be astringent and unpleasant.

There was nothing to lose by finely chopping or coarsely slicing all this parsley (saving the stems for the previously mentioned Tomorrow Soup) and spreading it over the bottom of the baking foil. *Some garlic slivers* could go here and there among the green. I then laid the fish on top of the bed of parsley after rubbing them all over with thyme, which goes as well with fish as tarragon does with chicken. (Tarragon is very nice with fish, too; and so are a lot of other things. See Chapter 17.) I sprinkled some salt over the trout and sliced some mushrooms to go into nooks and crannies around and about during the cooking.

This parsley bed thing has probably been used for thousands of years by cooks who have had too much parsley left over. Something special happens to it as a result of being cooked and soaking up juices from the trout and, in this case, the sauce.

But if you don't want to get into all this, why not put the parsley *inside* the fish? And put some onions in with them. (And that extra celery diced up with bread crumbs?) Why not!

There is another way to cope with a superabundance of parsley: *Parsley, when stored in an airtight container in the icebox — for example, tightly wrapped in a plastic bag — keeps longer than you think.* A couple of weeks.

Incidentally, you will find various directions in cookbooks for making a bed of something called *mirepoix.* (In English, this rhymes with *irifoy!*) But it's not the same thing. Mirepoix is a bed of herbs and diced aromatic vegetables, like carrots and onions, that go under meat and whose primary function is only *to flavor it.*

It's too bad that calling something by an unusual name — though it's a perfectly good name — can put off many a cook. "Gosh, I can't do *that!*" Fortunately, though, some of them have been making mirepoix, oblivious to the fact that someone else has given it a fancy name.

As we've said before, a name can be a help in recalling to mind whatever has the name; it can also be restrictive. The main thing is, if you're preparing this kind of accompaniment to a meat course, to get some carrots, onions, celery — and maybe turnips? — under there. Anything else? Herbs?

### Cooking the Fish

I put some lightly buttered aluminum foil on the oven broiling tray and curled the sides so the juices wouldn't run off. I made a bed of parsley with slivers of garlic here and there and placed the trout on top, putting dots of butter every 3 inches or so on each fish. Then I put it in the oven.

After the trout had been cooking a minute or two, they needed *basting.* I poured some of the sauce all over the trout, which of course were developing their own juices in the cooking, and thereafter I basted the fish with the pan juices, and sometimes with more of the sauce, every couple of minutes with a big spoon. Besides permeating the fish with essences of the sauce, basting keeps them from drying out. A little of the sauce was saved for later. At some point, I sprinkled the mushrooms in and around. (Mushrooms don't take long to cook, maybe 4 or 5 minutes.)

Meanwhile, the broccoli and the potatoes were — EGAD! The garlic bread was burning. I mean, it smelled like it was starting to . . . I quickly snatched the loaf (ouch! hot!) and tossed it onto a counter as though it were a live coal! The bottom part was very brown, but not yet burnt; it still looked intact, but I wasn't sure. I decided to chance it.

### Mustard Sauce

With the vegetable and potatoes coming on, I still had a burner left on the stove. I melted some more butter, added some lemon (but for some reason not as much as I did for the fish) and some French Dijon mustard. (There are also other interesting mustards to try.) Usually I use Grey Poupon or some other smooth type when I want to put it in things, but I had just bought a rougher, more granulated kind for a change. I put in a few dabs of mustard — not too much. I just glunked some out from the jar with a butter knife. (Depending on your style, you may prefer using, say, a tiny golden-colored mustard spoon for more elegant glunking.) Some salt and a dash of freshly grated pepper. I tasted it. Good.

Then I lifted the broccoli-filled steamer out of the pot. I drained the onions in a colander. After gently tumbling the broccoli with the onions in the colander (which was now on top of the original pot) I poured the butter-lemon-mustard sauce over it. I was just about to dish the vegetables onto the plates when a certain insecurity, and lack of experience, prompted me to taste again. Since the sauce no longer existed independently, having merged into the vegetables, I tasted a doused morsel of broccoli. It was all right, but it needed just a bit more . . . lemon! I dashed some over. I tasted. It was perfect. Being of thin consistency, it was an "invisible" sauce, so it gave the impression of being more subtle than it actually was. By itself, it wasn't outstanding, but the broccoli and onion combination, inspired by the sauce, *was.*

After one has cooked for a while, these last two tastings — especially the last one after more lemon went in — will not always be necessary.

Why not? People always say you have to taste everything.

Absolutely *not!* One cooks as much by touching, looking, even listening (remember about hearing things that go on inside ovens? They go on inside pots and skillets, too) and smelling. (Ever since you were a child, you knew that when aromas in the kitchen reached their peak, it meant that the food was *just about ready.*)

What most cooks do taste, however, are sauces, soups, and the liquid part of stews. Let's be sensible. These are the easiest to taste without leaving gauche traces. And the simplest way is to stick — I mean, introduce — your finger into the liquid and then put it to your tongue, just as you see in all those cartoon pictures. (Sometimes, though, it's not enough and you need to use a spoon.) And if you think there's something unseemly about finger dipping, why don't you hang out for a while in the kitchen of your favorite restaurant — the more exclusive and discriminating, the better — and observe the chef.

These particular foods — the sauces, soups, etc. — are also the very ones in which it is usually desirable that the commingling of their ingredients produce a *balanced* result, as in a salad dressing in which no one ingredient stands out.

Because of the need for "fine tuning" to achieve this balance, tasting the sauce or soup proves to be the most effective way. Later, the appearance, consistency, or even the aroma may be enough, but especially for soups and stews, certain imponderables like "more salt, maybe?" are too often present. And why *not* taste? Tasting a sauce or a soup in an imperfect state and gradually bringing it into balance is one of the most keenly satisfying activities in all of cooking.

This is the general idea, but there is a spectrum of nice distinctions between a *suffused ingredient*, like a bay leaf in a stew, and an *accent*, like chives scattered on a cup of vichyssoise.

The potatoes were ready; they were to be simply dressed with butter, salt, and pepper. But everything had to be keyed around when the trout was going to be ready. Now this is the moment of almost unbelievable panic, **especially if you're not used to it.** But not necessarily. An inevitable speeding up seems part of the natural process, so it's not a question of preventing it. But we can live through it — and even enjoy it. It's all culminating — the broccoli and onions, the potatoes, the fish . . . the BREAD! What do I do with the bread?! I put it back in the oven to heat up a little; everything is happening faster and faster. So what are you going to do? Sit down and have a smoke?

No, but you'll manage — because *you have to.*

### Doneness
The trout goes onto the plates — but how do you know they're done? You use the Method of Noah. He took a tooth-

pick (whatever toothpicks were then) or a fork and poked at the skin or lifted it up. If it *flaked easily,* it was done. However, I should point out that Noah was not impetuous. He didn't just barge (!) in there and start poking. If he had any doubts, he used the Method of Noah's Wife.* He first pressed a finger against the skin of the fish. If it felt firm, but not hard, and sprang back into shape with resilience, it was a good indication that it was ready. (This also happens to be a basic way to tell whether a roast, a loaf of bread, or a cake is done.) Noah also noticed that when fish is done, the flesh turns from translucent to opaque. Noah knew about fish.

The trout goes onto the plates delicately, and preferably with a *long* spatula to avoid breaking them up. The potatoes (which, after draining, I shook briefly in the pot with a little butter and covered with a dishtowel so they wouldn't get soggy). Simple. Next, the vegetables. Some lemon slices and parsley around the fish for garnish.

The garlic bread — which you're not supposed to reheat. I slit the loaf open lengthwise, *but without cutting all the way through the bottom* (I think this is important), and dribbled butter with some thyme in it (the same herb as the one on the fish) but without any garlic; the outside garlic does *all* the work. I cut the loaf into crosswise hunks — but again, not quite all the way through, so the diners had to tear off the pieces (your basic Viking Garlic Bread) — and put it all in a straw breadbasket (with a napkin underneath the loaf).

It was *good.*

I must say that with all the butter in the meal, I'm sure glad I made a salad to "cut" it. (When did I do *that?*)

The last remaining touch: I took the pan with the bit of sauce that remained and poured a little over the fish.

Neither the applesauce nor the vodka stood out in the sauce; only when it was pointed out did anyone realize what was in it.

Of course, inventing a sauce, or any number of other kinds of things in cooking, is what many — if not most — cooks do all the time without making such a big fuss. (There *are*

---

*I searched Genesis in vain for the name of the great-grandmother of us all.

exceptions; otherwise there wouldn't be any famous dishes.)
And the parsley bed, even though it was all drenched, was a
treat.

### Fish Treatment
People have strong opinions about which fish should get
which treatment. Almost all of them disagree.

I'm not even going to give *general* indications because it
might hamper your experimental approach. But you should
know that fish take well to herbal treatments, even quite
strong ones. *Capers* (they really perk up a bland fish like, say,
butterfish); scallions; lemon and, if poaching, white wine is
almost obligatory; various seasonings (fennel is a classic, tarragon, thyme, rosemary, always parsley or watercress, and three
thousand other things). Guides are included at the end of the
chapter for baking, broiling, poaching, steaming, and sautéing a
fish. Fish can also be broiled or baked or deep-fried. (Okay, the
guides do give a few general indications.)

### Dessert
For dessert, I had a nectarine and some good pears. Before I
started the meal, I whipped up some heavy cream with a decent dribble of vanilla and no sugar — maybe I did put a pitch
or two in, but it's not necessary. It would have been fine to
serve the pears *au naturel*, cored and sliced lengthwise with a
dollop of whipped cream.

But this is what actually happened. After the main course, I
went into the kitchen and turned the oven back on (350°), then
quickly cored and sliced — but did not peel — two pears and
the nectarine (the best way to learn to do this is just to do it and
learn afterward). The slices were bite-sized, about the thickness of half-dollars (remember half-dollars?). I layered them
casually on the bottom of a Pyrex loaf pan. I poured some
Amaretto over them — not a whole lot, but more than just a
little; plenty of leeway here. Another liqueur could have been
substituted. What flavor do you want? (Amaretto, though
made from apricots, has an almondy taste.) What flavor would
*you* like?

The Amaretto by itself would have been splendid, but I wanted a special zing. I took some ground ginger (fresh ginger would have been nice, but I didn't have any) and sprinkled some over the top, but not *too* much because ginger is *noticeable*. How much? Better here to be moderate. However, if you overdo the first time, you'll *know* how much to put in after that. (This is called *the ginger principle*.)

I didn't want a naked ginger dish. So I took coriander, a spice reminiscent of nutmeg, but more exotic, and put in at least as much of it as the ginger — actually, a little more. Then, with my hands, carefully so as not to bruise them, I mingled the pears with the liqueur and the spices.

The entire procedure from the coring and the slicing to the putting in the oven (which is what I did next) took less than a *few minutes*. The oven was already warm from the meal, so it would quickly reach 350°. I put the dish in even though it hadn't quite attained the desired temperature. (Usually one waits.) No cover. Then I announced to my guests that we were going to have Pears . . . *Touché!*

The pears were in at least 15 minutes, maybe 20. This depends on the ripeness of the pears, and how you like them. I prefer them fairly soft but not *too* soft, so I try not to use fruit that is too ripe. You can poke a fork in one and try it when you think they're ready. But as I've pointed out from time to time, it's better in most situations when you're not sure to test a dish just *before* you think it's ready. Ease into it instead of snatching things off the stove or grabbing things out of the oven to cram into dishes (or baskets) because they're just *past* being done.

So, what if it had been 25 minutes even? Fine, fine. Out they came. To be dished out into bowls with a spoon (because flat pieces on a flat plate — yuthh!), a little whipped cream on top of each (but I didn't drown them), and the final touch: a sprinkle of coriander on the top of each dollop.

Now these are *pears*.

The juices from the pears and the nectarine (or all pears, or all nectarines, or all peaches, or . . .), the Amaretto, the spices, the cream, the *vanilla*, all blend into an indescribable elixir.

A pear is heaven.

. . . . . . . . . . . . . . . . . . . . . . . . . . . . . . . . . . . . . . . . . . . .

GUIDE TO
**Baking Trout**

TROUT, rubbed with thyme or tarragon or . . . ?
Foil, lightly BUTTERED
PARSLEY BED — if you've got a lot of parsley (or *watercress*) —
with slivers of GARLIC betwixt and between.
Dab BUTTER on top of each fish every few inches.
Bake at 350° to 500°. (Preheat the oven.)
Baste a few times with BUTTER. (You may prefer it with but-
ter and something tangy like LEMON JUICE, VERMOUTH, GRAPE-
FRUIT JUICE, APPLESAUCE-VODKA (now that's a weird one!), etc.
Put other things in and around — your choice.
When it flakes easily with a fork, it's done. The flesh will be
opaque. Do not overcook or you'll be sorry.
You can garnish the plate with LEMON, WATERCRESS . . .

. . . . . . . . . . . . . . . . . . . . . . . . . . . . . . . . . . . . . . . . . . . .
. . . . . . . . . . . . . . . . . . . . . . . . . . . . . . . . . . . . . . . . . . . .

NOTE ON
**Fish Forms**

What I had gotten from the butcher were luscious whole fish
— including the heads and tails — that had been scaled and
gutted (or "drawn"). "Unbutchered" fish can be cooked just as
well, and fish in various other forms, such as fillets (which are
boneless slices of fish), fish "steaks," etc. (Fish with head and
tail intact will have a richer flavor.)
I could just as easily have broiled the fish (trout) underneath
the direct flame (or direct heat if my oven were electric). The
fish can be placed on aluminum foil with the edges curled up to
save the juices — or better yet, in a cast iron or other heavy
skillet.
Fish should be washed or rinsed before using.

. . . . . . . . . . . . . . . . . . . . . . . . . . . . . . . . . . . . . . . . . . . .

. . . . . . . . . . . . . . . . . . . . . . . . . . . . . . . . . . . . . . . . . . . . . .

GUIDE TO
## Broiling Trout

Same as BAKING TROUT, except you'll turn the fish once if it's
more than, say, ½ inch thick, which is probably the case. It's
best to use a long spatula.

Don't forget to include the PAN JUICES in basting if possible.

Oh, yes — place about 3 or 4 inches from the heat. When
broiling, you can go all the way up to 550° — in fact, 500° to
550° is probably best.

Be sure to remove just when — or just before — done. Serve
right away.

. . . . . . . . . . . . . . . . . . . . . . . . . . . . . . . . . . . . . . . . . . . . . .
. . . . . . . . . . . . . . . . . . . . . . . . . . . . . . . . . . . . . . . . . . . . . .

GUIDE TO
## More Fish

Fish can be *poached*. Try doing it in a COURT BOUILLON,
which means a quick or "short" bouillon. For a base, use a DRY
WHITE WINE, or WATER cut with wine, or WINE AND VERMOUTH.
Add PARSLEY, a BAY LEAF, and THYME, an ONION stuck with a
few CLOVES, SALT, and PEPPERCORNS. (This is the "grand bouquet garni" mentioned on page 120.) Bring to a boil and let
simmer for about 20 minutes. You can add to this things like
chopped CELERY, a cut-up CARROT, and some WATERCRESS. You
can also subtract, using only water, wine, and some seasoning.
(GARLIC is not forbidden, either.) Eventually we get hungry,
though, and it's time to put in the fish. If it's small, put it in
gently and cook approximately 5 to 8 minutes a pound. Never
overcook fish. (I mean try not to.) If the fish is large, wrap it in
cheesecloth for easy handling. Poaching should be done on a
rack for best results, though I have even done it on a romaine
lettuce leaf. If you allow the stock to cool to lukewarm, it will
be easier to lift the fish out without breaking it up.

To *steam*, keep the fish above *boiling* liquid in a steamer.

To *sauté*, you can dust a small WHOLE FISH, or a FILLET, with a light coating of flour — or dip in MILK, then in FLOUR, or in dry BREAD CRUMBS. Turn once in the middle of cooking. You're supposed to throw away the BUTTER (and maybe OIL) in which you sautéed the fish and start with another big lump or two. But I confess that sometimes I use the same substance that's in the pan (maybe pouring a little off), mixing it with a little more BUTTER, and, of course, LEMON JUICE and minced PARSLEY. (Let the parsley cook a little in the pan.) It depends on my mood, I guess.

I know you may not believe me when I tell you that everything important to learn about fish cookery, enabling you to feel free to try many different things (or just a few things that you like a lot), is based on *not overcooking fish*. It also helps to know that bland fish, like butterfish, for example, need seasoning, pepping up, and fast cooking. One of your great helpers in fish cooking is your bottle of CAPERS. And always LEMON. And forever PARSLEY and WATERCRESS. And don't forget WHITE WINE. Or VERMOUTH (use more cautiously than wine; it's excellent with fish).

. . . . . . . . . . . . . . . . . . . . . . . . . . . . . . . . . . . . . . . . . . . . . . . .
. . . . . . . . . . . . . . . . . . . . . . . . . . . . . . . . . . . . . . . . . . . . . . . .

GUIDE TO
**My Actual Great-Grandmother Eva's Poached Halibut**

Use an iron frying pan large enough to keep the fish separated (or use a Dutch oven). Brown a large, thinly sliced ONION in 2 tablespoons (globs) BUTTER until golden. Place 2 HALIBUT STEAKS in the pan and pour enough MILK over to cover the fish. Reduce heat to a simmer, add a BAY LEAF, 6 BLACK PEPPERCORNS, and SALT. Cover and simmer for about 20 minutes or until done. If necessary, more milk may be added during the cooking. Do not cook too fast or allow the fish to get dry. You may also add ¼ cup DRY SAUTERNE.

. . . . . . . . . . . . . . . . . . . . . . . . . . . . . . . . . . . . . . . . . . . . . . . .

. . . . . . . . . . . . . . . . . . . . . . . . . . . . . . . . . . . . . . . . . . . . . . . . . . .

GUIDE TO
## Good Plain Boiled New Potatoes

POTATOES — unpeeled, unsliced (unless they're big) — placed in boiling water. When fork-piercing tender (but it's better to use a knifepoint — less damage), they're done. Do not overcook to a mushy stage.

Drain and put pack in the pot with BUTTER, SALT, and PEPPER.

Do not leave in a covered pot to await serving unless it's covered with a dishtowel. Otherwise, steam will be driven back into the potatoes and make them soggy instead of mealy.

If desired, almost anything can be added. But how about just salt, pepper, and butter — and maybe fresh CHIVES?

. . . . . . . . . . . . . . . . . . . . . . . . . . . . . . . . . . . . . . . . . . . . . . . . . . .
. . . . . . . . . . . . . . . . . . . . . . . . . . . . . . . . . . . . . . . . . . . . . . . . . . .

GUIDE TO
## Onion-Broccoli Minglement

Little white boiling ONIONS — boil, covered.

BROCCOLI — steam or boil — salt and pepper with a little garlic (optional).

Mingle them when cooked (the onions will take longer than the broccoli).

Pour melted BUTTER-LEMON-MUSTARD SAUCE (in order of decreasing proportions) over the vegetables. Use a good mustard, like Dijon.

Taste before serving.

. . . . . . . . . . . . . . . . . . . . . . . . . . . . . . . . . . . . . . . . . . . . . . . . . . .
. . . . . . . . . . . . . . . . . . . . . . . . . . . . . . . . . . . . . . . . . . . . . . . . . . .

GUIDE TO
## Herb Butter

(There are at least Thirteen Ways of Making Herb Butter)

SWEET BUTTER. Melt on low heat — or cream.*

*Arm and Hand Movement.

HERB. Use about three times as much for a fresh herb as dried. Experiment with proportions. You can't miss. You could start with a quarter as much herb as butter.

LEMON. A dash or so. Optional, but do it.

(Dried herbs, when not having the advantage of being cooked, will benefit from being heated for a minute or so in hot cooking oil — or, for herb butter, in simmering water. Strain and dry them gently with a towel.)

. . . . . . . . . . . . . . . . . . . . . . . . . . . . . . . . . . . . . . . . . . . . . .
. . . . . . . . . . . . . . . . . . . . . . . . . . . . . . . . . . . . . . . . . . . . . .

GUIDE TO
**Viking Garlic Bread**

Saturate the *outside* of the LOAF with GARLIC by r-u-b-b-i-n-g peeled cloves all over it until they disappear (about 1 clove per small loaf). Do this immoderately, extravagantly, and foolishly. Do not skimp.

Bake at 350° until crusty (10 minutes or longer).

Slice lengthwise but not all the way through.

Pour herb butter down the middle of the "boat."

Slice crossways in big hunks but not all the way through.

You don't need any garlic on the inside of the bread.

. . . . . . . . . . . . . . . . . . . . . . . . . . . . . . . . . . . . . . . . . . . . . .
. . . . . . . . . . . . . . . . . . . . . . . . . . . . . . . . . . . . . . . . . . . . . .

GUIDE TO
**Pears Touché**

PEARS, cored, unpeeled, sliced bite-sized, half-dollar thin
AMARETTO (or . . .)

A bit more CORIANDER (ground) than GINGER (grated or ground)

Mingle all carefully in baking dish.

Bake at 350° until tender but *not* mushy.

Top with a dollop of whipped cream (that had some vanilla added) and a sprinkle of coriander. (If a pinch of sugar went into the whipped cream, it would not be a crime.)

. . . . . . . . . . . . . . . . . . . . . . . . . . . . . . . . . . . . . . . . . . . . . .

. . . . . . . . . . . . . . . . . . . . . . . . . . . . . . . . . . . . . . . . . . . . . .

NOTE ON
**Whipped Cream**

Made by beating air into HEAVY CREAM ("heavy" cream is simply real cream).

Additions of VANILLA and SUGAR are *optional*.

. . . . . . . . . . . . . . . . . . . . . . . . . . . . . . . . . . . . . . . . . . . . . .

# 20
# *The Overall Three*

Good food has a magic appeal. You may grow old, even
ugly, but if you are a good cook, people will always find
the path to your door.
— James Beard, *The James Beard Cookbook*

This is about the Overall Three: *Flavor, Texture, Appearance*
(F.T.A.).

**Getting flavors into the food** is a profound principle in cooking. Some flavors penetrate and permeate from outside, from
other elements, such as the tarragon we rubbed on the Chicken
Rustique; and some develop more from inside, as in the making of stock. The underlying notion the beginning cook needs
to remember is that in the earnest desire to produce a meal
within a given time span, the flavor need not suffer as long as
the cook doesn't *forget* about it. (That actually happens, so
don't laugh.)

Flavor and Texture together comprise a whole complex of
characteristics including hotness, dryness, and juiciness as
well as other familiar aspects.

Texture is closely bound up with Flavor, both being experienced together, and is probably the least equivocal of the
Overall Three. I mean if something's limp, it's *limp*. If it's
stringy, it's stringy. Tough is tough. There's nothing wrong, of
course, with limp, tough, stringy, gooey food. (Dates are gooey,
celery is stringy, taffy is tough — and gooey!) It depends on

what it is. (You want gooey bread, stringy eggplant, tough goose?)

The commonest contributing factor to these outcomes is *too much cooking*. This is not the same as *fast* cooking, as in many a sauté, for example, which is a prized culinary procedure. But boiling meat, even for a short time — instead of simmering it for even a much longer time — toughens it; and cooking vegetables too long, no matter by what method, makes them mushy and limp.

We're interested in bringing F.T.A. into our cooking world, not as a fear-producing standard to measure up to, but as a help to the cook to attain desirable results. By really being attentive to the Flavor and the Texture instead of just following a mindless, insensitive procedure, the cook will more quickly arrive at an intuitive or organic sense of timing and temperature control, as well as the combining and seasoning of foods. Through these, we can bring out shy or hidden flavors; take bland foods (like beans) and, if need be, imbue them with something more appealing; or tenderize tough, stubborn food (parboil it first? marinate it? use something acidic in the cooking, like wine?).

Appearance, in this context, refers to the appearance of the individual dishes themselves. Though many people have a natural flair for this, there are those who need to be reminded of the importance of how things appear. Appearance *is* a reality. Once you have an *interest* in this side of cooking, half the work is done.

This doesn't mean that every dish has to have uniformly designed morsels of whatever in rose-petal-shaped beds of rice or anything like that. The entire range is open. Some days, a carefully designed dish is just right; other days, it's a rough-and-tumble rice and vegetable dish (or side dish). The vegetables can be submerged in a sauce or can retain their own individual fresh appearance. No rule, no pronouncement. Only accept that Flavor, Texture, and Appearance are all influential and interdependent.

F.T.A. is an excellent "pocket guide" to cooking. Supported both by the knowledge of cooking methods that, in general, help to preserve the nutrient content of the food (any responsible cookbook helps here), and by the recollection of good and nourishing meals, let the Overall Three guide your efforts. As your taste and discrimination develop, the results, subtly but noticeably, will too.

It's the only real way to cook.

# PART FIVE

# FOCUSING IN

# 21
# Cooking Vegetables

"The Welshman did good service in a garden where
leeks did grow, wearing leeks in their Monmouth caps;
which, your majesty know, to this hour is an honour-
able badge of the service."

— Shakespeare, *Henry V*

Vegetables, including cereals and grains, are really the underlying foodbed of our existence. The lopsided care lavished on
the meat course, with the vegetable treated merely as an
attractive garnish, is finally becoming old-fashioned. Vegetables, of course, certainly are attractive and exist in a great
variety of forms. There are bean-shaped vegetables; zucchini-,
squash-, and cucumber-shaped vegetables; broccoli and cauliflower shapes; and so on.

And colors! Magenta, red, orange, yellow, green, brown,
white . . .

Happy cooks, responsible cooks, and profound cooks — they
all love vegetables.

Vegetables can be prepared by all of the basic methods —
boiling, steaming, braising, sautéing, frying, baking — and in a
variety of combinations. They can even be stuffed in a fish or
set alongside meat, for broiling. (Or, having been cooked by one
of the other methods, they can be placed by themselves under
the broiler for a few minutes — not too close to the flame —
with a topping of bread crumbs dotted with butter for a
finishing, au gratin touch. Grated cheese mixed in is optional.)

But instead of lists of the best ways to cook this or that

vegetable (about which various cooks flatly contradict one another), I'm going to give some general indications with just a few specific suggestions. In this way, other possibilities open up. For example, many things can be sautéed or braised that one might never have considered.

### Boiling

Almost all vegetables (even lettuce, with suitable seasoning) can be boiled. However, in order not to wash out much of the flavor, the color, and the nutrients, some care must be taken. If you just run a lot of water in a pot, boil it up, and clunk some vegetables in it, you might actually get a nice dish. Or a mushy disaster.

*Boiling* is a code word in cooking. Those in the know know that sometimes *boiling* means a rapid, rolling boil — when cooking pasta, for example, or reducing a wine-laced gravy. But most vegetables respond best to a more gentle treatment.

Immerse the vegetables in rapidly boiling water, enough just to cover them. Even a little less, the more young and tender they are. An inch or so of water may be enough. Estimate. More or less water won't hurt anything. As soon as the water is boiling again, reduce the heat to a more quiet, companionable boil. In most cases, the pot should be covered. Cook until the vegetables are just tender when you insert a fork or a toothpick. Or taste a piece of whatever it is. Drain immediately and serve with salt, pepper, and some soft butter, which will melt over the top.

Various cooking authorities give you various indications about which vegetables to cover while cooking. Approach boiling with the idea that covering is usually desirable because more of the flavor is retained. But if you're cooking strong-flavored vegetables such as whole cabbage, broccoli (especially older stalks), cauliflower, artichokes, Brussels sprouts, then you may want to cook them in an open pot with a good deal more water.

Little white boiling onions and new potatoes (do not peel) — as well as larger potatoes, which can be quartered for faster cooking — are usually cooked covered but with plenty of water. (But small potatoes, or sliced larger ones, can be cooked in a *small* quantity of water.) The same is true for any of the firm, strong-flavored vegetables.

What can you say about the size of the pieces?

Well, the smaller you cut things up, the faster they cook. But this means exposing more of the vegetable's surface, which then causes more vitamins and minerals, not to mention flavors, to escape into the cooking medium. This doesn't mean you're not allowed to boil little circlets of carrots or slivers of green beans, but be careful not to overcook them. (I prefer steaming them.)

What can you say about boiling times?

If I tell you that a medium potato takes 30 minutes, give or take 10 minutes, then by using Irifoy you can judge beets and onions. (To refresh your memory: Irifoy means "It's right in front of you.") A little faster in the cooking might be cauliflower, broccoli, and carrots. And so on. The fastest group is the more delicate leafy vegetables, which need only a minute or two to cook using only the water that clings to the leaves when you wash them.

About salt. The debate rages on: Is it really necessary to salt the cooking water when boiling vegetables? Some say absolutely, that the salt helps bring out the flavor. Others say no, that it leeches out vitamins, doesn't flavor anything, and is just a habit.

I'm not going to get involved in this. Salt the potato water; for the rest, do what you like.

There is room for choice in cooking.

Now what if my green vegetables don't keep their nice green color and I *swear* I'm not overcooking them?

Keep the lid off the pan for the first few minutes of cooking; or lift the lid for a few minutes in the middle of cooking; or leave the lid off entirely. If the vegetables are going to sit before serving (fie on you!), *partially* covering the pot will help them preserve their green.

Another way: Cook them in *milk* in a heavy pan.

While on the subject of color, if your water is hard, your green vegetables may fade and the whitish ones, like potatoes and cabbage, as well as white grains such as rice, may tend to yellow. Stop this immediately by adding something acidic, like lemon juice or vinegar — or even a sour apple — to the cooking water.

### Steaming

A tasty and more nutritious way to cook vegetables. Fish, thinner cuts of meat, and other foods can also be steamed. It takes a little longer than boiling, and strong-flavored vegetables like broccoli will tend to retain more of their body and flavor. However, this means that overcooking may not only be a limp or mushy disaster but also a smelly disaster. Still, steaming fresh broccoli — cut up — is one of the perfect ways to cook it. But do not overcook it or you'll have gray-looking broccoli.

Get a metal steamer at the supermarket or a bamboo one in a bamboo store. If you don't have one, use a colander or strainer. Insert in a pot and cover the top with a tight lid. The vegetables should not be put in the steamer until the water is boiling, and the water should not come up high enough to touch the vegetables; leave a small gap. You can even steam things over water that has something else, like pasta, cooking in it.

Salt in the middle of steaming or afterward.

### Sautéing

Not only is sautéing a flavorful way to cook vegetables, it gives you the feeling that you're in charge because you get to toss things and move them around. There are many variations on the theme of sautéing.

Strictly speaking, pure sautéing takes place in a shallow, open pan with a little oil, butter, or a combination of both. If you first heat the pan slowly, and then put the oil in, you'll find that very little will go a long way, spreading beautifully over the surface of the pan. The tendency for butter to burn when things get hot is reduced by the addition of some oil. Approximately half and half is a good combination. And sweet butter, which is *always* preferred, is less likely to burn than salted.

Vegetables should be reduced to at least a manageable size in the pan. They can also be cut up in small (equal-sized) pieces, too. Firmer ones like turnips, broccoli, cauliflower, and green beans (green beans have a tougher coating than you might think; Irifoy may fool you here) are often parboiled (this means partially boiled) for 4 or 5 minutes to take their hard "edge" off. Drain them well, and if you don't plan to sauté them right away, plunge them into cold water to stop the cooking. Potatoes are best sautéed after being cooked through but just to the point of tenderness, about 20 minutes of boiling. Sliced and sautéed until browned (turn them once), they are most delicious.

You can sauté over moderately high heat, shaking the pan often, tossing, or stirring with a wooden spoon — whatever seems appropriate. You can also sauté over very high heat. For this, it is essential to keep things moving. This method resembles the Chinese stir-fry that takes place in a wok, a remarkable large, conical pan. Garlic and ginger are often companions to the stir-fry, and tasty they are, too. (But I wonder why some cooks never deviate from this formula.)

Simmering in butter, or, "the more butter than you might think" method. Many vegetables perform beautifully with this treatment, which is not strictly sautéing. Since the pan is covered, they are partly *steamed*. You're allowed to do it anyway.

This is the generic guide of which Country Carrots is an example. (See the Guide at the end of the chapter.) Melt a fair amount of butter over low heat, a little more than you might think for a straight sauté. Up to four servings, about half a stick. When the butter is foaming, put the vegetables in. If they are more than, say, an inch thick, slice them in half. Cook over low to moderately low heat in a covered pan; shake the pan occasionally during cooking. Add seasoning from the middle to the end of cooking, depending on whether they are robust or more delicate herbs. You can quicken this method a little by adding a splash or two of water or chicken broth. You can even add quite a bit more than a splash and you'll get a different result — less firm. A touch of white wine now and then — or some other daring experiment — won't brand you as bizarre if you don't overdo it. The main thing is not to burn or overcook the food.

\*

Suppose you have some zucchini. Heat up some olive oil, or any oil of your choice — or butter — in a skillet. Add minced garlic or a whole, peeled clove (or how about this: an *unpeeled* clove!), which you can discard at the end. The garlic should turn golden, but don't let it burn.

Slice off the ends of the zucchini. Then either make thin coins or slice them in half lengthwise — if they're quite large, in quarters — and then cut in, say, 2- or 3-inch pieces. By using larger pieces, if you want to brown the zucchini a little, you won't overcook them. Sauté them in an open pan. Or brown them in the pan, and then cover and steam them for a couple minutes (only!) while they're sautéing. Or cover from the start. If the zucchini is the larger, somewhat less flavorful kind, use an *herb* like basil or marjoram or oregano. If it is small and tender, it's not necessary (but it's allowed!).

A bit of lemon can always be squeezed over it toward the end of cooking. A touch of whole wheat flour will aid the browning and give the zucchini a nice color. This is the general idea, but here is the main point:

*Do not overcook the zucchini.* Various books will give you various times, which can serve as a guide until you get your own cooking tempo down. But you know what? The best guide is . . . You guessed it — and it's really the easiest. You taste it, and if it's just beginning to be tender, stop the cooking. Remember, it's always best to remove vegetables from the heat on the early side, since they will keep on cooking by their own heat. (Like eggs, remember? Only it's not as critical as with eggs, which very suddenly become tough.)

You can use a certain time as a guide, but to some extent it depends on the size of your slices, on how much zucchini you're cooking, on the size of your pan, on the people who are going to eat it, on . . .

After a while, you'll know when things are done more by looking and smelling and by just being there.

Can one leave this subject without mentioning onions? The number of dishes that begin with the sautéing of onions in oil or butter until they are transparent, or golden, may outnumber all the rest combined. Not too high heat; don't rush them; keep moving them around; watch them. Add garlic?

Sautéing sometimes precedes the *baking* of a vegetable, just as parboiling may precede sautéing, especially for older, tougher, more fibrous stalks.

### Baking
Except for the obvious potato, whose skin is oiled and pricked with a fork (especially for higher oven temperatures), which goes into an oven of any heat 350° or higher, baking does not come readily to mind as being a normal alternative for cooking vegetables by themselves. Unless they're mingled with noodles or grains or meat or whatever — people call these dishes casseroles — baking vegetables may seem a little odd.

"Wait a moment, please. I have a question about the potato."

Okay.

"One book I looked in said you had to bake a potato at 425°."

I like that book.

"Why?"

Because that's the temperature I like to bake potatoes in. Even 450° sometimes. It makes the texture . . . Well, you should try it.

"But you said —"

I know, but you see, everyone doesn't like everything cooked the same way. It's important, especially in the case of potatoes, to point out that you can get a very acceptable potato if you bake it at 350° or 383° and so on up.

"Why is it especially important in the case of potatoes?"

I'm glad you asked that. You see, very often you're roasting some meat or you're baking something else —

"Baking and roasting in an oven — are they the same? Sorry to interrupt."

There's something about each of them that feels different. But as far as what you do in the oven to bake or roast — preheat it to a certain temperature, then put uncovered food in it — they're the same. Anyway, in the case of potatoes, it's good to know that you can put them in with other things that may be baking at 350°. Of course, they'll take a little longer. You can tell when they're done by squeezing them gently. When they give a little, they're done.

"I baked a potato once — *without* oiling the skin."

Oh, my God! What happened?

"It was *delicious.* The skin was more crinkly and crusty. *That* was a potato."

But all the books . . .

"Yes, yes. And I cooked it a very long time."

Well I'll be.

Potatoes, carrots, onions, and turnips are traditionally put alongside the meat when it's roasting. The potatoes are usually peeled, then halved or, if large, quartered. Be sure and turn them in the middle of roasting. In my opinion, the best onions for baking are the little white ones, which should be peeled. If the carrots are large, you may want to cut them up, too. Many good cooks prefer cooking these vegetables separately, then serving them with the meat. I have tried both and I believe the good cooks are right. The vegetables retain more of their individual flavors. Nevertheless, I often roast the potatoes *with* the meat — after parboiling them for 10 or 20 minutes depending on their size. Thirty to 45 minutes in the oven depending on Irifoy — even an hour — roasting at, say, 325° or 350° won't hurt a bit. Turn them once.

Onions are surprisingly good baked alone just like a potato, but for not quite as long. Most vegetables can be parboiled or sautéed and then put into a baking dish with some butter or other fat and some chicken broth, then left to bake at 350°. It will take about twice as long as boiling them.

But if you do this, I will have tricked you into believing that you were being asked to perform some ordinary process like baking or frying when I asked you to put some water, chicken broth, or a lot of fat in a covered pan.

But this is really *braising.*

### Braising

Endive can be braised. It's a famous dish that you can look up in many a cookbook. But believe it or not, it can also be sautéed! So can lettuce. I tried it for a midnight snack with fried eggs (which probably should have been poached).

Dry the lettuce. Sauté over fairly high heat, flavoring the fat with a clove of garlic or a shallot. Add a touch of tarragon or some other herb. Lemon juice squeezed over. Once in your life you should do this. They laughed when I got up to fry lettuce! Egad!

"But this is supposed to be about brais——"

Cooking can't always be contained in such neat packages. We pass on now to the dreaded . . .

### Fear of Frying

Deep frying, that is. If you are just beginning to cook, I don't expect you to do a lot of deep-fat frying. And I'm not recommending that you should because in my opinion there are other, more flexible methods to explore first. But deep frying is such a fascinating side of cooking that you might want to dispel whatever Fear of Complexity or Fear of Equipment — or Fear of Spattering — that you might have absorbed with regard to it.

*Note:* 375° is the number to remember for deep frying most foods — all of which should be wiped *dry.* (Potatoes are easy to dry.) If something resists drying, coat it with F.E.C. (flour first, then lightly beaten egg, then bread crumbs). You can let it rest to allow the coating to harden — about 30 minutes. But you don't have to. Parsley doesn't need a coating, and it is so tenuous and delicate that you can reduce the temperature by 10 to 30 degrees. In a moment, I'll take you through parsley — it's spectacular and easy — and then you're on your own.

Use any vegetable oil except olive (its smoking point is too low); for example, corn, peanut, or all-purpose. Put the oil in a deep, heavy pan or pot — not more than half full. Heat slowly. The oil should never smoke because that means it's too hot and is already disintegrating into some evil substance. Either use a fry thermometer, or else drop a 1-inch, day-old bread cube into the oil. If it browns in about a minute, you're close to 375°. A more "dangerous" way is to wait until the oil *just begins* to smoke. Immediately immerse the morsels and the temperature should quickly fall below the smoke point. You can use a fry basket to insert the food; it's practically essential if you're cooking a large quantity, but otherwise not. Food for deep frying should be in small pieces, not more than an inch or so thick, and should be at room temperature. (Potatoes may be sliced thin.)

Each time food goes into the oil, it lowers the temperature. Therefore, you should wait for the oil to heat back up in between batches. When using temperatures near the smoking point, some foods, like potatoes, will need two immersions, as the first time the oil will cool off before the potatoes are finished inside. If the oil is heated again, the potatoes only need a few more minutes to be fried to a good crisp.

Finally, don't crowd the pan.

Coated food may take from 2 to 8 minutes to cook. But parsley will take from a few *seconds* to a minute, depending mainly on the temperature of the oil. By the way, no matter how much fried parsley you prepare, all of it will be eaten immediately.

Drop sprigs of dry, stemmed parsley into oil that is anywhere from 340° to 365°. Stand back. When it stops sizzling, remove it immediately with a slotted spoon (your special deep-fry companion), and drain on paper towels. The parsley should be crisp, green, and delicious. Experiment with different temperatures and eat the results. Deep-fried parsley — who would believe that's how you got started!

Your frying oil can be reused as long as it hasn't turned dark and doesn't smell rancid (use Irifoy). Strain through several thicknesses of cheesecloth after each use. The oil won't last forever because the smoke point is lowered a little after each use.

If for some (bad) reason the oil gets so hot that it starts burning, never use water to dowse the fire. It won't work. Baking soda is okay. Or smothering it with a lid — probably the easiest to do under the circumstances. (I don't really know since it's never happened to me.)

### Mixing Vegetables

Though obvious, many cooks forget that vegetables can be *combined* to produce visually pleasing and tasty blends. Some cooks, often very vegetable-oriented people, mix anything with

everything with results that are not necessarily satisfying.
(There's more leeway in a soup or a stew.)

It's useful to begin with just two or three vegetables, paying
attention to the harmonies of flavor, texture, and color. (Beets
with spinach? or squash?) Suppose, for example, that you were
going to pick two vegetables from the following group: beets,
carrots, celery, spinach, green beans, cauliflower, peas, and
potatoes. Pick out a couple of compatible pairs. Then choose
some triplets.

Of course there are no right answers. (There might be wrong
answers, though.* What do you think?) This is something the
cook can actually practice in his or her mind's taste — like
learning to remember the taste of an herb — before putting a
single morsel in a pot or on a plate.

### Tips

Trim off any weird protrusions or strings at the tips, such as
you might find in green beans or carrots. This procedure could
be called Dwobbing — "doing what's obvious." Tough, thick
ends of some vegetables, like asparagus (break off where stalk
naturally snaps) and broccoli, need to have their ends cut off or
pared down.

Many items that people tell you to throw away — like the
leaves around the broccoli stalk — are perfectly fine when put
into a soup. Some like them cooked with the vegetable itself.
You won't know unless you try. No one could possibly argue
against learning to use these stray leaves, or slightly blemished
and leftover thicknesses of stalk, and so on, which, out of the
Fear of Getting Too Involved in Cooking, we throw away.
What makes it possible for those people who have been used to
throwing such items away eventually to incorporate them into
their cooking is that they do it gradually. Your current cooking
system — or your idea of what a cooking system is — won't
permit you to suddenly start saving every castaway and scrap
and begin using them in all of your meals. But if you make the

---

*In my book (this book) if you picked carrots with peas, you lost. (I know it's
supposed to be a famous duo.) In some other book, though, you may win.

effort to incorporate one or two things that normally you would pitch, you'll see very quickly how useful it is.

### This and That but Not Every Vegetable

No one would recommend that you buy limp, wilted, tired-looking vegetables. But if that's what you've got, soak them in ice cold water for some minutes before cooking.

*Artichokes.* One way is to cook them uncovered with lots of salted water. A little lemon juice in the cooking water is good. And try an experiment. Imagine what artichoke tastes like. Imagine an infusion of garlicness. Pretaste the two together. They work. So put a peeled garlic clove in the cooking water.

The chokes are done when the outer leaves pull away easily and the stem is somewhat tender. (You sliced off the toughest part of the stem before you started cooking them.) Drain artichokes upside down. (That's fairly obvious.) Everybody knows how he or she likes to eat their artichokes, so I won't give you my little speech on simple, salted, melted butter.

Cast iron or aluminum cookware tends to discolor highly acidic vegetables like *artichokes, asparagus,* or *eggplant.* (Many vegetables and other foods — like egg yolks — that have a soft, somewhat oleaginous texture are acidic.)

*Asparagus.* Most books tell you to stand a bunch upright in a tall, covered pot (your coffeepot?) with water covering the stalks, which will boil them, while the tips, which require less cooking (Irifoy), are being steamed. Personally, I prefer boiling asparagus flat in an open pan with water just to cover. They're done when the tips are *just* tender, not the slightest bit mushy. Remember, they'll continue cooking a little after you remove them from the pan. Yes, I know that the stalks will be ever so slightly firmer. I like them that way. But maybe you won't. (I also admit that if the stalks are *much* thicker than the tips, I pare them down a little.)

*Beets.* One way is to boil them with skins intact and a couple inches of stem left on. Otherwise, red water and pinkish beets! Skin and stem them afterward, but you'll want to cool them off a little first. See if you can invent some method to prevent this from being a messy job. There's always a way. Do you think

you could sauté — or braise — beets? How would you do it?
Try it — unless you don't like beets.

*Carrots.* The only time I ever even consider adding sugar
when cooking carrots is when they're big, old, tough, woody
carrots. To my palate, young carrots are plentifully sweet.

*Eggplant.* Peel and slice the eggplant into manageable strips.
Coat them with flour seasoned with salt and pepper, because
eggplant tends to be very watery. Sauté or simmer the strips in
butter and olive oil, but don't cover the pan. Turn them once.
They don't take long to brown on both sides. Eggplant likes
cheese grated over it toward the end of cooking. And onions are
an age-old friend.

After being cooked a little bit this way, eggplant can also
become part of a baked casserole with any number of other
things in it (tomatoes, *onions*, bread crumbs, and so on).

*Green beans.* Great cooked with bacon. If you cut the beans,
do it diagonally. It happens that more nutrients are preserved
this way than when they are cut straight across. Of course you
can sliver them lengthwise. Some people swear this is the most
flavorful way of cooking them. I don't believe that, but they
must have some clout because there exists a tool whose only
function is to sliver green beans lengthwise!

You can also leave them whole — unless they're gigantic. A
gigantic green bean on a plate! Why not?

*Lima beans.* Many people dislike lima beans because they
had to eat canned limas when they were tots. As in so many
other cases, consider fresh lima beans to be an entirely different food, quietly sweet with an earthy, satisfying texture —
and without that ghastly canned, metallic taste that we all try
to pretend doesn't exist.

Shell the beans just before cooking. Serve with salt, pepper,
and definitely butter, which it tenderly absorbs.

*Jicama.* Remember the jicama! ("Remember it? I've never
heard of it.") You can cook it, but I like it raw in salads cut into
comfortable, ½-inch-wide strips. It's mild, pleasing, and fresh.
Great with lemon or lime juice; with toasted sesame seeds in
the salad — outstanding! Remember the jicama!

*Potatoes.* The potato, in its role of "receiver," accepts in
combination a great variety of foods. (Hey — most foods do!) It

has a distinctive texture that is especially appealing when blended with "mushy-mealy," "mushy-grainy," or other soft foods. (Can you think of one or two? Like turnips?*)

Larger potatoes when boiled — or even the small new potatoes — favor being "mealed." The commonest way to do this is to put them back into a covered pot, having drained them, and shake the pot for a couple of minutes over low heat, which dries them out and, at the same time, "meals" them. But if you let them sit in a covered pot before serving, steam will accumulate and make them all soggy again. Use a dishtowel to cover the pot.

*Spinach, Swiss chard.* Irifoy can fool you here on quantity. These greens shrink down considerably. When I'm eating greens, a regular bunch serves only two because I eat a lot of them.

Some bunches need to be washed more thoroughly to remove sand and grit. Others do not. In either case, the water clinging to the leaves from washing *is all you need* to cook them in. Chop small, tear medium, or leave whole.

Add little salt (because they're somewhat salty by nature) and pepper. *A grating of nutmeg or mace.* Cover. Cook a minute or two. *Squeeze some lemon or lime juice over the top.*

You can cook other, stronger-tasting greens the same way; or, to weaken their flavor, boil them longer in a little more liquid.

*Bok choy.* (What's bok choy?) Boil in some chicken broth with or without some garlic and find out.

*Mushrooms.* They are wonderful. They go with practically everything. I like them sautéed, but they find themselves baked and broiled in stuffings, in casseroles, and on and on. They love a bit of lemon. (Occasionally a few drops of Worcestershire sauce.)

One thing I've never understood about mushrooms. Most

---

*Why am I putting in *turnips* all the time? Because many people who don't cook don't realize how much they are used, and how interesting their blended flavor is, used sparingly. This holds even if you don't happen to like turnips by themselves. (Small, young turnips can be sliced, then peeled and steamed — or sautéed in butter.)

cooking experts implore you never to wash them, merely to wipe off the caps. They say that you will wash away the nutrients, and maybe even the flavor.

Well, I try to follow that advice; but sometimes I have had mushrooms that were so crammed with dirt — for example, where the stem meets the cap (and as you must have gleaned by now, I do not go into shock when I see a few specks of dirt somewhere) — that I have felt obligated to *wash* the mushrooms. And each time this happens, I reflect: How can water ruin mushrooms? Doesn't it rain on them?

The most sensible reason is that mushrooms readily absorb a good deal of water, which means if you do find it necessary to wash them, be conservative about it. If you don't have time to let them drain, be sure to use fairly high heat when you sauté them.

### Mustard Family

The following are all part of the mustard family, and they seem to have a certain strong flavor component in common. If any of them are overcooked, this particular element gets angry, and unfortunately you will notice it.

*Brussels sprouts.* Another undeservedly maligned vegetable. Universally overcooked to the mushy stage.

Try steaming them with a little oregano or sage. **Do not overcook.**

You may never have had Brussels sprouts before! Look, they're bright green!

*Cabbage.* A popular and good way that people cook cabbage — in order to avoid the unpleasant odor of boiling cabbage — is to shred it as for coleslaw, then put it into boiling water. Cook briefly, 3 or 4 minutes or whatever, and remove it. But you can still do it the old way, boiling a whole head or a head cut into quarters, if you parboil it first. What this amounts to is that you boil it for about 5 minutes, then you dump the water — and you can even rinse off the cabbage — and start off again with a fresh quantity of boiling water. Each time you do this, you neutralize some of the odor and the strong flavor. The traditional way of toning down "aromas" of the Mustard Family is to toss some bread crusts in the cooking water. Rye bread with *caraway seeds* is best. Caraway by itself seems to have a neutralizing effect on these vegetables.

*Broccoli.* Buy stalks with tight buds. No flowerets should appear. But if that's what you have, then there might be a cream of broccoli soup in your future. Or perhaps you will spread a substantial sauce over the aging bush.

Broccoli always appreciates garlic. But don't use it all the time.

*Cauliflower.* This is an off-white food. So (remember Chapter 17?) a grating of nutmeg is an appreciated addition.

Many folks say that you should soak cauliflower and, especially, broccoli in cold salted water for at least 10 minutes before cooking in order to draw out the hordes of bugs and other entities that are supposed to be hiding there. That may be. But I often just cook them without this preliminary, realizing I may keel over at any moment from insect invasion.

One excellent way to cook broccoli and cauliflower is the way some people cook asparagus: boiling the stalks while steaming the buds.

Broccoli, cauliflower, and asparagus are often traditionally served with a hollandaise sauce. They all seem to share a certain oleaginous texture and baritone flavor (that's a ridiculous description) that welcomes the hollandaise. Another traditional sauce for these vegetables is brown butter (*beurre noir*, page 129).

*Turnips.* As with most vegetables, the smaller they are, usually the more tender. The best way to peel them is to slice them into rounds, then peel each one. (This works for any awkwardly shaped vegetable.) The simmering in butter method is delicious, but if the turnips are older, keep the lid off so they don't develop too strong a flavor. Steaming is another way to prepare nice turnips.

### Chombas

Sometimes it helps to be reminded that you can add certain traditional things to vegetables (and other foods). So at the risk of overburdening you with funny little words, here's one more: *chombas*. Just say once or twice: "I can add *chombas* to things."

CHeese (grated or not — baked or broiled until just bubbly)
Onions (green, yellow, white — sautéed)
Mushrooms (sautéed for 4 or 5 minutes, say)
Bacon (cooked, and broken into pieces or little bits; or cook the food with the bacon)
Almonds (skinned, slivered, toasted in — or not in — butter or oil)
Sesame seeds (toasted; excellent on greens).

These are the *chombas* — to give you something to get started with. Not all of them can be added to everything. You're a human being and you know about eating. Let your "pretaste" be your guide. You can do it already quite well.

*Note:* Try sometimes adding *two* chombas to a dish.

*Another note:* Chombas B.C. includes Bread Crumbs.

### *It's Better to Love Your Plants Than to Overwater Them*

The essential "secret" of cooking vegetables, the one overriding consideration, is not to overcook them — but also not to *undercook* them. Each vegetable has its "range of doneness." Young peas have a relatively short range; some have a larger one, like carrots. Of course this depends to some extent on your preference. A person's taste preference, however, may be spoiled either through years of consuming badly cooked vegetables or too little experience with authentically cooked vegetables. But these difficulties will simply dissolve with a couple of weeks of decent vegetable eating.

It's very satisfying to cook something, like a carrot, just the right amount. And I *assure* you that if you've never eaten carrots when they've *just* begun to be tender, then you may never have eaten *carrots*.

It's simply cheating to read in some modern (and rightminded) cookbook that you mustn't overcook vegetables and then proceed to cook them any old half-baked (half-boiled, half-steamed) way. Sure, it's better for you than cooking them to pieces, but what's going to happen when some scientist discovers in the next century that certain vegetables need to be cooked to a *certain* degree of doneness in order for us to be able to obtain a decent amount of vitamin W, or whatever the new substance is that will have become so essential to our health?

What's going to happen is that all the cookbooks will have to be changed.

So what to go on? Our own experiences, of course, and those of our friends, as well as the common sense and discriminating taste of the best cooks we have. You can go for whatever you want. I'll go for these.

In order not to overcook vegetables, you need to know two things:

1. When they're done, and that
2. Vegetables will keep cooking after they've been removed from the heat. So depending on when they're to be served, you have to gauge this. **There is no other simple way.** And fortunately, for some reason I can't explain, it turns out to be very possible to do after a few attentive attempts. It's not exactly like learning to drive; it's more like learning how much water to put on your plants.

You can avoid *undercooking* vegetables simply by not wanting to undercook them.

### A Super Experience
The next time you go to a supermarket, wander attentively through the produce section (if you think I'm trying to get you to pay attention to the produce, you're right) and pick out some utterly unknown item, buy it, and go home after you get the other things you need.

By now, you should be able to COOK IT.

You'll look at it, smell it, feel its heft. Do an Irifoy on it. Maybe you'll slice it? Will you boil it? Parboil it in order to peel it more easily, or to make it more amenable to, say, sautéing or baking? How long? Steam it? Bake it? Fry it? What?

Well, what does it seem to be like? An onion? A potato? A pea pod? Broccoli? Spinach? Do you think it's bitter? Mild?

Do something! Remember, if it turns out inedible (it won't, I'll bet) see if you can doctor it (or nurse it).

Of course you can! (1) Mix it or blend it with something. (2) Will bread crumbs sautéed in butter help? (3) Mush it and sneak it into the salad. Surprisingly good! Or look in your cupboard, and in your *other* cupboard. See all those things

there? Or in the icebox? There are at least a dozen ways to get
from a pot to a table.

## The Need for Variety

Variety — at least in its subtler, milder forms — with regard
to flavor, strength of taste, texture and tenderness, appearance,
cooking methods, and presentation, should be a permanent
consideration for any cook. For one thing, variety is necessary
in order to guard against vitamin and mineral deficiencies
known *and as yet unknown*. Different cooking methods tend
to destroy different vitamins, minerals, and who knows what
else. For example, boiling is generally destructive to vitamin C,
a water-soluble vitamin, and many minerals. The more water
used and the longer the cooking period, the more is lost. Most
of it goes into the cooking liquid, *which is one of the reasons
we should be finding uses for it*. (The major reason is that it
adds real flavor and zip to soups, stews, sauces, and other
boiled and braised vegetables.) Baking, which retains the vitamin C, loses, for example, vitamin A to heat and oxidation.

Variety doesn't mean wild abandon to the promiscuous sampling of every which thing. Within every style of cuisine, there
is ample variety if we only avail ourselves of it. This means,
specifically, variety in: **what we cook, the way we cook it, and
what it's cooked or combined with.**

## The Dark Side of Vegetables

*Dark.* Some vegetables and fruits discolor almost immediately when their cut surfaces are exposed to the air. As we
do so often in cooking, we call upon the magic of *lemon* (or
vinegar) to help us. Sprinkle the following with this elixir immediately upon slicing and they will not be subject to such a
pedestrian misfortune: apples and other fruits, artichokes,
bananas, celery root, eggplants, Jerusalem artichokes, mushrooms. Cold water will serve for potatoes and avocados.

*Darker.* You can be sure that wherever fresh vegetables are
kept — whether in the icebox, in a cupboard, or hanging up —
most likely it's cool and *dark*. Most vegetables are placed in
the crisper, which is the "warmest" part of the refrigerator, to
keep them cool without danger of freezing them. Potatoes and

their cousins, turnips and rutabagas, should be stored outside the icebox where it's cool and shady. Onions, garlic, shallots — the same. But these two families are not on good terms in their raw state. Onions, in fact, will make potatoes spoil faster if they're stored next to each other.

*Darkest.* How to deal with the guilt connected with dumping the vegetable cooking water because you *really* don't want to drink it. This guilt is a good thing because it's important eventually to incorporate some of this semivaluable material into your cooking system.

That's right, *system.* Maybe you didn't know you had one. I mean, look, if you're more or less an everyday cook, you're not just cooking this meal or that meal, you're cooking for yesterday and tomorrow and the day after tomorrow — every meal is connected. Cooking isn't like a dip in the pond or even a plunge in the bay. It's an oceanic kingdom.

Yapping at you to use the vegetable water probably isn't going to make you do anything.

Start expanding your system, first by thinking about the possibility of doing it, then by trying in vain to imagine what catastrophe would befall you if you risked trying something like saving some vegetable water just one time.

"But what can I use this, this weird-looking water for?"

For making vegetable soup, or putting in meat stock, or in a cream sauce, or using it to boil or braise other vegetables in. Start with a small attempt. Just pour the cooking water from any vegetable — except those of the mustard family, which may be too strong — into a covered container in the refrigerator (or any cool dark spot); use appropriately.

You have to make room for the *concept of vegetable stock* in your cooking world. (Try asparagus juices, mushroom juices, etc.)

### *"Mystery" Vegetables*

Just because a beginning cook doesn't consider certain vegetables as *basic, worthy,* or even *plausible* doesn't mean that he or she is right. Why not look at it from the vegetable's point of view? Do you think for one moment that red chard doesn't consider itself as real and important as *peas*? Perhaps it says,

"Peas? Those are funny little pod things growing on my, uh, somewhere around here." (I don't think plants have a very good sense of direction.)

The problem is the cook's, not the vegetable's. (Of course, maybe the cook *really* doesn't like red chard.)

Child's Vegetable Question Number One (*pointing at a celery root*): What is *that*?"

The fastest way to move in on the Fear of Strange Vegetables is to find a market that sells *celery root,* known also as *celeriac.* Its flavor and texture are pleasantly mild — it can even be eaten raw — and its appearance when cooked arouses little or no repugnance. But uncooked and unpeeled, it is one of the strangest and most fascinating objects you'll ever gaze upon. It looks like something right out of a story full of owls. GET A CELERY ROOT AND COOK IT. Failing that, or in addition to that, obtain some Jerusalem artichokes, also called sunchokes since they are the root of the sunflower.

Here is a good way to cook them. They are delicious.

. . . . . . . . . . . . . . . . . . . . . . . . . . . . . . . . . . . . . . . . . . . .

GUIDE TO
**A Jerusalem Artichoke and Swiss Chard Salad**

In enough SALTED WATER to cover, boil SUNCHOKES (JERUSALEM ARTICHOKES) until *just* tender, not too tender. *Do not overcook,* even a little. They get mushy and then toughen up. Start testing with a fork or a toothpick after about 10 or 12 minutes.

Pour the water out of the pot and fill it with cold water to stop the cooking and to cool the chokes so you can hold them in your hand while peeling.

Peel and slice them into bite-size rounds. (You may find it easier to **slice them first,** *then* peel each slice.) The rounds should not be too thick (about half the thickness of typical zucchini). Drop each one immediately into another bowl of cool water that has enough RED WINE VINEGAR in it to make the water a little pink.

Let them sit in the vinegar water until ready to serve. (This will also keep them from darkening.)

Wash the CHARD well (green or red, or use SPINACH), but please, don't overdo it like all those books say. How long can it take to get some grit out of the leaves? Do not dry them.

Cover the bottom of the skillet with OLIVE OIL and some minced GARLIC — one clove for one or two people.

Put the chard in whole or coarsely chop.

PEPPER the leaves with NUTMEG or MACE.

These greens contain a lot of SALT, so try half as much. Or salt and pepper them afterward the first time.

Cook covered over medium heat (steamier) or uncovered over higher heat (crisp). Keep the chard moving, turning frequently, especially when uncovered. Roughly, 5 minutes' cooking time.

Dopple a few LEMON drops over them just before serving. The sparing use of NUTMEG and LEMON will make these greens come alive.

When the chard is ready, under cool water quickly rinse off the excess vinegar from the Jerusalem artichokes and place the chokes on top of the chard.

Serve as a salad.* Notice how the two different textures complement one another.

This is complete in itself. However, you may want to experiment with a dab of Dijon or other good MUSTARD — straight, or in a creamy dressing — on the chokes.

. . . . . . . . . . . . . . . . . . . . . . . . . . . . . . . . . . . . . . . . . . . . .
. . . . . . . . . . . . . . . . . . . . . . . . . . . . . . . . . . . . . . . . . . . .

GUIDE TO
**Country Carrots**

Someone said, "Carrots are boring." But these carrots are never boring.

Use small baby CARROTS (or regular large ones sliced in half lengthwise).

---

*Slices of *raw* Jerusalem artichokes are also very good and often used in salads.

Melt about ½ stick BUTTER in an 8 to 10-inch skillet. Keep the heat quite low.

Get the carrots all buttery (use your hands).

Add SALT, and little or no PEPPER.

*Cover* the pan so that the carrots sauté and steam at the same time.

About halfway through the cooking (no earlier), scatter crushed TARRAGON over the buttery carrots; (actually, I *rub* it on — ouch! hot! — but I'm a little crazy).

A few minutes later, sprinkle powdered or grated FRESH GINGER all over the carrots.

It's 9 to 19 minutes cooking time altogether, depending on the carrots, the heat, your skillet.

You can tell when they're done just by touching them or poking them gently with a fork.

Remove them when they're *just beginning* to get tender.

Put them on a warm serving dish or on the plates.

Don't let them sit around in the hot pan or they'll overcook and will look ugly and taste mushy (unless you took this into account and turned the heat off early).

Sprinkle some minced PARSLEY about if you like. Or you can let the TARRAGON and GINGER carry it.

. . . . . . . . . . . . . . . . . . . . . . . . . . . . . . . . . . . . . . . . . . . . . . . .

# 22
# The Artful Use
# of Nuts and Seeds

Touches of magic.

The crunchy texture of nuts and seeds, and their pleasant taste, often provide just the right complement to a dish, a simple yet intriguing means of varying the flavor, texture, or appearance of something you may have made many times. (Walnuts or almonds in your pasta?) There are, in fact, few places where nuts and seeds are not welcome and delicious — with grains, pasta, numerous vegetables, desserts of all types, salads, meat, fish, poultry . . . Since these small but important cooking aids are mentioned elsewhere (for example, in the last chapter), here we will concentrate on how to prepare them for use.

Some good basic nuts are almonds, walnuts, cashews, peanuts, and filberts (and more that you can think of). Among the popular seeds are sesame, poppy, and sunflower (as distinguished from, for example, caraway, fennel, and anise seeds, which are more traditionally thought of as spices; the lines, of course, are fictitious, especially in the case of sesame).

Almonds and peanuts (shelled) are frequently *blanched* before use. A twofold Arm and Hand Body Movement consisting of **dropping** (into boiling or very hot water) and **slipping** the skins OFF (with your thumbs). If you are going to sliver the nuts — almonds are frequently prepared this way before mingling them with something else — do it while they're warm.

It's much easier. Nuts can be slivered and chopped with your chef's knife. (Though nutgrinders do exist.)

To toast nuts and seeds, which really improves their flavor, spread them on a baking sheet and place in a 350° oven for 10 to 20 minutes, turning or stirring them about every 5 minutes and *watching carefully*. They should brown but not burn. It takes a little cooling for the crisp texture to set in.

Though the following will be obvious to anyone who has come this far with us, I shall specifically mention a very handy way to toast nuts and to *butter* them: Do it in a heavy skillet with butter. It's very convenient for blending with, say, vegetables, in which case the latter can be added to the blanched, slivered, buttered, toasted almonds already in the skillet. Yum!

. . . . . . . . . . . . . . . . . . . . . . . . . . . . . . . . . . . . . . . . . . . . . .

GUIDE TO
## Nut Loaf

Grind in blender (or chop) about 1 cup WALNUTS. Add an equal amount of grated CHEDDAR CHEESE. Sauté some ONIONS in BUTTER. Add ½ cup TOMATO JUICE, ½ cup WHEAT GERM, 1 or 2 EGGS, SALT, and PEPPER. Combine all together in a baking dish like a meat loaf.

Cook for 25 to 30 minutes in a 350° oven.

. . . . . . . . . . . . . . . . . . . . . . . . . . . . . . . . . . . . . . . . . . . . . .

# 23
# *Salad*

Put the required number of whole tomatoes into boiling
water to remove the skins. Arrange them in a shallow
bowl or silver dish.

Pour over them a dressing consisting simply of thick
fresh cream into which is stirred a little salt and a tablespoon of chopped tarragon or fresh sweet basil.

A splendid accompaniment for a cold or, for that matter, a hot chicken.

— Elizabeth David, *French Country Cooking*

A salad embodies the entire cooking process in miniature.
Generally speaking, the only element excluded is heat. Besides
greens, legumes, and other vegetables, salads contain grains,
pasta, seeds, nuts, meat, fish, fruit, dairy foods, and condiments of every kind. At this, the mind staggers and falls into a
pool of vinaigrette while innumerable salads, hitherto submerged in the endless flora of cookbook pages, swim into view.

Are we going to shield our eyes and our palates from this
profusion of possibilities and retreat into making one salad
forever? Some kind of an iceberg lettuce and tomato salad with
a bottled dressing?

Tragic!

We begin at home. As far as salad is concerned, lettuce is
"home." (Sometimes we leave home; for example, to eat
potato salad.) Discover how refreshing and elegant a presentation of nice, crisp (non-iceberg) lettuce with a vinaigrette sauce
can be. Butter lettuce, bibb, red, romaine, are some of the ones
to choose from. So when you go to the store, don't just squint

when you pass all those strange greens in the produce section. Take one home.

To crisp lettuce 15 or 20 minutes before using, wash the leaves separately — and check for grit. Dry gently with towels or in a salad dryer (a most worthwhile utensil); salad greens must be dry, otherwise the oil won't cling properly to the leaves. Put in a bowl or wrap in a towel, and place in the refrigerator.

You can make an attractive combination of contrasting greens using different kinds of lettuce, spinach, or watercress. (Iceberg lettuce can be included in a combination. But look, it's not even cheaper than many other kinds. It just keeps longer, has fewer nutrients, and less flavor — though it does have a nice crisp texture.) Some of your combinations will be more successful than others; experiment. Contrast is good, but a very strong and a very delicate lettuce would obviously not work together too well.

A few obvious additions: Radishes — use the whole red part or slice into rounds. Cucumbers — peel (unless you have the kind that doesn't have this nauseating, meaningless wax all over it, put there to make the cucumbers look more *appetizing* — can you believe that?). If you wish to draw some of the bitterness out of the slices, salt them and let them stand in cold water for an hour or so; I happen to like them the way they are, sliced thick or thin. Tomatoes — these are w-a-t-e-r-y, so slice them or cut them into wedges and put them in just before tossing; otherwise, they'll wilt your lettuce. Grated carrots. Sliced beets. Chopped celery; or slit the stalks lengthwise for a decorative curl. Raw mushrooms. Scallions.

But instead of adding things straight off, take a moment to wonder about what a salad is.

Salads, above all, convey freshness — even if you are using leftovers. Salads, in fact, are one of the primary ways of using up leftovers.

Fresh, cool, crisp. The salad should be a complement to the usual warm and tender foods that are the heart of most meals. And when the salad is the focus of the meal, it should be a complement to the rest of the meals of the day. It's not enough to be reminded that you can make all kinds of simple and wonderful salads. You may still find yourself hastening to snuggle back up to a safe bed of lettuce with perhaps a few small black olives or cherry tomatoes tossed into it. (Sounds delicious.)

Keep coming back to the salad as one part of the meal at hand. This is what can open up many possibilities in a manageable way. To complement doesn't mean to repeat but to bring something colorful, crisp, or tart that will appropriately set off the other dishes.

The word *salad* means "to salt." That's a surprise, isn't it? But it makes sense; for I believe here it alludes to the sharpening of our senses, the freshening of the entire meal.

To the basic barefoot lettuce salad you can add almost anything else that's in your refrigerator. Consider vegetables such as broccoli or cauliflower. These are firm and sometimes even a little bitter when raw. You may wish to partially cook them by submerging them in boiling water for about 5 minutes. If you serve them raw, try soaking them first in ice water for 15 or so minutes to crisp them or use them, washed, just as they are. And there are things you've never thought of — like slivering just the tips of *raw* asparagus and adding them (with some toasted sesame seeds? some *jicama?*). Delicious.

A luncheon salad can be made with thin slices of beef (that aren't all gristly) in a mayonnaise-type dressing with or without the ubiquitous lettuce leaves or with rice. Pretend that the rice is lettuce and top it with tomatoes, sliced olives, and so on. Cook the rice a few minutes less than usual to be sure it's not mushy. Add to it some nutmeg or ground ginger. For best results, dress it while warm, even *hot*. Beans in a salad should also be dressed when warm even if served cold, and, similarly, mixed vegetables when they constitute the main ingredients of the salad. The same applies to potato salad. You remember that one of the basic principles of cooking is to get the flavors into the food. This gives more time for the sauce to soak in.

For a simple salad, boil new potatoes in their skins (don't use big Idaho potatoes for this!), slice (peel, if you must), let them cool down, but dress them while still warm. Chill. Add chives and/or parsley just before serving. You can add the familiar chopped celery, hard-boiled eggs, pickle, and other things you can think of as easily as I. Or discover something new; potatoes are very accepting. These all should be added while the potatoes are still warm. (But do you always have to add so many different things? Or even anything?) You can use a homemade mayonnaise or an herb-vinaigrette dressing, with capers or even a touch of curry powder once in a while. (Of course, you won't serve potato salad if potatoes are included elsewhere in the meal.)

Now I'm not suggesting that you run wild and start putting together canteloupe and oatmeal salads or other strange concoctions for every occasion. But meander from "home" to explore now and then, to bring variety into your meals in a colorful and upbeat way.

And don't forget to include frequently something crunchy like toasted sesame seeds (excellent with greens) or toasted almonds, chopped or slivered. There are walnuts, cashews — and caraway seeds (great in coleslaw sometimes).

At first be conservative. Understate. Why? Because coolness, crunchiness, and freshness have an incisive effect on the taster without your having to mingle too many ingredients or to rely on odd combinations, like onions sliced very thin with peeled orange slices. (Sorry, this one happens to work beautifully. Try "pretasting" it and you'll see.)

Observe also that some salads are tossed and some are arranged. These latter can be simple — and visually striking — or evolve into elaborate geometrical or layered compositions that are a feast for the eye as well as the palate.

### Dressing the Salad

Just as important as the dressing's ingredients and proportions is the way you approach it. If you are a pussyfooter, consider making a dressing an opportunity to be decisive, even bold. Standing squarely (or seated solidly on a kitchen stool), pour the oil in one smooth motion. Though one has to be sparing here, be assertive with the vinegar. (Try often using *lemon juice* with or without a dash of vinegar. Excellent on fruit salad, fish, or vegetable salad.) Add seasonings. Shake. Taste. Correct boldly. No shilly-shallying with a little oil, then more vinegar, then more oil. You'll lose track; your taste buds will get confused. Your salad will lack zest.

Now you must know I have tricked you. The quick and tasty salad dressing you put together at the last moment in Chapter 12 is, in fact, your basic vinaigrette sauce or French dressing. Even more basic is that same dressing without the garlic or mustard.

To remind you of this primordial combination: oil, vinegar (or lemon juice; or a combination), salt, pepper.

*Oil.* The best is good olive oil; a poor grade of olive oil will not be pleasing in a salad. A combination of olive and a mild vegetable oil like safflower or corn is very acceptable.

*Vinegar.* You should have on hand a mild red and mild white vinegar — the white for a less tart dressing. Obtain good vinegar. I know fine cooks who can produce culinary wonders with so-called second-rate produce and first-rate condiments such as vinegar or herbs. Also, I suggest you have apple cider vinegar. Not only for an occasional variation, but, like wine vinegar, it has other last-moment uses in cooking. I also find *rice vinegar* to have a wonderfully different and pleasing flavor, especially compatible with fruit salads.

There are excellent herb vinegars — notably, tarragon vinegar — but delightful though these can be, you can produce a dressing as fine as you please by applying your own herbs to a good wine vinegar dressing. (However, I'll enjoy every bottle of good herb vinegar that comes my way.)

*Salt.* Any salt is okay, but kosher or sea salt is best.

*Pepper.* You will get black peppercorns and grind them with your pepper mill. And though you may be reduced to poverty, you will never relinquish your pepper mill. It stands in your kitchen as a courageous warrior defeating, at least in your own domain, the vast battalions of flavor and aroma-destroying pepper-grinding machinery of the contemporary food industry. Ground black pepper has a place. But not in your kitchen.

You can also crush peppercorns simply with something heavy. And sometimes it is nice to use white pepper, both for disguising the presence of pepper (say, in a fruit salad) and because it is milder than the freshly ground black peppercorns.

*Proportions.* I have talked about using too much vinegar, especially in milder, delicate salads. But there is another even more basic misunderstanding that is continually strengthened by the careless practice of many restaurants: salads drowning in dressing. A little dressing goes a long way. Put those nice big wooden salad-tossing forks up in an inaccessible cupboard for a while and use your hands to toss the salad. They will tell you, without measuring, that you need much less dressing than you think to coat all those leaves.

In adding the vinegar, eyeball a third to a quarter of the amount of oil. It's better to start with a little less vinegar than too much and add if necessary. If you do add garlic, try one clove minced up fine for up to a teacup's worth of dressing. (The indication "one clove of garlic" is not very precise until you have an idea of what an average clove looks like. Garlic cloves vary considerably in size. In this particular situation my advice is: Do not worry.) Rubbing the salad bowl with a cut clove of garlic is another good way to flavor the dressing.

*Mustard.* For dry mustard, start out with a little more than half the amount of a normal salting. If you're using prepared mustard (Dijon is good; never use bright yellow hot dog mustard in a dressing), use about twice as much as the dried. After you do it a few times, you'll see that worrying over measuring spoons is not necessary.

Now you can think of this as a basic vinaigrette that can be suitably varied. On fruit salads — or on any other salad that you might have doubts about — leave out the garlic and mustard. Experiment with using lemon juice for the vinegar. Or mix the two.

Many other things can be added to a dressing for variety: *onion juice* — just ream an onion (you don't even have to peel it) on an orange or lemon squeezer (aren't onions incredible!), capers (don't forget about these), paprika, Maggi (a drop or two only!), ground ginger. TRY THEM.

In my own basic dressing I almost always include an herb, fresh if possible. (I try to keep a few little plants on my windowsill.) You remember from Chapter 17 that certain herbs — namely, parsley, chives, and chervil — can accompany practically any of the stronger herbs you might use. Of course, any of these can be used singly and very effectively in a salad. Many individual herbs, fresh or leaf-dried, are commonly used. In salads, as opposed to in certain other dishes — such as soups, stews, and grains — the taste of single, distinct herbs such as tarragon, basil, marjoram, oregano (especially when fresh), rosemary (try on fruit salad, sparingly), and occasionally mint or dill weed is a distinctive voice that "fine tunes" the dressing, bringing the composition into sharp focus. This is not meant to be a rigid pronouncement, but as a basic rule of thumb — especially when you're just beginning — it holds up. (Parsley can always be sneaked in.)

The herbs I just mentioned are traditional salad herbs, and for good reason, though others can be used successfully. If you are starting out, I suggest you use tarragon at the earliest opportunity. And with tomatoes, the most frequent choice is basil, but marjoram and oregano are also superb. Dill, as you doubtless have observed, is a frequent friend of cucumber. But try fresh mint, too.

After the dressing is mixed, shake v-i-g-o-r-o-u-s-l-y. Really shake. There are laws of physics that pertain to the need to shake this sauce (yes, a dressing is a sauce) in order to get the vinegar and oil to blend together.

### Balancing the Dressing: When All the Ingredients Blend So That No One of Them Can Be Tasted Separately Without Especially Trying

As pointed out in Chapter 19, this is a basic principle in cooking.

Many folks have an unfortunate habit: They always add a pinch of sugar to a basic vinaigrette. It is not generally necessary. Sometimes it even covers up the true marriage of ingredients. The original intelligent reason for using a bit of sugar or a dab of honey was, I believe, to bring out the sweetness latent in certain foods like carrots, beets, cabbage, even lettuce, and fruits. However, I think many people began to overuse this sweet infusion as a fast-food method of balancing a dressing, especially one that was afflicted with too much salt. (When this happens, try adding fresh parsley. If that doesn't work, try a little sugar, brown or white.)

I certainly do not mean that sugar or honey has no place in a vinaigrette. I have had a fine dressing, for example, on a salad of *avocado, grapefruit, white onions sliced very thin,* and *mild lettuce* that was made with *olive oil, rice vinegar, salt, white pepper, a little honey, fresh basil,* and just a touch of *mint.*

### The Bypass

After you've had some experience with mixing the dressing, another excellent way to make it — and a flashy way if you do it in front of company — is to rub the bowl with a garlic clove, then put only the *oil* on the greens. By this time you know how much is enough. To toss, use your hands to be sure. Tossing is important. Lift the greens up and let them topple back into the bowl until all the leaves have a shiny coating. Then add herbs, vinegar and/or lemon juice, and finally the heavy or goopy substances (like mayonnaise, buttermilk, etc.). Toss after *each* of the above additions.

Then add garnishes, including some finely shaved or cut raw vegetables.

There should then be applause — unless they saw you use your hands. Or maybe because they saw you use your hands.

### Wise Words

There are two age-old sayings that have accompanied the creation of salad dressings for generations. They have been quoted by father, mother, grandparents, even uncles and aunts, and they are worth setting down again and again. You will find each of these in other books.

I. The Persian (or Italian) Saying. It takes four people to make a salad: A spendthrift to supply the oil. A miser to put in the vinegar. A wise man to season it. And a fool to toss it.

Take this seriously. It is the key to good salad dressing.

II. The French (Turkish or Chinese) Saying. If the dressing lacks body, add salt. If it lacks bite, add mustard. If it lacks flavor, add garlic (*Tassajara Cooking*, Edward Espe Brown).

This saying, interpreted broadly, applies to cooking across the board. (Your curry powder lacks bite? Try adding a bit of dry mustard.) If you forget everything else, with these two sayings, you can make salad dressing.

### Texture

You remember from Chapter 18 that the texture of a sauce is one of its most significant attributes.

It is helpful to think of dressings as falling within a kind of spectrum. At one end, the more vinegary types (hence *vinaigrette*); at the other, the creamy, dairy type, the extreme being simply buttermilk or cream.

So now all these apparently random creations that you read in recipes begin to make sense.

You can add almost anything "googy" or creamy or thick and dairy-like to the vinaigrette: cheese (Cheddar, Gruyère, Swiss, Parmesan), yogurt, sour cream, hard-boiled egg mashed up, and similar things in texture like mashed avocado (with lemon or lime juice), and mayonnaise, a world in itself to which you can add any of the above (for example, mayonnaise with whipped cream for a fruit salad).

Or, you can substitute part or all of the oil with one or more of these oleaginous substances. If you don't want the creamier sauce to be quite so tart, subtract some of the vinegar. Or use lemon juice. Try some things on your own. As a guide, the creamier, heavier dressings, such as mayonnaise, would be used on more substantial salads: on fruit, tuna, and mixed vegetables. But the lighter vinaigrette is really more versatile than many people realize. Obviously appropriate on a more delicate salad, with suitable seasoning it can be used on weightier vegetable salads, even fruit salads, tuna salad, and the like.

And within the vinaigrette itself, you can simply subtract some of the vinegar, for a smoother dressing, or some of the oil, for one that is more tart.

With regard to mayonnaise, do not fall into the weary repetition of plastering glunks of it over all your delectables. Use it with discretion. Think elegantly. Mayonnaise can be visually appealing too. Should I place it pleasingly in the center of the salad? Or do I always do that? (The guide to homemade mayo is on page 137.)

### Relationships
The dressing is made to blend with the salad. When the salad is considered in relation to the rest of the meal that something magical most frequently happens. You're having a quiche for Saturday lunch. One of the nicest salads I know is slightly undercooked asparagus or green beans marinated (soaked for an hour or so) in olive oil and lemon juice with herbs.

### What If All I Have Is Chicken Broth and Lemon Juice?
Fine. Use a small amount of lemon juice. It works. The fatty texture and the tartness are both here.

GUIDE TO
## Hard-Boiled Eggs (Also, Soft-Boiled)

There are many ways; the following is one of the gentler methods.

Put room temperature EGGS in COLD WATER. (If they're not at room temperature, warm them. Or just proceed. If they tend to crack, try piercing the large end with a needle.) Bring water to a boil and immediately turn off the heat and let the eggs stand (covered) for 22 to 25 minutes, depending on the size of your eggs. Then immediately *plunge into cold water*. This is the best time to shell them.

For SOFT-BOILED EGGS, 2 to 4 minutes should be enough. The cold-water plunge is not essential, but it helps to stop the cooking and makes handling easier.

GUIDE TO
## Dressing Yourself

Some creamy, oleaginous ingredients: MAYONNAISE, SOUR CREAM, YOGURT, BUTTERMILK, CREAM, WHIPPED CREAM, MASHED AVOCADO, HARD-BOILED EGGS.

Some tart ingredients: LEMON JUICE, VINEGAR, MUSTARD (which is also a little oily).

Think of a spectrum from VERY CREAMY (maybe cut with just a little lemon juice) to MIDDLE (which is VINAIGRETTE of 3 PARTS OIL to 1 PART VINEGAR) to TART (maybe just lemon juice). And all in between.

So a rice salad and a spinach salad might take vinaigrette (of some kind); a fish salad could go all, or almost all, tart; potato salad or chicken salad could go creamy or vinaigrette; cole slaw runs the gamut.

Look at all those ingredients out there! Puréed potato, for example. Of course it doesn't really fit that neatly onto this spectrum, but I warned you earlier (Nonlinear Eggs, page 51) that the spectrums we make up are never perfect. But they can still help guide us.

Examples. A *creamy* dressing: 2 MASHED HARD-BOILED EGGS, 1 teaspoon (guess) MUSTARD, 2 tablespoons OIL or **cream,** 1 tablespoon VINEGAR or LEMON JUICE. *Creamy/tart:* HARD-BOILED EGGS mixed in VINAIGRETTE.

And just MAYONNAISE mixed with WHIPPED CREAM is great on fruit salad (and very famous).

*Tart?* You can think of some, I'm sure.

. . . . . . . . . . . . . . . . . . . . . . . . . . . . . . . . . . . . . . . . . .
. . . . . . . . . . . . . . . . . . . . . . . . . . . . . . . . . . . . . . . .

GUIDE TO
**Chicken Salad**

Dice up lots of COLD CHICKEN (cold food is just as nutritious as hot food).

Add ALMONDS or WALNUTS, ONION, DICED HARD-BOILED EGG, LEMON JUICE — CAPERS? You can add PIMIENTO and GREEN PEPPER if no one is allergic to them. Oh yes, TOMATOES and all that. Dress with MAYONNAISE.

You could start over again and to the CHICKEN add DICED APPLE, some PINEAPPLE SLICES, CURRY POWDER, MAYONNAISE, ALMONDS (or PEANUTS!). Put some fresh CILANTRO LEAVES on it.

It's all too complex. Just CHICKEN, CELERY, PEANUTS, toasted SESAME SEEDS, and CILANTRO.

. . . . . . . . . . . . . . . . . . . . . . . . . . . . . . . . . . . . . . . . . .
. . . . . . . . . . . . . . . . . . . . . . . . . . . . . . . . . . . . . . . .

GUIDE TO
**Spinach Salad**

A lot of SPINACH, well cleaned.

Sliced, beautiful RAW MUSHROOMS, a couple HARD-BOILED EGGS, chopped. A touch of SUGAR isn't bad here. A VINAIGRETTE with MUSTARD — or a TART VINAIGRETTE (2 parts OIL/1 part VINEGAR) — sometimes try 1 part OIL/1 part LEMON JUICE.

After dressing it, crumble BACON over it.

. . . . . . . . . . . . . . . . . . . . . . . . . . . . . . . . . . . . . . . . . .

GUIDE TO
## Lentil Salad

Cook the LENTILS. While still warm add VINAIGRETTE (with MUSTARD) and a bit of minced ONION. Mix in chopped-up PARSLEY and, if you have some, FRESH OREGANO.

GUIDE TO
## A Nice Salad

APPLE SLICES, CUCUMBER SLICES, YOGURT, FRESH MINT (easy on the mint — it can be overpowering).
Another idea is to put small slices of PEAR (why peel them?) in a salad with CRUMBLED BLEU CHEESE on it.

GUIDE TO
## Fish Salad

What could be better than COLD POACHED SALMON with SOUR CREAM? Garnish with something GREEN (WATERCRESS), and, naturally, LEMON WEDGES.

GUIDE TO
## A Fruit Salad (to Encourage You to Make Your Own)

PEACHES, PEARS, BLUEBERRIES, BANANAS, LEMON JUICE, a touch of SUGAR (if necessary). A baking spice like NUTMEG or CARDAMOM.
Do you have any CRÈME FRAÎCHE left from the duck (page 104)?

# 24
## The Store

Remember the jicama!
— Chapter 21

Everyone at some time or other asks, "How do I pick out the best produce?" When in doubt, use Irifoy. If it looks good, it probably is good. Suppose it's a green vegetable. If it's firm, crisp, "filled out" — and *green* — you're probably on to a good thing. More indications: compact, tight buds or leaves; heavy for its size. If it looks like a no-good, rotten, squushy thing, maybe it is. Avoid wrinkled fruit, limp or discolored vegetables (broccoli can have some purple showing in the buds, but yellow is not a good sign), leaves that are loose and spreading. Iceberg lettuce should not be colorless and hard, and both iceberg and romaine should be crisp. Other lettuce may be tender but not wilting. Potatoes should be firm, unwrinkled, and without green tinges or sprouts growing out of them. For juicy oranges and grapefruits, look for thin-skinned, heavy fruit (because liquid is heavier than fiber by volume), though thick-skinned ones may be fine for eating.

Irifoy is a good elementary guide. With it, you can get beyond the Fear of Rotten Food.

But let's eliminate one absurd misconception. *Large size* has nothing to do with this. If anything, it means less density of flavor, especially for cucumbers, eggplant, zucchini and other squashes, carrots, and turnips. When in doubt, look for the *small*.

After you gain some experience, your concept of edible, cookable food will broaden, especially regarding *blemishes*. This is an intriguing side of what a cook eventually learns. Instead of automatically recoiling at imperfect appearances — **which is okay in the beginning** — little by little, by trying, by asking grandmothers and neighbors, one discovers new ways to disguise, to transform, to combine.

One of the best ways to get inspired and discover new things, and even new ways to cook old things, is to look around the store. Walk by the produce bins and look, handle, and smell. Wander down unfamiliar aisles and poke around. Shop with a notion instead of an ironclad plan because some things are fresh one day — meat, *fish*, vegetables, fruit,* bread — and not fresh the next. And sale items may fluctuate daily.

Find a store you like — whatever that means for you. Maybe it's the quality of its produce or its meat or fish. The prices, of course; the general atmosphere; the people. If you walk into a store and you don't have a good feeling about it, walk out (if possible).

Convenience and cost overwhelmingly affect us all. But consider your time. A store that's a little farther away, that has more of what you want, at better prices, possibly with more efficient service, may be more practical in the long run. Midweek is the best time to shop. Stores are less crowded, and there are usually more sale items.

Get to know your store. That way you don't have to constantly retrace your steps. And usually, as I pointed out earlier, it's important to remember what you came to get and not dawdle about needlessly.

Don't be fooled by the products stacked on the ends of aisles in supermarkets. Sometimes they are genuine sale items, but usually they're being pushed for reasons not necessarily favorable to you. (And don't complain. If you owned the store, you'd probably do the same thing.) Try to resist just grabbing something because it's at shoulder level on the shelves. The best

---

*The best way to ripen fruit — including avocados — is to store in a paper bag.

buy may be way down below. (Another sales technique.)

The store is challenging you. Shop in that spirit, and it will eventually yield its best — that is, what's most appropriate for *you*.

*Buy in bulk when practical.* It saves money, time, and hassle. This is one of the most useful counsels. More and more stores are providing bulk foods, and the saving in money and sometimes even the higher quality of the raw, bulk food — for example, some grains — makes it very worthwhile. The amount we all pay for packaging and packaging design sometimes reaches the ludicrous. What do I mean? When you come across a bag that contains eight or nine fried chiplike substances with packaging that obviously costs more than the food, you will know.

We are being encouraged more and more now to observe the ingredient listings on labels (which list the contents in order of quantity). This is a good thing, but only if these ingredients mean anything to you. You might begin your ingredient survey project with a very simple notion: When I buy this container of something that I'm going to put inside my body (and my family's bodies), I'd like to get some sort of inkling about what's really in there. We're not talking about becoming food activists or health-crazed Californians or something; no, we're just trying to keep abreast of the times. And in our time, there is a growing awareness and concern about food additives, excessive sugar, and (for some) salt, to name a few.

Another useful label message is the *weight.* When wondering about which bread to buy, this is a truer indication of quantity than size.

With regard to bread, only "whole wheat" bread is *whole wheat* bread. If it just says "wheat" bread, or even if the package is labeled Real Country Kitchen Oven Grandmother Honest-to-Goodness Heartland Fresh-Baked Homemade Health Food Wheat Bread, it may be fit only for rodents. Read labels.

If something you got from the store is no good, take it back. A responsible store manager will really appreciate this. This is consumer feedback that benefits everyone. (I have this fantasy that one fine day, everyone in the world who bought a waxed cucumber, a waxed apple, a lousy tomato, and a chemically saturated orange will take them back at the same time. No, that wouldn't work; the freeways would collapse.)

### Fear of Lists — II
No matter how clever you are, don't be embarrassed to make a *list* of what you need at the store. Okay, so don't make a list. You know what will happen? You will definitely forget something (the butter? the paper goods?) or else you will spend more money than you should. I can tell by your smile you know what I mean.

### Imagination Practice
Think of any three people you know. Then look at and actually pick up loose vegetables in one of the produce bins (e.g., green beans, asparagus, carrots, broccoli, turnips . . . well, whatever). Try to *imagine* how much you would have to buy to serve as part of a meal for those people. To help you, here is a fascinating tip:

### The Hand Is More Dependable Than the Eye
*Look* at the vegetable in question (green beans are good for starters) and gather up with your left hand (left-handers use their right hands) the size bunch that your eye tells you is about right for three people. With the other hand, pick up what your *hand* tells you is about right. Notice the difference. Most of us, deciding visually, will buy *too much.* The hand not only knows better, it knows best; it even knows more than the cookbook that told you to buy so many pounds for so many persons. (You may have forgotten, however, that the cookbook probably took the trouble to tell you that it was offering its formula only as a guide.)

It's a very freeing experience when you discover this. There are a few tricky ones (like spinach), and if you need further help — say, with turnips — just imagine what you're going to do to the vegetable, how you're going to slice it, for example. You can estimate pretty simply and directly, if you just try it.

How did my hand get so smart?

# 25
# Meat

If you learn the two basic principles of meat cooking and something about the cuts of meat, then you can certainly cook meat.

**The First Principle:** *There are tender cuts of meat and there are tough, stringy cuts. Tender meat is cooked with dry heat. Tough, stringy meat* — which generally is more flavorful — *usually needs moist heat and prolonged cooking.*
Dry heat means roasting, broiling (under the broiler or in a pan), and sautéing. Moist heat means braising or stewing.
Other ways to render tough meat more cooperative are grinding (as in hamburgers), pounding (as in veal scallopine), scoring (a London broil), or marinating (stewing meat, for example). Generally, meat is sliced across the grain, which helps tenderize it by breaking down the connective tissue.

**The Last Principle:** *Slow cooking, by and large, is a good thing. But overcooking is not.*
Slow cooking produces a tender product with less shrinkage (and actually less consumption of fuel in spite of the longer time). The less tender the cut, the more it benefits from slower cooking.

There are some notable exceptions to the slow-cooking process, the most obvious being when you have *thin* cuts of meat, ½ inch or less. These are usually sautéed quickly in a pan on top of the stove.

The Last Principle does not preclude an initial searing or browning of a roast, steak, or stew over high heat or in hot fat. The function of this preparatory process is to seal in the juices while imparting the characteristic crusty texture and caramel-flavored coating to the meat before it is then roasted, broiled, braised, or stewed more slowly.

The main thing is to get started. This chapter will give you enough material to make a good beginning. After you've tried a few things, you will learn even more quickly *by making friends with your butcher* — another basic principle in meat cooking.

Let your butcher educate you a little at a time, as you go. Not only can he assist you in buying meat intelligently, but he can also advise you about how to prepare the different cuts. A good butcher, and a smart one, will appreciate your efforts and will help you. Take notes if you want, but the best way is to try a particular thing. Like learning a new word, you have to use a cooking process to make it yours.

But what if your butcher . . . well, I know he wouldn't do it on purpose, but suppose he's tired or mad — or maybe the fellow just isn't a very good butcher — anyhow, suppose he gives you a bum steer? No, I don't mean he gives you some bad meat. I mean he gives you lousy information on some particular cut.

In that case, consider yourself lucky. I've told you that you can learn fast from mistakes. Next time you'll know, for example, to braise a piece like that instead of trying to broil it.

Although all butchers know more about meat than any of us, some, by nature, are going to be better at giving advice than others. Since the butcher is a busy man, allow me to conserve some of his time by pointing out that raw meat should be stored in the refrigerator loosely wrapped in butcher paper for ventilation. Ground meat, fresh sausage, and variety meats (liver, sweetbreads, and the like) should be used within 24 hours. Steaks can be held for two or three days; roasts from three to five days. Cooked meat is best refrigerated immediately, tightly wrapped in aluminum foil; but if it sits out cooling for a couple of hours, it's still safe.

Ultimately, it is desirable to be able to pick out each cut of meat on sight. But it's not essential. In the beginning it's enough simply to learn the *name* of the basic cuts and to remember the best methods of cooking them. This is because at most butchers' and meat counters the cuts are named, and you'll find that as you roast and broil and stew, you'll automatically learn what the various cuts look like.

We'll begin with a primer on the cuts of beef, and afterward include a few suggestions for cooking other types of meat: veal (young calf), lamb, and pork — all of which follow a similar pattern. This is in no way a statement that beef is better than other kinds of meat. It depends on you. In fact, as you cook, you may find your tastes gradually changing or at least broadening. It's nothing to be afraid of.

The logical approach to learning the basic cuts is to draw a picture of a cow and divide it up in regions like a map (though I have never met anyone who memorized one of these maps and went right into the butcher's and started snapping up all the best cuts of meat with a clear conception of how to cook each of them). Once you know the cuts, however, the diagram is a big help. It suggests that you are wise in the ways of meat, and this gives you the confidence to cook any cut whatever.

Therefore, no matter how you look at it, it is worthwhile to know one of these maps. But embarking on such a study is fraught with dangers. My sincere attempt at "teaching you a map" may prove frustrating and, even worse, boring.

I've decided, nevertheless, that the advantages outweigh the risks and that I will face our common Fear of Geography and go through with this simplified primer.

### The Cuts of Meat

First, look at the following picture of a compressed beef carcass:

*Compressed beef carcass*

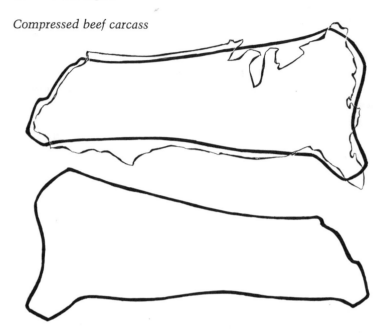

If you like, think of it as a map of the continental United States that's been squushed down. If that's disturbing, how about facing it the other way?

Now, look at the next diagram.

This represents the **rib** and both **loins: the short loin and the sirloin,** the ones I recommend you learn first. Why? Because some of the most famous cuts of beef come from these areas, and that will make them easier for you to learn.

These are the parts of the animal that are exercised least and therefore are the most tender cuts. They are candidates for roasting, broiling, or sautéing — i.e., dry heat.

Various rib roasts come from the Rib. Four well-known steaks come from the Short Loin: club, T-bone, Porterhouse (the choicest), and the tenderloin or beef fillet (the most tender, but lacking in flavor). Sirloin steak comes from the Sirloin.

Right below the Loin is the not-so-tender Flank, from which the true, and best, London broil comes. (Today you frequently find it being cut from the Top Round. I told you to make friends with your butcher.)

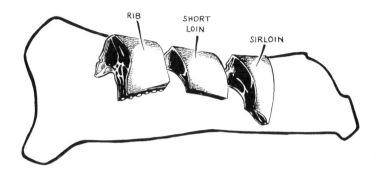

Now everyone knows more or less where the ribs are located, and that loins are below ribs, and so on. So if you don't feel overtaxed, I'd like to go on just a little; otherwise, you may get the impression that some of the other cuts are not equally tasty if prepared properly (maybe they're tastier).

Think of the **chuck** as the **shoulder** and **neck** area (which includes the **arm** and shoulder **blade**); the **brisket** and **plate** as constituting the **breast;** the **round** as the upper portion of the **leg;** the **shank,** of course, is the **shin;** and the **rump,** the **rump** — and it all becomes very obvious. If you learn it this way, these names carry right over into veal and lamb. Only a few changes are required for pork (for instance, **rump** becomes **ham; shank** becomes **hock**). Yes, there are also brains, tongue,

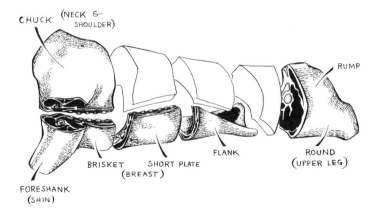

heart, kidneys, liver, sweetbreads, and tail, but concentrate first on the larger portions of the animal; the rest is easy.

This second group of cuts is more often braised or stewed. But this is not rigid doctrine. The rump, which borders the more tender sirloin, can still make a very good roast, though it's chewier than a rib roast.

It's also useful to know that the Round — which is always a lean cut — consists of Top of the Round, Eye of the Round, and Bottom Round (the least tender of the three). Round steak is more expensive than chuck or shoulder. But chuck generally has more fat, and if it includes the blade bone, there is more waste. (Not total waste, though. All meat bones can flavor stocks, soups, and stews.)

### Familiar Things

You probably would like to know which cuts are used to make things you've known and eaten since you were a toddler. (But you don't have to memorize any of these. Right now it's more useful to learn the "map.")

*Hamburger* most often comes from the Chuck or Top of the Round. The latter gives a leaner burger, but many prefer the chuck — and much of the fat is rendered out during cooking. Which do you like? You'll never know until you stop buying that prepackaged hamburger, which has God knows what in it.

*Chateaubriand, tournedos,* and *filet mignon* are cut from the Tenderloin. They're very tender, but lacking in flavor. Sauce it up.

*Swiss steak* is floured, pounded, and *braised,* not broiled or sautéed. (But you know something? I sautéed it once, after pounding it like the dickens, and it was excellent.) It comes from the Bottom Round or Chuck. Bottom Round is the best buy if the Chuck has a lot of waste.

A few of the preferred cuts for each of the following:

*Pot Roast* — Chuck, Shoulder, Rump, Brisket.

*Boiled Beef* — Brisket, Flank, Shank.

*Stew* — Lean Chuck (try the Neck for cubing); or get a Blade steak and have the butcher cut part of it up for stew and grind the rest for hamburger. Butchers will do this for you even if you don't know them. And remember to keep the trimmings; they are rightfully yours. Beef fat is most appropriate for greasing pans for cooking meat, potatoes, or whatever beef flavor is compatible with. Pork fat, including bacon fat, is superb for cooking a whole range of foods such as eggs and vegetables and for the browning of beef, lamb, or veal for stew. (**To render any fat,** break it into small pieces, melt over low heat, and strain through cheesecloth. Store the fat in the refrigerator.) Top Round, which is already lean, and many other cuts trimmed of excess fat are also used for stew.

*Corned Beef* — Brisket.

*Soup* — The Shank is famous for soup and stock because of its gelatinous quality. (Shank and Knuckle of **veal** are highly prized.)

One of the first things your friend the butcher will tell you is that you should look for cuts that are *well marbled*. Marbling is the fat that is "marbled" throughout the meat. It is a sign of juiciness and flavor. The U.S. Government grades meat starting with *Prime* (expensive, and bought up mostly by hotels and restaurants); *Choice* (with less fat than Prime, makes excellent eating, the recommended buy); *Good* (okay for braising and stewing); and so on down.

Beef varies in color from bright red to a darker red with an almost purplish cast. The latter, if it has been aged properly, may prove to be a better cut. Talk to your butcher.

Meat should be removed from the refrigerator long enough before cooking to bring it to room temperature. About 2 to 3 hours for thick steaks; 2 to 4 hours for roasts, depending on size.

### Roasting

For your first roasting experiment, I suggest a Standing Rib Roast — the larger, the better. And though expensive, the results will be fine enough to give you the bravado to roast anything.

You have left the roast out of the refrigerator for a couple of hours; if it's large, 4 or 5 hours won't hurt. Trim the excess fat if there is any, leaving about ½ inch. Wipe the roast dry.

Place in a pan with shallow sides, enough to hold the juices. Use the smallest pan that will comfortably accommodate the meat (a general principle in cooking). The broiler pan will do, with an edge of aluminum foil all around to catch the drippings.

Grease the pan lightly. Do not salt. (You can if you want, though.) In fact, *don't do anything.* Just place in your preheated oven standing on its ribs, fat side up, and close the oven door. The roast will baste itself.

How hot should the oven be? There are many "best temperatures." However, since I am not trying to tell you every possible thing but just one or two methods that really work, I suggest that you preheat the oven to 275°.

You should know that excellent roast beef can be produced in a 250° up to 350° even 375° oven. Some sear the beef at 450° for half an hour (often salting it at the beginning), then reduce the heat to, say, 325°. This gives a nice crust, meat that is rarer in the middle and more done on the outside portions (a plus or a minus depending on your diners) — and more shrinkage.

A rare roast takes roughly 18 to 20 minutes a pound to cook. But there are so many variables that no general time rule can be given. Fatter and less aged meat, for instance, cooks slower. Chunky-shaped roasts cook faster than oblong-shaped ones.

In every case, a roast *must* rest for 15 to 20 minutes before carving. This not only makes it easier to carve, but it gives the juices time to diffuse throughout the meat. This means you should remove the roast just before it reaches the desired stage, as it will continue cooking by its own internal heat. And don't worry, the roast won't cool off (unless it is small). In such cases, 10 minutes may be enough. Use Irifoy.

### When Is the Meat Done?

If you look at many modern cookbooks, you get the impression that before the invention of the meat thermometer, nobody was able to roast or broil anything without scorching it or causing some other disaster.

For example, your great-grandmama Sophie is cooking a roast for a dozen dinner guests to celebrate your grandmother's engagement announcement. Poor Sophie, she doesn't have a meat thermometer. She's going to blow it **because she doesn't**

**have a meat thermometer.** The poor thing is dumping the roast in the garbage (for the fifth time in a row) and she's baking turnips for dinner. It's all right, Sophie; the guests understand. They don't have meat thermometers either.

Now why did I ask you to ditch your thermometer for a while? Isn't it one of the most helpful tools devised by modern science? Yes, surely. But I believe that if you learn to cook a roast without one, you will appreciate the meat thermometer as a helper, not a tyrant.

Did you know that there are thousands of unenlightened but nevertheless very good cooks right in your neighborhood who don't have a meat thermometer (or can't remember which drawer it's in)? If you don't believe me, ask around. Judging a roast's doneness by look, smell, and feel is learned through experience. But I'm not just going to leave you out in the cold with nothing to go on.

Use your finger. Push into the side of the roast. If it's soft and squushy, it's not done. If it has a certain resiliency, springing back like a done cake, it's medium rare. If it's firm to the touch — oh Lord, you blew it! — it's well done. In the beginning, if you feel you need more assurance, you may prick the meat near the bone. If the juices run red, it's rare; pink, medium rare; colorless, well done. For poultry, it's different. Where the leg joins the body, the juices should run clear. You don't want to lose precious juice, so be conservative about this; on the other hand, where do the juices go? Into the pan, where they'll become part of a delicious gravy. Don't hesitate to look inside the meat, if in doubt. If you learn this way, you'll discover later on, when you're using your meat thermometer, that sometimes your own judgment will urge you to keep on cooking (or to stop the cooking) in spite of what your meat thermometer tells you. (Incidentally, when using a meat thermometer pay no mind whatever to the "recommended" temperatures on it. They're all too high. Life is full of little traps.)

Now just when I think I'm explaining everything, along come the American National Cow Belles. These are the wives of U.S. ranchers, and if they don't know how to make really good Roast Beef, I quit. Their method deserves much more recognition, for it produces superb roast beef. And guess what? It doesn't conform to any of my temperature suggestions. In fact, you can't even tell what temperature it's cooking at!

Never mind. Just cook your next (or first) rib roast the way they say:

"To prepare perfect roast beef, preheat the oven to 375°. Salt and pepper the roast, which should have been removed from the refrigerator the first thing in the morning to be at room temperature. Place the roast on a rack in a shallow baking pan and put it in the oven. Roast for 1 hour. Then turn off the oven, but do not open the oven door. If you do, you'll let out all the heat and louse up the whole process. Trust me, it works — **do not open the oven!** Allow a total of 3 hours in the oven to complete the cooking. (That includes the first hour with the heat on.) You can even let it go a bit longer if need be. About 20 minutes before you want dinner on the table, turn the oven back on to 300° to warm up the roast. While it's warming, you can finish the rest of the meal . . . .

"Start the roast at two or three o'clock in the afternoon and finish it off when the guests arrive. It works with any size roast. I have used the process with equal success on a 4-pound sirloin tip and a 10-pound rolled cross rib.* It even seems to help tenderize the tougher cuts. A boneless rolled chuck roast cooked this way is fantastic. The procedure even works with a roast that's frozen solid; simply roast it for 1½ hours before turning off the oven."

And it is essential that all roasts and steaks be served on warm, even hot, dinner plates.

### *Broiling — 1 Inch, Preferably 1½ to 3 Inches Thick*
Flame, distance, meat. Done, season, eat. Simple, fine.

Look for well-marbled meat. Trim off the excess fat. (If you wish to leave some of it on, slash it every inch or so to prevent the meat from curling.) Dry the meat with a towel.

---

*A rolled rib roast has been boned and rolled by the butcher. It's not as splendid as a standing rib, but it's easier to carve. It takes 10 minutes longer per pound to cook (because bone conducts heat better than meat).

For charcoal broiling, multiply distances from the heat by 1½. Adjust to suit yourself.

Be patient and watchful when broiling. (You can always cut into the meat to see if it's done.)

### *Pan Broiling — 1 to 1½ Inches Thick*

For a steak this size, you'll get superior results if you broil it on top of the stove in a heavy pan. Dry the meat. For well-marbled cuts use no oil; otherwise, just a light greasing. Heat the pan until it is hot — use the "water drop disappearing almost at once" method. Put in the meat and sear until juices appear on top of the meat. Salt and turn. Brown the second side, then *reduce the heat* and cook until done if it's less than 1 inch thick. Up to 1½ inches turn once more — carefully, with tongs or a fork stuck in the fat, so you don't lose the juices. How long? Figure about 15 minutes altogether for a rare steak, but it could vary a good deal. If you have doubts, cut into it near the bone, or outer fat, and look.

A combination method is to brown the meat on top of the stove (with or without oil) and then put it under the broiler.

Whatever method you use, *be sure to pour off any fat that accumulates* or your meat will be fried.

### *Sautéing — 0 to 1½ Inches Thick*

Similar to pan broiling, this method is ideal for thin cuts from less than ¼ inch to *no more than* 1 or 1½ inches thick. Cuts with little or no fat, such as veal or beef tenderloin, or cuts that may toughen under a broiler — pork chops, for example — are ideal for this method.

The fundamental difference between sautéing and pan broiling is that for this method the pan contains a small amount of fat. Dry the meat, trimming any excess fat. Slash the fat every inch or so. Heat some fat in a heavy pan, using the fat from the meat itself or oil. For veal, you can use butter (or butter and oil so the butter won't burn) in order not to overwhelm the veal's delicate flavor.

When the oil is hot enough to look wavy (this is pretty hot), but not so hot that it smokes (never let it smoke), put the meat in and brown it, and then proceed as in pan broiling.

When sautéing chops and cutlets, some people say you should always cover the pan; others will insist you should never cover it. Either way works, but you'll get different results. For chops less than 1 inch thick, you get a nice, crisp result if you leave it uncovered, which I almost always do. For 1 inch or more, I often cover and generally find myself adding some interesting substance, like wine or a little broth to the pan. Suddenly, I'm braising! Ah, well, I couldn't help it. It's so delicious. I'm sorry. Tomorrow I'll try again to sauté.

### Seasoning — Dry Heat Methods

Roast beef doesn't really need any seasoning, except pepper and salt, but this doesn't mean you can't. Rub rosemary or thyme over the roast for something different.

Other cooking methods, I think, can benefit from a garlic/herbal treatment. A few suggestions have been given for each, but only as a beginning.

For broiling: Rub garlic over the meat (it's even better if you do it ½ hour or so ahead of time). Smear good mustard on beefsteak. When there are pan juices, deglaze with wine or cognac and pour over meat. Try other spirits as well. One of the best sauces for broiled meats is simply herb butter, which will melt over the top by itself. Just plain butter is fine, too.

Of course, gravy can be made from drippings and juices (Chapter 18), and seasoning the gravy is an excellent way to incorporate seasoning into a roast, should you wish to do so. A good way to start thinking about it is to consider the three different types of blended seasoning that were discussed in Chapter 17: herbal, oniony, and spicy (page 119).

### Veal

Veal has little fat. Its color is milky white with a touch of pink. Rosy veal is probably not veal anymore, but beef. Except when cut thin and pounded (from the previous section you know instantly that such a cut would be sautéed), it is usually cooked slowly in moist heat. Veal should be cooked medium well to well, until the juices just run clear — but never overcooked. Overcooked veal is a misunderstanding (it's all tough).

Veal is never broiled because of its tendency to toughen. Large cuts like the shoulder or breast can be roasted (325°), but because of their lack of fat, such cuts are often *barded*. They are covered with fat, such as salt pork or bacon. Lean cuts of any kind of meat can be treated this way to keep them from drying out. Veal can also be basted every 15 minutes or so with a butter–white wine mixture.

But veal really takes to *braising*. One of the best buys is veal breast, easily braised right on top of the stove. (Veal shoulder is fine, too.) Veal, as well as lamb and pork, is favored by a rubbing of garlic. Herbs that are nice to try with veal are tarragon, thyme, or rosemary (go easy). So rub one of these on if you like — or even just a cut lemon.

Brown the meat in butter on all sides, remove, and put garlic or other herbs into the pan to cook for a few minutes. Then add about a cup of dry white wine, or sour cream, or sour cream cut with a little wine. The veal is then added, the pot covered, and everything is simmered over low heat for 1½ to 2½ hours (depending on size) until tender and the juices just run clear.

Veal's soft flavor harmonizes wonderfully with dry white wine, sour cream, butter, lemon, and *Marsala,* an Italian wine that has a truly magical rapport with veal. Of course, mushrooms and tomatoes are always welcome.

### Confession: Eye à la Veal

One day the supermarket had a special on "breakfast steaks," very thin cuts of eye of the round (beef). Almost no fat, all meat. They were less than ¼ inch thick.

Once home, I put them under wax paper and pounded them even thinner. I dried them. I could also have dredged them with flour, but I didn't. I sautéed them two at a time in sweet butter, with a little olive oil to keep the butter from scorching — a minute or two on a side; no more. I transferred them to a warm platter, put a little dry white wine in the pan (it could have been red) and let it heat through for a bit, bubbling. I deglazed (scraped) the pan and poured the juices over the meat with a trace of basil and some minced parsley I had tossed in earlier. A few drops of lemon squeezed over completed the dish. (A little sour cream could have been stirred in the pan, off the heat, at the end, yes?) My guest and I were both pleased. Surprisingly filling it was, too.

Eye à la Veal! Be my guest. (Another famous substitute for veal scallops are skinned and boned chicken breasts pounded thin. Should you possess actual veal scallops, cook them the above way. You can use Marsala instead of white wine. You may like it better if you put the meat back into the pan for a minute or two after the Marsala has cooked a little.) Another similar way to cook these eyelets of the round is given in the Guides (Eye-cooked Beef).

### Lamb

Lamb is very tender. Look for pink to bright red meat with a fine grain. Many of its cuts can be roasted. The rib, often called the rack, is highly prized, but the leg is probably the best known. However, the shoulder, which doesn't have the same firm texture, is a very tasty roast and can be braised as well.

What are called steaks with regard to beef are usually referred to as chops when speaking of veal, lamb, or pork. Those cut from the loin are the most choice, and they are usually broiled. Rib chops are a close second and can also be broiled, but are often braised. When roasting, the same applies to lamb as to beef: either roast at low heat (say, 325°) or sear at 450° for a little less time than roast beef — say, 15 minutes — then reduce to 325°; this will give you a tasty crust, but the doneness of the meat will vary, depending on how near the surface it is. Lamb does not need to be basted.

Lamb stews are good (if they don't have a lot of fat floating around) and are usually prepared with lean shoulder or breast. Moist heat cooking is reserved for Chapter 31.

Lamb is fine. But I suggest you do not overcook it. If you overcook lamb, if you even cook it well done, as far as I'm concerned you have not gotten the best from it. I don't care if you've eaten stringy, overcooked lamb roast all your life and you like it that way. Try at least twice to eat it medium rare. If you still don't like to eat anything but well-done lamb, well, who am I to tell you how you should like your meat?

Lamb, like veal, benefits greatly by a rubbing of garlic — or *lemon*. Garlic slivers can also be poked into incisions in the meat, as in the Guide to Sherwood Forest Lamb. Rosemary and thyme are ancient accompaniments to lamb.

### Pork

Pork offers a great variety: ham, sausage, spare ribs, bacon, chops, and so forth. Pork, of course, has to be cooked well in order to destroy the trichinosis-bearing creatures that might be lurking deep within it. But as many excellent chefs have pleaded, this does not mean to cook the animal to extinction. When the meat has just lost its pinkishness (if there is pink, put it back in!), it is very tasty — and entirely safe.

Pork also likes its rubbing of garlic. Personally, I think roast pork should always have some seasoning treatment. Rosemary is excellent; sage is traditional. A 325° oven is fine for roasting pork. Basting is unnecessary.

Why are pork chops so popular? Because they're very satisfying and taste incredibly good. If you cook them the following way, they're beyond belief. (Before beginning this, I must admit that so many people say that some way or other they have of cooking pork chops is "so incredibly good, it's beyond belief" that it makes me wonder if it's the pork chops themselves that are somehow what's good — as long as we don't mess them up too much.)

After browning pork loin chops fairly slowly — maybe 5 minutes on a side — and pouring off the fat, put in enough red wine to come halfway up the chops, a bay leaf or two, and some garlic. Cover the pan and cook on low heat for about 45 minutes.

Beyond-belief-pork-chops #576.

．．．．．．．．．．．．．．．．．．．．．．．．．．．．．．．．．．．．．．．．．．．．．．．

GUIDE TO
### London Broil

Use FLANK STEAK with the excess fat cut off. In this special case you may cook it directly from the refrigerator. SALT and PEPPER it (and rub with GARLIC, if you want). You may score the meat (crisscross incisions), but you don't have to. (If it's really not flank, you might want to.) Put on an oiled rack *close* to the flame, about 2 inches, no more.

It is cooked rare — no other way. Cook 3 to 4 minutes on a side. Carve diagonally across the grain in thin slices.

. . . . . . . . . . . . . . . . . . . . . . . . . . . . . . . . . . . . . . . . . . . . . . . . .
. . . . . . . . . . . . . . . . . . . . . . . . . . . . . . . . . . . . . . . . . . . . . . . .

GUIDE TO
## The Meat Loaf of Your Choice

A couple pounds of GROUND BEEF, but it's better if about a third of it is GROUND PORK or PORK and VEAL. A large ONION chopped, 2 EGGS. You want GARLIC? Put in 1 or 2 cloves. Some DRY BREAD CRUMBS, ½ cup to a cup, or OATMEAL! (right from the box). Seasoning is a must — but what? SALT, PEPPER, maybe THYME and/or MARJORAM, SAGE? A little WORCESTERSHIRE (sometimes), TOMATO JUICE if you want (like it says on the oatmeal box). Endless things.

Work the ingredients together with your hands, shape the loaf, and put into a baking dish. A few strips of BACON over the top helps keep it moist. At least put some BUTTER over it. (Basting with butter is permitted.) Bake at 325°, uncovered, for 1¼ to 1½ hours, until cooked through. It's good to eat at almost any temperature.

. . . . . . . . . . . . . . . . . . . . . . . . . . . . . . . . . . . . . . . . . . . . . . . . .
. . . . . . . . . . . . . . . . . . . . . . . . . . . . . . . . . . . . . . . . . . . . . . . .

GUIDE TO
## Eye-cooked Beef

A variation on Eye à la Veal in the text. Don't pound the meat. Heat up a skillet and add BUTTER — and a little OIL to keep it from burning and a dash of WINE VINEGAR (a good time to use that tarragon vinegar someone gave you). Add a minced clove of GARLIC and sauté it for a minute — don't let the garlic brown. Add the meat, but don't crowd the pan. A *pinch* of SAGE on each roundlet (and a hint of TARRAGON if you didn't have it in the vinegar). Cook over fairly high heat for a minute or less per side. As soon as the meat is cooked through it's done. Deglaze the pan with a little wine, or just scrape it with a wooden spoon. These are very tasty.

. . . . . . . . . . . . . . . . . . . . . . . . . . . . . . . . . . . . . . . . . . . . .
. . . . . . . . . . . . . . . . . . . . . . . . . . . . . . . . . . . . . . . . . . . . .

GUIDE TO
**Wanda's 18-Hour Turkey with (Optional) Co-Star Dressing**

I'm not asking you necessarily to make this. It's here because you should know that every twenty years or so, food fashions change, and what was considered excellent cooking then, is often snubbed as out of date. Here is an example of doing things the way "you're not supposed to." But if you tasted Wanda's 25-POUND TURKEY (it's made every Christmas), you'd have to reconsider some of these things that aren't supposed to work.

First of all, instead of a shallow roasting pan (which I personally believe is generally best), Wanda uses an old-fashioned "turkey roasting pan," with sides that are much too high for good roasting. She covers the bird with aluminum foil — more like steaming than roasting. And she puts the turkey in breast side down — rubbing it all over with GARLIC and BUTTER — even though, currently, breast side up is the way. Anyway, she does one thing that is popular in some circles now — she roasts it for 12 to 14 hours at *125°*. When the juices start to appear, she bastes every hour, turning the heat up at this point to about 200°. About 2 hours from the end, she kicks the heat up to 300°, loosening the foil at the ends and a little all over. A half-hour before the end, the heat goes to 400°–425° with the foil off, to brown. Toward the end, she may baste more frequently.

*Co-Star Big Production Dressing:* 4 kinds of BREADS — CORNBREAD, RYE, WHITE, and WHEAT — all crumbed. At least 3 cups. Another cup of a good COMMERCIAL STUFFING (like Pepperidge Farm). Also chopped CELERY, LEEKS, ONIONS, WHOLE PARSLEY SPRIGS, BASIL, MINCED GARLIC, THYME, PAPRIKA, SALT, PEPPER, and 2 cups WHOLE OYSTERS that have been SMOKED by wrapping them in foil and putting them in a charcoal fire for about 10 minutes. Then they are put into a frying pan to sauté with BUTTER and GARLIC. Everything gets mixed together and bound with 2 to 4 sticks of BUTTER. It should not be too sticky or wet. Put in cavity and sew up with a *needle*.

Such juiciness of turkey, even after days, is a legend in Wanda's neighborhood.

There's nothing wrong, of course, with a basic ONION, CELERY, and SEASONED BREAD CRUMB STUFFING. Another endless area for improvising.

Really, people should cook turkey more often.

. . . . . . . . . . . . . . . . . . . . . . . . . . . . . . . . . . . . . . . . . . . . . . . . . . .

# 26
# *Cheese*

Nobody can simply bring together a country that has
265 kinds of cheese.

— Charles de Gaulle

Entire libraries could be written about cheese. There are
cheeses to accompany almost any occasion — with wine and
crusty bread for picnicking under oaks, with pears for the perfect finish to a superb supper, for just nibbling as you rest by
the Thames on a Saturday afternoon, with omelets, sauces,
fondues, casseroles, quiches, soufflés, and for lunch.

Here are only the basic counsels for using cheese in cooking.
Well, there are a few other items. (This means I won't even
mention those outstanding soft cheeses that are strictly for
eating, such as Camembert and Brie.)

You know that you go to a butcher to buy meat. Well, you
can go to a butcher to buy cheese, too. Some butchers, that is.
However, it is probably best if you can find a good cheese store,
one that stores its cheeses properly — not just to catch your
eye. Then get to know your cheese person.

I'm going to resist giving you lots of opinions about using a
particular cheese in a particular dish. Experience here is instantly rewarded. If you read a recipe that tells you to use
Cheddar, you can try Parmesan, or a *mixture*, say, with Gruyère (this is an excellent combination) or some other cheese.
(Get to know your cheese person.)

### Cheese Counsels

The fundamental fact about cheese in cooking is this: If you subject cheese to prolonged cooking, it will get all rubbery and tough and stringy. You may also be told not to use high cooking temperatures with cheese, but you can if it's only for a short time.

Cheese should be added to a dish as close to the end of cooking as possible; it should be at room temperature (remove from the refrigerator an hour before using). If it's a semisoft cheese, it should be cut up into small pieces or grated in slivers for faster melting; if it's a hard cheese, it should be grated fine for the same reason. When melting cheese by itself, as for a sauce, it should be done over very low heat. A double boiler (or an improvised double boiler) makes it easy.

There are two categories of cooking cheeses: semisoft and hard. Theoretically, cheeses within each category can be substituted for one another. My advice is: Get to know your cheese person — if only to sample a new cheese before you go ahead with it.

The most useful cheeses to know about are the all-purpose cooking cheeses because they grate easily, melt easily, and are used in cheese dishes generally.

For example, an aged, sharp Cheddar will perform all these wonders and taste good, too.

So will Gruyère, a nutty-flavored Swiss cheese. (This kind does not come in little triangular foil shapes. You have to get some from the cheese store or your butcher.) Emmenthaler Swiss is another excellent all-purpose cheese that's somewhat milder than Gruyère. Though these cheeses start out as semisoft, through aging they become hard. (This is a good thing.) But there are other good "melting" cheeses. (Try Fontina.)

Of the naturally hard cheeses, strictly for grating, practically everyone knows about Parmesan, which is an outstanding cheese. Avoid those expensive shakers of gratings and *buy the real thing and grate it yourself.* What a difference! Like a whole other cheese! (Cheaper, too.) You should also try the subtle tang of Romano.

Though it's not always possible, try to resist buying the packaged processed cheeses. Some really aren't bad, but especially if you haven't had much experience with naturally ripened cheeses, make the effort to get some.

### *Familiar Things*

While I won't mention cottage cheese, Monterey jack, blue cheese, ricotta (one of the lasagna ingredients at the end of this chapter — a bland cheese with good body used in baking and for stuffing pasta), or many others we are all familiar with, I will point out that many common cheeses vary widely in quality. For example, if you think that cream cheese always comes in a slippery, silver wrapper with the name of a big city on it, you may be surprised to learn that cream cheese from a good cheese shop is not only *pure* cream cheese (without vegetable gum) but is quite a different order of cheese. Or try Neufchâtel, a flavorful cheese that resembles cream cheese.

The best feta cheese — the main attraction in many a Greek salad, and great for eating just with bread once you get past the salt barrier — may lie waiting, not in your supermarket, but in a cheese store or in a Greek or Middle Eastern specialty shop.

### *Storage*

Cheese should be wrapped tightly — in foil, in a plastic bag, whatever keeps air out — and stored in a cool place like your refrigerator. If a cheese begins to dry out, you can put a damp cloth around it. Leftover cheese should be returned to the icebox as soon as convenient. (Please don't be rude to your guests.)

"Okay, when is he going to get to the good part? When is he going to face the Fear of Mold?"

This is it, brother. And perhaps it's the parting of the ways. I hope not, but for just this once you may have to go on trust. You see, after a while cheese *gets moldy on the outside,* even though you are keeping it tightly wrapped. But do not pitch it out. Why? Because inside that mold is *good cheese.*

"No, it can't be. There's mold there. It's horrible."

Did you ever consider how cheese is made?

"Oh, come on, I don't want your big lecture on the technology of cheese production."

Just one point. Cheese comes about as a result of a mold.

"No!"

And when you make some cheeses you actually get all this mold that is peeled away, revealing cheese inside.

"Really?"

So when *your* cheese at home gets moldy, consider it a sign that what you have inside is still cheese.

"No kidding?"

No kidding. But I'm not saying that you should encourage this crummy mold to hang around the outside of your cheese. Sooner or later it's inevitable. The cheese gets lonely or something. But to ward off mold for as long as possible, keep it wrapped tightly.

"Okay. I am not afraid of you, mold. Bring on the mold! My knife is at the ready."

### *The Power of Cheese: The Great Buttermilk Conversion*
If you know someone who detests buttermilk — you? — this adventure will provide an experience both stupefying and deeply significant. For the scenario about to be described suggests that some, perhaps many, of our abhorrences are not based on physiological incompatibilities or even psychological repugnance, but upon irrelevant associations.

This is what you do.

Fill a drinking glass with **buttermilk** and hand it to the potential convert, the confirmed and probably skeptical buttermilk detester. While he is holding the glass, ask the following question:

"Do you like cottage cheese?"

The answer to this will almost invariably be yes. (In case it is no, take back the glass, drink it yourself, and tell him that it won't work.)

If the answer is yes, then simply announce in firm and steady tones that he is about to drink **liquid cottage cheese** and *immediately* have him take *one sip.*

That is all. Sip — and presto! He now likes buttermilk. (Conversions can even take place over the telephone, but it's not as enjoyable.) The conversion is real and permanent.

Now this story may seem laughable or frivolous, but actually it is quite serious. What does it mean when we don't like something? Are there different kinds of not liking, all of which we tend to lump together into one type of unpleasantness?

I have since discovered that in reality there are very few foods that are actually repelled by my organism on the basis of taste in all of its elaborations, including flavor, aroma, texture, and so on.

Food for thought, perhaps.*

### *At the End*
All cheeses, not just those for cooking, should be brought to room temperature before serving — except cottage cheese and

*One of the benefits of this conversion is not wasting buttermilk after only part of a container has been used for baking something or after an even smaller amount has gone into making the miraculous *crème fraîche* (page 104).

yogurt. When the cheese is cold, much of its flavor remains in suspended animation.

A final word on buying cheese. There are splendid cheeses that I have purposely not even mentioned by name, such as Stilton, Port du Salut, Muenster, Gouda, Gorgonzola, Finnish Lappi, and on and on. (There are hundreds.) Discover them yourself. Don't wait for some book to tell you what cheese is best. Also, cheeses that you don't like at first may eventually become favorites, so don't be too uppity.

Almost no one ever likes Norwegian goat's milk cheese on the very first bite.

. . . . . . . . . . . . . . . . . . . . . . . . . . . . . . . . . . . . . . . . . . . . . . . . . .

GUIDE TO
## Quiche of Many Kinds

Sauté diced ONIONS in BUTTER with a CRUSHED GARLIC CLOVE, some CHOPPED CELERY, WHITE WINE, and some LEMON JUICE. Beat 2 EGGS lightly with 1½ cups half-and-half (3 EGGS for a very rich filling), and add along with a cup each of either GRUYÈRE AND CHEDDAR or GRUYÈRE AND PARMESAN (all grated), SALT, PEPPER, CINNAMON (not too much), NUTMEG (a big pinch, only), CAYENNE (a small pinch). Sprinkle PAPRIKA on top.

Make a PASTRY CRUST (see page 235). You can use UN-BLEACHED WHITE FLOUR, or ¾ WHOLE WHEAT AND ¼ UN-BLEACHED WHITE. After rolling out, put waxed paper over the crust and some RAW DRIED BEANS to hold it down (this is traditional; obviously there are many other things that will work, such as hard cash). Put in a 400° oven for 10 minutes. Remove the waxed paper and put back for 5 or 10 more minutes at 375° until *just* turning brown. This way your crust will never be soggy.

Pour in the filling and bake in a 350° oven for 35 to 45 minutes, until a knife comes out clean (it's okay if it's a little sweaty).

For an ASPARAGUS QUICHE, use 2 or 3 inches of the tips and season with TARRAGON.

For a ZUCCHINI QUICHE, cut into rounds and salt them to

draw out the water (this is important). Then add to sauté (with BASIL, maybe?).

For a CRAB QUICHE, CANNED CRAB will have to do for most of us, and it's fine.

Here's a curious one: SPINACH AND RAISIN.

Also, invent your own.

. . . . . . . . . . . . . . . . . . . . . . . . . . . . . . . . . . . . . . . . . . . . .
. . . . . . . . . . . . . . . . . . . . . . . . . . . . . . . . . . . . . . . . . . . . .

GUIDE TO
**Pastry Crust (for Quiche and Pies)**

For a SINGLE 9-INCH CRUST: Mix about a cup and a half of FLOUR with about ¼ teaspoon SALT (estimate) and cut in a cool stick (½ cup) of BUTTER. You can use a pastry blender or two butter knives, but I prefer floured fingers. Don't let your palms come in contact with the dough; keep your fingers cold. You can use the trick of *running cold water on the main artery of your wrist.* Work quickly and lightly, reducing the butter to pieces the size of coarse cornmeal, or slightly larger. Uniformity is not important. Sprinkle ice water over the mixture a tablespoon at a time, mixing lightly with your fingers (or a fork). Use *just enough* water (no more than ¼ cup, probably less) to shape the dough gently into a ball that holds together. Roll it into waxed paper and let it chill in the refrigerator for half an hour.

Flour the board — or use a cold countertop. (Marble is the ideal. Hunt around for a slab.) Dust some flour on a rolling pin and roll out gently from the center to the edge in four directions, turning to shape it into a circle. Be careful about rolling out to the very end, for you will crack the dough. (Any holes in the dough should be patched with the dough itself.) Occasionally lift the dough so it doesn't stick. You can even turn it over if you like. Roll *only* outward, never toward the center. When it's a couple of inches larger than the pan, lift it either by folding it in quarters or by rolling it back on the rolling pin, and transport it to the pie pan. For a single crust, flute the edge. For a double crust, leave enough extra to join the upper crust. Prick the bottom all over with a fork.

Try to avoid *shiny* metal pans for quiche and pies.

For a DOUBLE CRUST, you don't have to double the amount. 2½ cups UNSIFTED FLOUR, ¾ cup BUTTER (or other shortening), ½ teaspoon SALT, should do. Roll out separately, of course. Though it's a bit heavier — and a little more velvety — I prefer UNBLEACHED WHITE FLOUR. But you may not. (You can also use ¾ WHOLE WHEAT AND ¼ UNBLEACHED WHITE.)

. . . . . . . . . . . . . . . . . . . . . . . . . . . . . . . . . . . . . . . . . . . . . . . .
. . . . . . . . . . . . . . . . . . . . . . . . . . . . . . . . . . . . . . . . . . . . . .

GUIDE TO
**Making Cheese (Try This and Feel Ancient)**

Boil MILK, about ½ gallon. Remove from the heat and *slowly* add the JUICE FROM A LEMON just until the milk separates — no more, or the cheese will taste a little sour. Cover and let stand for 10 to 15 minutes. Pour (or ladle) into a dishcloth or a *cheesecloth!* (several thicknesses) over a bowl. In about an hour, you have CHEESE. If you can find a way to press the cheese as it's straining through (a tofu box with a hole in the bottom works), it will come out firmer, which makes it better for spreading.

. . . . . . . . . . . . . . . . . . . . . . . . . . . . . . . . . . . . . . . . . . . . . . . .

# 27
# Grains

I'm a veritable *nut* on grains. I love them, and I think most people do. A lot of folks are now discovering "new" grains, grains that are so old that many people thought they were too peculiar to eat. This was probably a cover-up for the Fear of Hardiness, behind which was an anxiety that these grains are so sturdy that they don't "respond properly" to modern bleaching methods.

As an example of an ancient grain, take millet. It's one thing when it's cooked alone (I'm not that crazy about it, but some people are); however, when combined it has an *entirely different* effect. If someone doesn't know this, he or she is liable to get some birdseed (millet) and cook it up and perhaps — pugh! — there goes the Great Millet Adventure. Too bad! Because when millet is cooked right along with, for example, brown rice (about 2 or 3 parts rice to 1 part millet), the result is very satisfying both in flavor and texture. A most amiable dish.

Interesting results can be achieved by simply mixing some of the current crop of pure grain cold cereals — those with *just* grains — with other grains like rice, bulgur, or kasha (buckwheat). This is a moderate way for persons to get into natural grains without immediately cutting themselves off from the

security of their packaged past. It would be unfortunate if too sudden a contact with a real, unmonkeyed-with, earth-cereal substance should put someone off who is trying to be more receptive to an essential, immemorial grain.

### Grain and Fear

Let's call up what is probably the major fear connected with cooking grain; perhaps by acknowledging it, we can proceed.

While we're waiting for it to appear, and while you are imagining an especially insidious batch of barley overflowing and swelling to fill the entire kitchen, I must warn you that the fear that I am speaking about is so inconsequential that we don't really believe it has much power over us even when it does come to light. It is the Fear of Confusion Because All These Grains Look Like Sort of Pale Brownish, Off-White Little Things — and What's the Difference in Cooking Whole Grains and Cereals *and Why Bother When I Can Buy Packages of Known Things?* Enough said.

## Whole Grains vs. Cereals

*Whole grains* are those grains that can be cooked up whole, of which there are only five: *brown or white rice, barley, buck-wheat or kasha* (which is not strictly a grain but looks and tastes like one), *millet,* and *bulgur wheat* (which, though a "cracked" grain, is prepared and served like other whole grains).

*Cereals* are grains that have been coarsely ground (when they're ground to a powder, you get *flour*), and they often have words like *cream* (because cereals cook to a creamier consistency than whole grains), *grits, flakes,* or *meal* attached to them; e.g., rice cream, soy grits, wheat flakes, cornmeal.

Amazing things happen in life! In one stroke half the Fear of Grain . . . dissolves.

### Ways to Cook Whole Grains

Common to all methods: (1) Unless the grain is prewashed, rinse it until the water runs clear. (2) Once boiling liquid has gotten into the act, do not stir unless you want things to get gummy. (Maybe you do.) (3) If possible, use heavy pots with tight lids (as usual). (4) You'll probably want to add salt — about ¼ teaspoon per cup of grain.

*Sauté first, then steam.* Sauté lightly in oil, butter, or both, with or without diced onions. Stir almost constantly, watching carefully so the grains don't burn. After a few minutes, when the particles are browning nicely, pour in salted, boiling water (or any kind of stock — use a bouillon cube at least; or for a milky texture use milk. Simmer over low heat — as low as possible — in a tightly covered pan. Seal with a dishtowel between lid and pot for an even fluffier result. When done, let stand for a few minutes; toss and fluff with a fork. This is the same basic method as for Rice à Gauche (page 82). Of course you're free to add anything you like to the pan, such as celery, garlic . . . you know.

An almost obligatory method for kasha and bulgur, it can be used successfully for millet, rice, and barley as well.

*Trickle, boil.* Trickle the grain into boiling, salted liquid, stirring the whole time. Then cover and proceed as above.

*Devil-may-care boil.* Use lots of boiling, salted water in an open pan, tossing the grain into it merrily (rice works especially well; so does barley). After it's cooked — or better yet, slightly undercooked and steamed and dried out over low heat — drain through a sieve. This way probably loses more of the nutrients to the cooking water, but I'm sure it can't be too disastrous since entire civilizations have thrived hardily while cooking rice this way.

Which method you use depends on your style, but also on the results you want. Sautéing first will give a nuttier flavor. Steaming, a more neutral flavor. (Incidentally, if you want a creamier texture, start with the grain in the cold liquid just before you begin bringing it to a boil.) Cooking in the open pot, similar to the conventional method of cooking pasta, gives a somewhat firmer, more separated grain, which is very good for immediate dining as well as for stuffing and for casseroles.

Yes, grains can be baked. It is accomplished in a medium (temperature, not size) oven. But it's nicer when there are other items mingled in, layered through, dotted on, and spread over. This is called a casserole and we'll visit them in Chapter 31.

### Proportions

Just a rough guide. Why? Because the grains simmered in liquid will, in due time, absorb all the liquid presented to them as long as it isn't outrageously in excess. Actually, it's more common that longer cooking is required, so more, not less, liquid is needed. (Just put more in.) If, by mistake, you should have extra water, it's better to drain it off before the grain gets too mushy. Use forks to handle the grain so you don't bruise it. If it's already been sautéed, less cooking will be needed — and less liquid.

The basic rule is: the faster the cooking, the less liquid you need. (Doesn't that make sense?) By the way, another reason why exact proportions can't be given is that the older the grain, the longer it takes to cook. But don't worry. There's leeway. When you hear things sputtering or cracking in the pot, it's probably done. At least all the water is absorbed. Don't let it burn, though it will be a bit browner on the bottom.

The approximate proportion of liquid for cooking most

whole grains (including the ones we called whole grains for practical purposes) is *twice as much liquid as grain* — if you like rice mushier, you can use 2½ cups. Barley and wild rice (I slipped this one in. It's actually not a grain, but a — costly — grass seed that grows in wet, northern climates): *three times* as much liquid as grain (though barley can take a little less).

**Times**
Kasha and bulgur (which I prefer sautéed first, then steamed), take about 15 minutes, sometimes a bit more. Millet, 30 to 45 minutes (it can cook right along with brown rice); barley, about 45 to 50 minutes; wild rice a little longer.

**A Sudden Summary**
Just remember that the quicker-cooking grains get roughly 2 cups liquid to 1 cup grain, and cook them fast: 15 to 20 minutes. The slower-cooking ones like brown rice (2½ cups liquid to 1 of grain) and barley and wild rice (3 to 1) take about 45 to 50 minutes, give or take 15 minutes. Taste.

**The Whole Grains**
*Brown rice.* Yes, everyone knows by now that this is "real" rice. The problem is, it's so "real" — that is, substantial — that for some it can be a bit heavy in a meal that is already weighted down with meat, bread and butter, vegetables, and other courses. I can't entirely disagree with this. It depends to a great extent on what you're used to. Brown rice with beans or cheese or tofu (soy bean curd) is also an excellent alternative to meat. (The word *substitute* is demeaning for such ancient and highly esteemed foods that have borne up whole civilizations.)

And if you're very hungry or it's cold out, or you're having a lighter meat such as chicken, brown rice can be a hearty addition.

As for flavor, I don't think anyone can deny that brown rice is stronger than white rice. Of course, one of the advantages of white rice is that its flavor is more adaptable for assimilating other flavors without intruding.

In view of the much greater nutritional value of whole

(brown) rice and its pleasing flavor, you might consider making it a staple in your diet.

*White rice.* Already a staple in your diet.

Rice comes in two general varieties: long grain, which is usually preferred for rice dishes, and short grain, the common choice for stuffings. But why not do the opposite sometimes? They're both good.

*Barley.* Most of us are familiar with it in Scotch barley soup — it's often used to thicken a soup — and it makes a fine combination with either white or brown rice (it can be cooked along with the latter) in a casserole or steamed on top of the stove. By itself, it's chewy and somewhat heavy; the rice combination (perhaps two or three times more rice than barley) will tone it down.

*Cracked wheat/bulgur.* To be precise, bulgur is cracked wheat that has been precooked and is therefore a little browner. (Ala is a trade name for bulgur.) True cracked wheat will take about 10 minutes longer to cook than bulgur. Tabbouleh is an ancient Middle Eastern *salad* made with bulgur (which merely soaks for an hour in cold water — no cooking), with parsley and mint as the major seasonings. Bulgur combines well with other grains, such as buckwheat or rice.

*Buckwheat/kasha.* Considering its hearty flavor, it cooks very rapidly. It is actually a Siberian grass seed. Although consumed in many climates, it has a very warming effect on the body, making it especially suitable in colder climes. Buckwheat "groats" are often cooked the following way, and for good reason — they're delicious.

Put the kasha in a heated pan and mix with *a lightly beaten egg.* Sauté over medium heat until *dry.* Then proceed as usual, pouring in the boiling liquid (which is really much nicer when stock or at least a bouillon cube is used). Toss with butter when cooked.

*Millet.* Supposedly, the only alkaline grain and very nutritious. Sauté it first (as on page 239). Mix it into bulgur. *Superb* cooked with brown rice. The crunchy little yellow particles make them a good blend in other grains and in bread. (Just toss them in.)

### Accompaniments

*Tiny ones.* Nuts and seeds (both toasted). Seasonings like celery seed (careful, just a pinch or two for a couple of servings), basil, thyme, marjoram, sage (very sparing), good Heavens! almost anything . . . but also try these grains without any seasoning at all except salt, pepper, butter — and perhaps a little lemon sprinkled over at the end.

*Larger ones.* After all we've been through together it seems hardly necessary to say anything about vegetables and such in grains. Onions, sautéed first in the skillet with or without garlic. The mighty trio (to be exalted in Chapter 30, on Soup): onions, carrots, and celery. Mushrooms put in near the end . . . Oh come on, I don't really have to tell you what to try. It's insulting. I won't.

A word, though, on a few combinations you might overlook. *Plain yogurt* is a refreshing addition.

Subtle and pleasing combinations of all kinds can be discovered, such as the corn tortilla, brown rice, mushroom, chopped spinach, avocado with lemon plate. (Simple guide at end of chapter.)

Beans go with grains.

And gravy, forever.

### For Breakfast: Cereal

Just cook with more water, over *very* low heat for best results. Cereal doesn't mind being stirred. The thinner the pot, the more you'll have to stir it to avoid burning. If you can't avoid it, use or improvise a double boiler; that is, a pot in which you have whatever it is you wish to keep hot, and a pot below with hot or, in this case, boiling water.

It's easy to remember what to do. A basic method is the one described earlier (page 5) for oatmeal and Wheatena. Trickle the cereal into boiling water, stirring all the time, and cook over medium heat for 2 or 3 minutes. Then either remove from the heat, cover tightly, and let stand (as in the case of the above two cereals; rolled oats cook quickly, and Wheatena is already partially cooked) or, with most other cereals, not precooked, put into the double boiler for about 20 minutes or so.

For a creamier texture, start with the grain in cold water.

For a nuttier flavor, sauté first (as on page 239).

Where have I heard all this before? (Whole grain cooking, earlier in this chapter.)

*Proportions.* Rolled oats and partially cooked cereals require *twice as much water as cereal.* For other uncooked cereals: *three and a half to four times as much water.*

*An Exception: Cornmeal.* To eliminate the granularity of the cornmeal, put it into an equal amount of cold water, say 1 cup each. Bring 3 more cups of salted water (no less) to the boil and add the cornmeal-water mixture. Cook over medium heat, stirring frequently. When it thickens, it's done. It doesn't take long — about 7 or 8 minutes. This is a famous substance: *cornmeal mush.* In my opinion, the best thing to do with it is either:

1. Spread it as thin as sliced bread and put it in the icebox. For breakfast the next day, fry it in bacon fat or butter and oil as you would French Toast. Serve the same delicious way.

2. Don't make the cornmeal mush exactly the way I said. Instead, put some red-pepperish things into it: a few pinches of paprika, a tiny smidgeon of cayenne. What you now have is the famous Italian dish *polenta.* You can cook it with some grated cheese; you can top it with tomato sauce; you can put diced onions . . . Oh, you know these things.

Corn (which is *maize* for English people since to them *corn* means "wheat") is a Native American food, America's gift to the world.

# 28
# Primo Pasta

I shall bite to the tooth.

A new and simple method of cooking anything is a big event. Because when good ways of cooking pasta — or anything else — materialize, they abide for millennia. But even though this new method was discovered in Italy (legitimizing factor), due to lack of publicity, the number of buoyant psychological states wrecked by the serving of mushy, overcooked pasta, the anxious hovering over hot, steamy pots, and all the rest have probably contributed as much as anything else to the present precariousness of the world situation.

In other words, after you find out how to cook pasta this way, you should inform other people.

I became privy to this particular contribution to the saving of the world when I purchased some imported Agnesi linguine. Right there on the side of the package was a revolutionary message direct from Italy.

I'm not going to quote these presumably perfectly clear instructions. Why? Because at the beginning of the world a gremlin (or *gremlinone*) was appointed to make sure that all package directions — even Italian ones — would be incomplete or misleading.

Here's how to cook pasta: Put a whole lot of water — I mean a *lot* — in a big pot and as much salt as you think you need for whatever amount of pasta you're going to cook. Then heat it until it's boiling rapidly. This gives the salt a chance to dissolve properly. If and only if it's really inferior pasta, to prevent sticking pitch a little olive oil into the cooking water. But if your pasta doesn't stick together, don't do it.

Immerse the pasta as quickly as possible without breaking it so that it cooks evenly. *Stir it around;* then cover the pot to bring the water back to a boil as fast as possible. Remove the lid. At this point, you may reduce the heat a little as long as the boiling remains rapid and rolling. Vigorous boiling in plenty of water will keep the pasta from sticking. As I said, if you're using an inferior grade of noodle, a tablespoon of oil helps, too.

Cook it uncovered for *2 minutes.* (For heavier pasta, like rigatoni or big macaroni, you'll need 3 minutes.) Then stir it around once or twice, *take the whole pot off the heat,* and cover it with a dishtowel and a lid. If you don't have a clean dishtowel, don't worry. A tight lid will do.

Now leave it and do something else.

How long? Well, when you cooked pasta the old way (which you will never do again), you had to watch very attentively because the shift from not being cooked to being overcooked happened quickly and *stealthily.* Of course, I'm talking about *al dente* (firm to the tooth) pasta, which is how pasta was created to be eaten. This new method is more gentle and doesn't require such tense hovering.

When you cooked pasta the old way, you probably knew that for a decent result, you cooked it only about three-quarters of the time it said on the package. If it said cook spaghetti for 12 minutes, you cooked it for 8 or 9 minutes. But with this new method, *you keep it covered and off the heat for the length of time stated on the package.*

There are many advantages to this method. Obviously, it saves fuel; and because the pasta doesn't degenerate into mush, it proves to be easier to cook to the right consistency. Above all, this still quite secret method produces a full-bodied, perfectly cooked, delicious pasta. Even leftovers — if there are any — taste better and are more wholesome.

That's right, more nutritious. Look at the water in which you have cooked the pasta. What do you notice — or rather, what do you *not* notice? The water is clear. THERE'S NO WHITE STUFF MILLING AROUND IN THERE. You know how it is, looking at all that foamy water pasta usually ends up in. Maybe you say something like, "Hey, that's *my* pasta. So how come you water bubbles are always scaring my noodles or beating them up or something and making them fork over their white stuff?" (Nobody seems to know what the white stuff is, exactly.) "There might be some vitamin W in there or traces of convivium" (these are substances essential to health that haven't been discovered yet) "and they're being destroyed by naked exposure to the elements." Even the package agrees: "It will be noticed that the water from the [pasta] is almost clear, evidence that it has retained its *valuable content* which, if cooked in any other way, is to a large extent lost" (Agnesi linguine package; italics mine).

Here are three ways to tell when the spaghetti, linguine, fettuccine, and so on, are done.

Method one: When the whitish starchy circle that takes up the entire cross section of the uncooked spaghetti noodle has *just* shrunk to nothing, the spaghetti (and so on) is *done*. However, this may seem to be too complicated (even though it isn't).

Method two: Throw a noodle against the wall. If it sticks, it's done. (No kidding.)

Method three: Taste it. It should be firm to the tooth.

When the pasta is ready, drain it, but do not rinse — or make it too dry. Be ready to toss immediately with softened butter, salt (if needed), and pepper; don't let it just sit around. Freshly chopped parsley? Maybe sprinkle some freshly grated Parmesan or Romano cheese over the top. Or heat some minced garlic slowly in pure olive oil until it turns golden, add some salt and pepper, and after mixing it with the pasta, you can toss with the parsley or the cheese. **Or great quantities of** *fresh* **basil.**

Cooking naked pasta will inspire any cook — new or old — to spread, to mingle, to blend. One day soon, you will arrive in eating heaven.

Where words fail.

GUIDE TO
## One of Many Ultimate Garlic Sauces

3–5 cloves of GARLIC, crushed, ½ cube of BUTTER, a *small dash* (only) of RED WINE VINEGAR (if you were measuring this, it would be about ¼ teaspoon), which will keep the butter from burning.
Cook until the garlic *just* begins to brown.

GUIDE TO
## Billy's Restoration Lasagna (and Real Spaghetti Sauce)

This will provide you with three mouthwatering but not inexpensive Lasagnas, enough for a good-sized gathering. To make just one, divide everything by three.

Sauté a chopped-up ONION, 5 or 6 cloves of crushed GARLIC, a HALF CARROT, diced, in OLIVE OIL and a little BUTTER. Add 6 *mild,* ITALIAN FENNEL SAUSAGES with skins peeled off (the sausages will break up immediately) and ¼ pound HAMBURGER. Cook until the sausages are gray and the hamburger loses its pink — about 5 minutes. Then add 5 cans of TOMATO PASTE (a good brand, like Contadina) and 2 large cans of ITALIAN PLUM TOMATOES. Rinse out the tomato paste cans by adding 4 or 5 cans of WATER, add 1½ cups of RED WINE (no more), a good pinch BASIL and MARJORAM, HALF A BAY LEAF, and about 20 ANISE SEEDS. This is the SAUCE, and it should, at this stage, be about the texture of cream of wheat; that is, *almost* liquid.

Simmer (occasional, wee bubbles only) for a good 1½ hours, stirring every 15 or 20 minutes so it doesn't burn. It should get nice and thick. You can always add more water if you need to.

In three loaf pans, 5 by 9 by 3 inches, put down a thin layer of sauce, a layer of LASAGNA NOODLES (see this chapter for cooking guide — being large, they'll require 3 minutes initial boiling), 3 squares of MOZZARELLA CHEESE, 4 rounds of MUENSTER, about 8 dollops (or some such number) of RICOTTA, a good layer of SAUCE, GRATED PARMESAN AND ROMANO CHEESE; then repeat starting with LASAGNA, then putting 4 squares of mozzarella and 3 rounds of Muenster. Repeat once more and on top of the last layer of Parmesan and Romano, ladle a couple of big spoons of sauce.

You'll need in all about 1½ pounds each of mozzarella and Muenster and about 2 pounds of ricotta.

Cook in a 350° oven for 45 minutes (maybe less), uncovered. One bold way to test for doneness is to hold back the top portion with a knife and dip your finger into the middle; if you cry out "Ouch!" it's done.

Lasagna freezes well and can be heated up in about half an hour (maybe less). The addition of the Muenster makes it extra hearty (and rich).

For a REAL SPAGHETTI SAUCE, instead of peeling the SAUSAGES, cut them into, say, THIRDS and then proceed as with the Lasagna Sauce.

GUIDE TO
**Homemade Pasta**

Try to get SEMOLINA FLOUR, 3 cups. Stir in a little SALT if desired. Make a well in the center and break 4 EGGS into it. Move the flour gradually into the eggs to combine. Knead on a lightly floured board for about 10 minutes, until the dough is smooth and elastic. If it's too dry, add a little water, if too wet, flour. But first, try to make do. Cover with a damp cloth and let rest for half an hour. Divide into thirds and roll out, one at a time, into 4-inch widths — paper thin — with a lightly floured rolling pin (using no more flour than necessary). Let it dry for half an hour. Before it's too dry, shape it into a long tubular roll, and slice across to make noodles.

These will cook about two thirds as fast as bought noodles, maybe less.

# PART SIX

# BLENDING

# 29
# How to Invent Food: Innovative Cookery

"What say you to a piece of beef, and mustard?"
— Shakespeare, *The Taming of the Shrew*

What does this mean, innovative cookery? I can tell you that it has nothing whatever to do with being a head chef in an expensive restaurant, though such a personage may indeed be and probably is such a cook.

Who is innovative? Anyone who cooks with what's available, with what's reasonable, with what a friend brought over, with variety, without being fussy about following someone else's procedure all the time. Just "being at home" with cooking.

It may surprise you that many so-called innovative cooks (like my grandmother) never considered cooking to be anything else. In fact, many folks would assume that a person who *all the time* measured out everything exactly as some other person ordered, never deviating, would be a strange person indeed.

You see, everyone is capable of feeling free about cooking, not just a few highly attuned persons. It begins with the physical, sensory contact with the food, experiencing its taste, texture, aroma, and how it looks.

Without this primary interest in food, which by nature all of us possess, we can't expect to get very far. But even a little genuine appreciation of food as it is cooked, sniffed, tasted, and touched can embolden the cook to try a reasonable "something different" or "Why didn't I do this before?" (Sprinkle chives over sautéed oysters; add some minced scallions to the rice that you sautéed and then simmered; maybe you'll even green it up more by adding a whole lot of minced parsley at the end . . . and so many other possibilities.)

Innovative cookery simply means that a cook might cook something differently than he or she has ever thought of doing. It may mean combining ingredients one never considered before. Even garnishing something a new way can qualify. It doesn't matter if someone else has done it. Someone probably has. But so what? The purpose is not to be awarded a decoration but to provide a fresh, tasty, and appropriate dish at the table.

I have just mentioned the two basic kinds of innovation. (But let's not get all puffed up. If we want to talk about *real* innovation, of another order, we have to look at something like the original use of Leavening. Or of Fire itself.)

One kind is the variation, combination, and elaboration of cooking *methods*, including how food is cut up, what medium it cooks in, and how it's cooked. One begins with a method of food preparation — a simple sauté or bake. Then after a while, through experiences that include following recipes, intentional deviations, even accidents, the cook begins to acquire a more flowing approach to methods. Food is parboiled, partially sautéed, various foods cooked perhaps differently are put together and baked, pastry crusts are filled with egg or fruit or other mixtures, and so on. More and more, small things, nuances, begin to be emphasized and even dominate, depending on the style and temperament of the cook.

The other basic innovation is the choice of ingredients for a particular dish. This is something that is easily practiced and can immediately give interesting and satisfying results.

But here again there are two life situations. Having food on hand and wondering what to prepare, or having a yen for something really different, whether or not you have all the ingredients, which may necessitate a trip to the store.

Suppose you have a number of disparate ingredients, for example, some of these: lima beans, rice, chocolate, anchovies, bacon, potatoes, apples, noodles, cold chicken, turnips, eggs, tomatoes, bananas (or just check what your situation is *now*), and of course onions, garlic, lemon, and parsley, all of which should be permanent inhabitants of your kitchen. The variety of dishes and subtle variants (even without the staples) an experienced cook could provide! And so can you. It all starts from doing it for the first time.

Common to most such innovations is the application of pretasting. Call into play your mind's taste (or your stomach's taste, or wherever you experience it). To sidestep the Fear of Being Overwhelmed by All the Possible Foods There Are, you might begin by combining any two or three items, one of which is a "receiver," like lettuce, rice, noodles, or let us take baby lima beans (not canned), which, relative to many other foods, are bland enough to be very receptive to many additions. Dried limas, which are cooked for a much longer time than fresh ones, are often simmered with a ham hock — as compatible a combination, surely, as bread and butter. Pretasting a fresh lima, you might modestly consider that some crumbled bacon would be a tasty addition. It doesn't matter that almost everyone who has cooked limas a fair number of times has probably cooked them this way — if it's new for *you*.

Shell some *baby* lima beans and immediately put them into boiling salted water, enough to just cover the beans. Cover and simmer them for 20 minutes or so, until just tender. Add the bacon bits. (Occasionally add sour cream and dill at the end of cooking with or without the bacon. To avoid curdling, don't boil the sour cream.) Or cook the bacon in a pan in which you add some chopped onion. When the beans are done, add them to this mixture.

"Wait a minute, here. Remember you told us about chombas when you were talking about cooking vegetables?"

Yes, certainly.

"Well, the bacon and onions are right out of chombas."

I appreciate this opportunity to remind you about chombas (page 182). Remember, fresh or appropriate for *you* (and your diners) — that's what counts. If it happens to be unusual, or even startling, well that's okay too — if it tastes good. The more you try, the more you'll begin to discover that some foods have flavors we often fail to discern.

These adventures in combining foods are not absolutely foolproof. (They wouldn't be adventures if they were, would they?) Pretasting itself is certainly not foolproof. But this is mainly in the positive sense. By that I mean, you will not often produce ill-tasting dishes, but there may be combinations that really do work that might surprise you. (Tomato juice — in a walnut loaf?) But any blend, once experienced in fact, can be recalled to the inner taste in a precise way later on.

If pretasting something gives you the willies, then leave it alone. (Anchovies and chocolate? Not for me.) We're not trying to discover a method for making the bizarre, even if some flashy gourmet cook makes it work. (That's okay too.) We need to discriminate between what is bizarre (chocolate anchovies) and what is fresh (Rice Going Bananas with Anise, at the end of the chapter. Or if that's too strange for you, how about bananas in cranberry sauce? or anchovies in a potato salad?)

### Enlarging the Vocabulary

I know the following suggestion may seem naive and even simple-minded, but this actually works as a method to discover country-road alternatives to the freeways each of us so often goes down.

Turn to the Index at random and point at something. (Sausage.) Then something else. (Scallops.) What do you think? I think that the sausage is likely to overwhelm the delicate scallops. But perhaps clams with a pasta like linguine or fettuccine with sausage added. Pretaste. Would you want to try this? Maybe you would, but someone else may not. Clams stuffed in eggplant? Oyster sauce in the tomato sauce? Feel free. The point is not to be always creating the unusual but what's reasonable. It may be something you've never had or simply have forgotten about. (Chicken livers and polenta.)

Instead of selecting two random ingredients and adding a third to bring the dish together, try (maybe just once) to choose *three* random ingredients and see if they can be harmonized into a pleasing chord. This is an intriguing experiment, but you have to be much more conservative here. Unpleasant dissonances do exist. Many things may not work. (Broccoli, ice cream, and watermelon? Okay, so you've discovered a way. I'm sorry I won't be able to partake of it with you. I have a pressing appointment on that particular day.)

### *Reality*
When you actually taste the real live dish, it will probably shock you a little. Not because it's bad, but because living food has a dimension (literally) of flavor and substance that imagined food can never have. By accepting this, and by experiencing the results of your pretasting experiment, you will become more confident. And the entire experience of pretasting will become more and more organic.

If you really try this, or something comparable, you'll even find that an occasional partial failure (complete failure? remember Lucifer Toast!) will be taken in stride.

### *Caution*
Certain basic combinations should be approached with the utmost care or even avoided, not only on grounds of incompatibility of taste, but also (according to some nutritionists) on gastrointestinal grounds. One such combination is fruit with vegetables. Obviously, there is fruit salad with lettuce and other examples we can all think of; and there are time-honored kinships like turnips, apples, and potatoes. Nevertheless, approach these combinations cautiously. Fruit with grain also needs a conservative approach until you gain some experience.

And of course there are avoidances that hardly need to be mentioned, such as most vegetables with desserts, and so on.

### *Not All Adventures Are Swashbuckling*
The more we go adventuring in cooking, truly adventuring — without necessarily giving up any interest we may have in conducting bolder experiments — the more we begin to appreciate subtler variations. For example, everyone understands that eggs basted with butter from a spoon, or turned over, or steamed with a lid are all slightly different. As long as the

ingredients are compatible and pleasing, a welcome, new experience may arise from the way something is cooked rather than some bold "new" harmony of flavors. (Consider the vast number of baked batters and doughs — almost infinite — composed essentially of the same few ingredients.)

When you begin to be actively interested in these finer distinctions, you have reached a new stage. Experimenting with different ingredients is important, but without sensitivity to the processes and microprocesses of cooking, it soon grows wearisome. Every cook knows what I'm talking about, and each in his own way has experienced something similar. Through cooking, through tasting, through planning meals, we gradually discover more of what exists even beyond the conscientious and loving preparation of the individual dishes.

Who knows the harmony of food and how it is revealed through the reality of cooking? The tradition that is *cooking* goes on developing, growing, and plugging its holes, encouraging those whose attempts are naive, not taken in by the merely flamboyant, and relatively unconcerned with fashions and revolutions of thought, handing down its lore through the centuries.

Did a scientist — or an artist — discover nutmeg and spinach? bacon and eggs? tabbouleh and mint? pears and cheese? duck and turnips? gingerbread with ham!

The lines between the scientist, the artist, and the cook are not always easy to distinguish.

· · · · · · · · · · · · · · · · · · · · · · · · · · · · · · · · · · · · · · · · · · · · · ·

GUIDE TO
### Rice Going Bananas with Anise

Norma left before giving me the recipe. Three ingredients. How about cooking the RICE with ANISE SEEDS, quickly and lightly sautéing the BANANAS, and, when the rice is done, stirring the bananas into it until thoroughly blended. Or maybe there's another way. Anyhow, try something. I don't think you'll be disappointed — the second time, at least.

· · · · · · · · · · · · · · · · · · · · · · · · · · · · · · · · · · · · · · · · · · · · · ·

GUIDE TO
## The Marriage of Cranberries and Bananas

Boil any amount of WATER (a cup?) with the equivalent amount of SUGAR for 5 minutes, uncovered, without stirring. Add twice the amount of CRANBERRIES (2 cups?) and *simmer* for about 4 or 5 minutes until the skins pop. You can add some grated ORANGE RIND if you want (about ¼ teaspoon per cup of cranberries is enough here). Chill.

Mix with (room temperature) BANANAS, sliced into the familiar rounds. Make any amount. You can even set up a chain of Cranberry-Banana Shops nationwide.

GUIDE TO
## Sausage and Clam Fettuccine

Cook cut-up SAUSAGES in a little water until they are gray, about 5 minutes, then continue cooking them, covered until they turn brown. Turn frequently. (If you cook them uncovered, they will be crisper, but for this dish you may prefer them softer.)

If you should have fresh CLAMS, you can cook them like mussels (page 377) with just a little lemon juice. For this dish, you can just use canned clams (which are okay and which you'll use anyway).

After the sausages have cooked, add the clams and some GREEN ONIONS (SCALLIONS) and THYME. Heat through, but don't boil the clams or they'll toughen. Toss with cooked FETTUCCINE (see page 245 for cooking pasta).

# 30
# Deep Soup

> In taking soup it is necessary to avoid lifting too much
> in the spoon, or filling the mouth so full as almost to
> stop the breath.
> — St. Jean Baptiste de La Salle,
> *The Rule of Christian Manners and Civility,* 1695

Soup is one of the most profound and important substances on
Earth. Even the stars, according to some, were crystallized out
of cosmic soup. Oh, immortal soup!

"How do you make soup?"

Begin with some water that has things in it; heat it up and
simmer until done.

"Okay, I'm going off to get up a quick batch of soup."

Hold your horses. You can't rush around with soup. It's a
process, and certain processes take time. Fortunately, though,
we aren't in charge of most of them. For example, we don't
actually extract the flavor from a carrot and instill it into the
cooking broth.

"You mean there are little beings hovering over the soup
who do these things?"

How you explain it depends on your cultural upbringing. In
any case, our job is to provide and maintain the working conditions — that is, to care for the soup — and to intervene at
certain times. And a time comes . . . and it's done. And it's
tasty and satisfying.

How to get started? You already have, but you've been
throwing it all away before you've gotten anywhere. Here is a

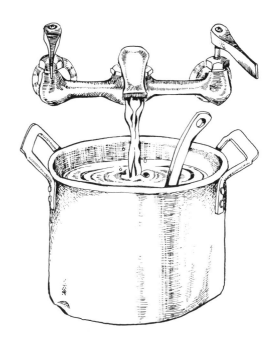

list of certain things you and I have both been throwing out: parsley and spinach stems, weird-looking lettuce and cabbage leaves, celery tops, asparagus stalks, the ends from green beans, from onions, carrots, and zucchini, ugly tomatoes, extra watercress, mushroom stems.

"I sure have been throwing these out. I don't have the time to mess with them."

Instead of throwing this *food* into a bucket, put it into a bag and save it.

"Does this mean that I throw anything at all in there? What about the leftover Brussels sprouts that have been sitting in my icebox for days?"

Certainly not. And one should be conservative in general about the strong-flavored vegetables, such as cabbage, Brussels sprouts, broccoli stalks, and bitter ones, like carrot tops or mustard greens. With gentle cooking and judicious seasoning, these can be delectable in their own right, but use them sparingly, as they may overwhelm more delicate flavors. Tomatoes, of course, will color anything in their favor. It depends on what you want. (I would never reject asparagus or leeks; they have great soup essences.)

Keep putting these little remnants of raw, fresh vegetables — which are actually pearls — into a designated bag. Later, we'll use them. Perhaps tomorrow. Now let's turn our attention to making *stock*.

"Stock. I've always wondered what that was, really."

Stock is the body and soul of a soup. By itself, in fact, it *is* soup, though often its goodness is further refined or enriched.

Beef, chicken, vegetables, fish — each can produce a stock. Soup making is a process. But it can also be viewed as a two-step process: *making stock,* then using the stock as a base for *making soup.* Both are easy, relaxed procedures. If you skip the stock step, what you've really done is to combine the two.

### Making Stock — Substitutes

Let's be honest. I know you're not going to be making stock from scratch very often unless you're cooking daily for a fair number of people, so I won't leave you high and dry. The fact is, you can get by very well with a good canned beef bouillon (not consommé; it's too sweet) or a chicken broth. Whichever one you use, you will dress it up with herbs (at least one should be fresh, like parsley) and maybe other seasoning, and possibly a bit of wine just before taking it off the heat. Hints are given throughout the chapter, and the Guide to Improving Canned Broth is repeated at the end because of its usefulness.

For what they are, taking into account their necessary limitations and their "condensed" flavor (even if the can doesn't say *condensed*), some of these are truly excellent products; I have named a few in the Guide. But there exists no true common measure between them and a good homemade stock — like a record versus a live performance.

For lack of one of these just-mentioned substitutes, a bouillon cube will have to do, and sometimes it does surprisingly well.

Most of the commercial preparations are salty; try to re-member this when adding your own salt.

### Stock (Real)

To make beef stock — also called brown stock — you can use tougher cuts of meat, which usually have more flavor than the more tender cuts and are less expensive. The shank, which includes the shinbone, is a good choice, or the shoulder. It's best to cut the meat into small pieces, *removing the excess fat*. (Excess fat is the enemy of soup.) Bones and their marrow added to the stock are desirable, as they gelatinize the stock while adding their own essences to the pot. As a general guide, use at least twice as much meat as bone, and the bones should be cut up or cracked. It's better to have too little bone than too much because they can make the soup too scummy or gluey for your liking.

Of course, splendid soups can be made with water, a few vegetables, seasoning, and, if you like, something to enrich it, like milk or cream. I mean *wonderful* soup (and we'll make some like this later). But meat stocks, which are easy to pro-duce, are one of the most profound substances employed in all of cooking. And the more people you cook for, the easier it is to have stock on hand because leftover meat and bones can be used.

Where do you get enough bones? A roast has bones in it; when you buy meat, save the bones. Use bones that are left on plates. If you don't have any bones, you can get "soup bones" in the market. A veal knuckle — buy one from your butcher — will thicken the soup beautifully because of its high gelatin content. But if you don't have any bones, you can still make stock. Stock made from cooked and uncooked bones will al-ways be cloudy and will not be the purest of stocks, but there's nothing wrong with it.

Put enough *cold*, salted water in the pot — a large pot, mind you, and preferably a tall one — to cover the bones and meat and a couple of inches more. You're going to cook all this for at least 3, or better, for 4 or 5 hours, so you may need to add more water later if the level drops below the ingredients. Before you tremble at such a commitment, you should know that chicken stock needs only 2 hours, and vegetable stock, only 1. A less well known fact is that if you considerably reduce the amount of stock you are making and cut the meat into small chunks, you can *halve* the time for chicken and beef stock.

How much salt? It depends. If you're going to use all of the stock for soup, then put in about a "pitch" (i.e., a tablespoon, page 41) of salt for about 4 or 5 pounds of meat and bone. Obviously, it's best to undersalt and underseason and adjust at the end; but salt put in at the beginning helps to draw out the juices and flavors from the meat into the stock. However, if you plan to reduce the stock further to use in a *sauce* or *gravy*, *then it's best not to salt it at all* — or very little — since you risk ruining the more concentrated stock with excess salt.

Let's assume for now that the entire stock is going to be used for (delicious) soup. Most likely you will add to the pot for flavoring the great trinity of aromatic vegetables: *onions, carrots*, and *celery*. Onions provide body; carrots, sweetness;* celery, a bit of tang. (Of course, there's much more to it than that.) Now I could specify so much of this and of those, but it's not that precise.

Start out with a large onion (yellow globe ones are excellent), even two, into which sometimes you should stick a couple of whole cloves (but you don't have to). *Do not peel the onion;* the skin will help give a rich color to the stock. A carrot or two chopped coarsely, and you can include a few of the tops if you like, though they are somewhat bitter. A couple stalks of celery, including the leaves. Chop them up in thirds or quarters. You really can't go wrong. These three vegetables are an especially well balanced trio that helps infuse a harmonious spectrum of flavors into the stock. You can always rely on onions, carrots, and celery. There are other excellent flavoring vegetables to consider, but let's get the stock started first.

When do you put all these into the pot? Although there are other ways (there are always other ways), the simplest is to put them all in at the beginning, before you heat the water.

---

*It's especially useful to remember that the natural sugar in carrots will sweeten whatever they're cooking in — as a reminder to use them, but sometimes as a reminder not to.

As far as seasoning goes, I like to put in a half-dozen or so black peppercorns and some herbs at the beginning. But go easy and add more later if need be. A small bay leaf crumbled, or half a large one. An estimated teaspoon or less of thyme — or a half each of thyme and marjoram. Or better yet, a few sprigs of fresh herbs. One or two parsley sprigs, minced or not. These are all very traditional European-American soup seasonings, but of course others can be used. Additional seasoning, however, can best wait until after the lengthy (but for the cook, leisurely) process of stock making. Then, depending on the kind of soup — or sauce — you want, season it accordingly. This certainly doesn't mean that you can't put in a crushed garlic clove (two?) right at the beginning.

The purpose of starting with cold water is to extract the maximum flavor into the stock, which is where you want it, not in the meat. If you have time, soaking the meat in the cold, salted water for a good hour before you begin helps even more.

Bring the entire mixture slowly to a boil. Though many experts suggest that you allow the stock to boil for 5 minutes before reducing it to a quiet simmer, you can reduce the heat immediately and still get excellent results. In either case, you will discover that what is referred to in the trade as scum will probably begin rising to the surface. Skim off this murky stuff with a big spoon for about 5 minutes. Then lower the heat so the stock *simmers.* You can keep skimming the scum occasionally for 20 or 30 minutes more, but a little in the stock won't hurt you; it just makes it murkier than you may like. At any rate, as soon as this brownish substance turns white, it's definitely time to retire the spoon if you haven't already done so, because just as when you cook cereal, the white stuff disappears somewhere into the pot.

The most important thing, along with cutting off the excess fat and not oversalting, is not to let the stock boil (except for those few minutes in the beginning). Once you have reduced the liquid to the required simmer — an occasional bubble gently breaking the surface — especially if you're not well acquainted with your stove, watch the stock to make sure it doesn't eventually return to a boil. This is your only duty during the long simmering process (except to add more water if the level should get lower than the meat). Boiling will toughen the meat and make it more difficult for the flavors to escape into the stock. (If it boils a little, don't get nervous. Just turn the heat down.)

Simmer the stock for at least 3 or 4 hours; in fact, you can let it brew all day (or overnight if your stove is reliable). You can start tasting it after a few hours.

Do you cover the pot or not? One of my favorite questions. No one ever answered it conclusively when I began, so I tried to make sure that I wouldn't make a mistake either way. Therefore, I discovered at first hand what most soup-making beings in the universe have also discovered. I *partially covered* it, leaving just an inch or so of unlidded top. And it works. The fact is, it will work any way you do it. Totally uncovered, more of the nutrients and flavors will escape into the atmosphere, and the liquid will cook down much more rapidly. But if your aim in a particular instance is to make a richer (that is, more concentrated) stock quickly, then leave the cover off. Covering the pot is a good way *as long as the additional pressure doesn't cause the stock to begin boiling*. It depends on how low and how steady you can keep the heat, on how much liquid there is in the pot, and on the pot itself. (Tall pots are better for soup making. Why? Because liquid evaporates faster in wider pots and you will have to keep adding liquid.) If necessary, you can try putting an asbestos pad over the heat, or raise the pot up on bricks, or train your pets to hold it up. But unless you're sure, leaving it a little uncovered is the safest method.

After the long simmering process, in which as much goodness as possible has permeated the stock (why don't you taste it?), remove the pot and strain the liquid through several thicknesses of moist cheesecloth — or a linen napkin. Cool the stock *uncovered*. (If you do it in the refrigerator, the heat may defrost it.) When cooled, chill *covered*. Due to a quirk in the cosmic laws of animosity, fat, which as I've said is the enemy of soup, also guards the sleeping stock by forming a protective coating over the top, a cake of fat that sits there until you are ready to use the stock. Then you merely lift off the cake. The bones and marrow will have caused the stock to gelatinize, giving it a luscious body. (If it didn't gelatinize, it's still good.)

For a richer colored beef stock (brown stock), you may brown the bones for about 10 minutes before putting them in, either under the broiler (far from the flame), in the oven, or on top of the stove, turning them frequently. Browning some of the meat also helps, though it will toughen it as well. (Don't brown more than half the meat.) *Simmer, strain, cool,* and *chill.*

You now have something that really makes you feel like you are *cooking.* It is as close to a magic elixir as any substance you are likely to use in the kitchen — subtle, rich, complex, full-bodied. It has power.

And here is some good news. You don't have to familiarize yourself with some entirely different procedure in order to make chicken stock — also called white stock. Just do the same as for beef stock; only substitute chicken backs, necks, wings, legs, hearts, gizzards (when removed, these latter can be eaten, or presented to the cat), and even feet (which contain a lot of gelatin). Old stewing chickens, not young fryers, are best for this purpose. A veal knuckle — or any other veal segment you might have — can go in, too.

Chicken stock need be cooked only 2 or 3 hours, but the longer you cook it, the more flavor will be extracted (up to a point). The herbs can stay the same, but they don't have to. How about marjoram, savory — a little rosemary, or garlic?

Yes, there are many fine points, but I think many are best left out because my choices may be different from yours. For example, perhaps there *is* something in chicken that responds to the bitterness in celery, so maybe you'll put an extra couple of stalks in the chicken stock. (Or maybe you won't.) Things like that. Other cooks don't hesitate to add pork meat, which is relatively rich and sweet, perhaps too much for some. Lamb meat is too strongly flavored to combine with other meat and tends to be fatty. (Lamb and mutton fat are among the unluckiest substances to discover in your soup.) If you have some lamb, though, by all means cut off the excess fat and use in stew or barley soup — or with beans.

Maybe some fastidious cook will be shocked at putting pork (or beef!) in a white stock, making it something else, but it might be useful to know if it works. (It will work if you don't require a purer flavored stock. For a soup or a stew, it may be just the right dish on a snowy night.) The most important thing is to experience the making of stock, and you'll discover quickly what *you* would like to try. But never put smoked, cured, or processed meat in a stock. Also, it helps to know that you can mix raw and cooked meats, though the stock will always be cloudy if you do (there's really nothing intrinsically bad about a cloudy stock). The minimum time for simmering cooked meat is half the time for raw meat, so if all of your stock consists of leftover meat, you can have a good stock in a couple of hours.

I have gone on about stock because I want you to *make some*. It's no good just reading about it. Not only that, if you cook consistently, daily or nearly so, especially for a number of folks, it's not at all difficult to do what's necessary to have it on hand, especially chicken stock. When you discover the amazing variety of possibilities, not only for soup, but as a base or an *extender* for sauces and gravies, as an addition to the cooking water for vegetables, rice, and other grains, you may actually come to make it *an important part of your cooking system*. (You can even use it in salad dressing.) The hardest part is just to get started. As a means to help the cook turn out delicious, heart-warming meals *while saving time*, stock is a boon companion. You may even cook a chicken dinner (or a boiled beef dinner; in this case don't cut the meat into little morsels) just to produce some good stock. You see, I didn't tell you, but you can also eat the chicken or beef as long as you remove the chicken after 1 or 1½ hours, the beef when it's tender, after about 2 to 2½ hours. Return the bones and skin (in the case of chicken) to the stock pot and continue simmering.

Let's take up some of the other flavoring vegetables that can be used in the stock including stock made from a good canned broth. There are many excellent ones, depending on such things as seasonal availability, your tastes, the weather, where you live, and so on.

*Leeks.* Use the white parts and just a little of the green, unless you're making leek soup. Clean carefully, because grit lurks. Slitting them lengthwise is the traditional method for ridding them of this substance, which is most unpleasant to meet in your mouth.

*Turnips.* There are different opinions, of course. I encourage you to peel and cut up one small turnip for a certain subtle addition to the stock pot. But too much turnip will probably disappoint you.

*Parsnips.* These are not just sepia-toned carrots; they are parsnips and are rather sweet. Try a maximum of one.

*Tomatoes.* The decision to use tomatoes depends on — guess what? Whether you want tomatoes in the soup or not. If you do, you can remove the skins by dropping one or two of them (or a whole bunch if you want a very tomatoey stock) into boiling water for a minute, then slip the skins off. Quarter the tomatoes and remove the seeds by squeezing them into your palm (or your fist), and put them in the pot.

### Tomorrow Soup

"So what about those odd remnants you had me save at the beginning of all this?"

*These can also go into the stock. Or, without meat, they can be used to make a stock of their own.* And therefore a soup. Tomorrow Soup.

"What does that mean, Tomorrow Soup?"

It's just to encourage you to use these scraps by tomorrow. It can be the day after tomorrow, but don't wait for the vegetables to get tired out. In fact, they can be used today. Having Tomorrow Soup today is one of the ironic pleasures of life.

Treat these bits and pieces just the way you would beef or chicken. Put them in a pot of cold water to cover plus a little more, with a bit of salt and a bouquet garni (parsley, bay, and thyme will qualify) or other herbs such as marjoram, summer savory, basil, oregano (if you have some stronger-flavored vegetables like broccoli stalks), caraway (also for cabbage or mustard family vegetables). Simmer the brew for no more than 1 hour, because vegetables alone cannot endure long cooking without releasing muggy, dank flavors.

The stock is strained through a strainer or colander, muush-ing it as you do to extract all the pithy juices. Every batch is a little different. A kaleidoscope of liquors!

This substance is *vegetable stock,* and so also is any liquid remaining from the cooking of one or more vegetables. Though for most cooks it is not as useful as a good chicken stock, these vegetable liquors, provided they are not too bitter or strong, can make very pleasing additions to rice water, sauces, and gravies (in place of chicken stock — or along with it), and are a base not only for soups but for extending other stocks and also for cooking *other* vegetables in. For example, *spinach* can acquire an intriguing flavor by being cooked in the same water you cooked *curly leaf cabbage* in. I know because I just did it the day before yesterday.

Of course, with all the business going on in your kitchen, you probably aren't going to save dozens of bottles of vegetable water. But one or two can be useful if you have the space.

If you plan to store the vegetable stock until tomorrow (or much later), you may want to simmer it for only about ½ hour. Then, when you resurrect it from the icebox to turn it into soup, you can simmer it for the remaining ½ hour.

To have Tomorrow Soup today, simmer for the full term — 45 minutes to 1 hour — season to taste, and strain. Or simmer about ½ hour, strain, and add other partially cooked vegetables that have been either parboiled or sautéed for, say, 5 to 10 minutes in butter. Rinse the pan out with some of the stock because the butter is pleasing in the soup. Season. Simmer 15 minutes more.

A further refinement is to strain out the "new" vegetables and mash them through a colander or food mill and return the purée to the soup to thicken it. The idea is to try three or four Tomorrow Soups so you get a sense of how the flavors intermingle. The seasoning will give it all a great lift, but if the stock is stale, smelly, and sour, no amount of rosemary can disguise it.

### Storing Stock

Heavier stocks and soups, such as those made with meat, taste better the day after they are made — and even better the second or third day. The flavors will continue to develop and blend and "marry." Vegetable stock, however, doesn't require a night of rest for its flavors to be fully elaborated. Immediately it's as good as it will get, though certainly you can store it like any other stock.

In order to preserve the stock — which, for easier handling, you probably divided into smaller batches to fit inside your refrigerator — boil it up again for a couple of minutes (an easy process) every three or four days to keep bad bacteria from souring it. You can play this game for several weeks. And whenever you want to add leftover gravy or more stock to it, boil it up again. Don't worry about making stock too concentrated. You can always add water to dilute it.

And you can *freeze* it — even into *ice cubes* to use in a bit of gravy or sauce. It will keep for *months*. Then, when you're ready, out comes the stock; you perform some very simple actions, and soup happens in full measure.

### Soup
It's so easy to make good soup from good stock that you don't even need advice. Hunger is all you need. But I'll point out a few things anyway.

Stock, which is a strained liquid with a certain body, becomes soup simply by adding the proper amount of salt, and perhaps some fresh parsley or other seasoning. If it is meat or chicken stock, the fat must be removed. (Congealed fat is the enemy of soup, remember?) If you don't have time to chill the stock quickly and lift off the cake of fat that surfaces and reheat, then just skim off the fat with a serving spoon and try to blot up some of the excess with absorbent paper towels. (Some towels definitely work better than others.) An ice cube in one of the towels may help. Lettuce leaves have also been commandeered for this purpose.

A garnish on top of the soup is always appropriate. (Lemon peel? grated cheese? diced hard-boiled egg? croutons? parsley? shavings of a raw vegetable?)

### An Infinity of Soups
It's true; there are. But I shall exercise some restraint.

1. Strained Soup; that is, bouillon or stock, which I just de-

scribed. Salt it, season it, and include some wine just before serving if you like. You've got it made, so to speak.

2. Soup With Things In It; say, vegetables. There are two general ways to add vegetables to soup (not counting any that may have gone in at the very beginning and whose flavor and body are already well diffused through the stock). Put them in raw, or cook them a little first, usually sautéing or parboiling. If you like the individual flavors of the vegetables to be well preserved, *cooking them first is the best way.*

It is helpful to realize that someone is doubtless going to partake of your soup employing a moderate-size soup spoon. Therefore, common sense dictates that morsels be in the bite-size range.

If you are putting the vegetables in raw — that is, you are using the soup as a cooking liquid — employ Irifoy as your guide — with one proviso: Since the vegetables need to be blended *with* the soup and not merely cooked *in* the soup, and since the heat is at the simmer, not the boil, everything should get cooked almost *twice as long* as you would normally cook it. But you know what? After you've done this once, you'll never have to think of it again. It's so obvious when you actually do it, and there's plenty of leeway.

Here are two examples to give you a sense of the flexibility that's possible. You can melt some butter in the bottom of the soup pot, put the cut vegetables in, and cook them for, say, 10 minutes, including some diced onions. Add the stock to the pot and let the entire brew simmer for about ½ hour.

Another way is simply to bring the stock to a boil, add the cut, sliced, or diced vegetables, and let the whole kettle simmer for a little bit longer since nothing has been cooked. Irifoy will inform you about the adjustments to make for slow- or fast-cooking vegetables. Look. Smell. Sample.

With beef stock you can produce a wide range of hearty soups from meat to vegetable; at least one substantial root vegetable such as onions (almost always) and maybe carrots will usually be found in such soups. Chicken stock or broth can also be transformed into a robust soup; however, it also serves as the base for most cream soups and especially delicate soups with lighter vegetables (when these are not made with vegetable stock, or simply water).

Chicken stock alone provides enough different soups for several lifetimes. Almost any vegetable soup can use chicken stock as its base. If you want the soup to be *chicken soup with vegetables*, you may not wish to dilute the stock. But if you want a *vegetable soup*, you most likely will want to use a weak chicken stock that, if necessary, has been diluted with water or vegetable stock. And as I've said, vegetable stock is a fascinating field for variety and experimentation. Stocks can usually be mixed freely when experimenting without danger of disaster. Now and then, you should even mix beef and chicken stock to taste what it's like. (You won't keel over.)

But you must also know that heaven-sent soups can be made simply using water as a base!

"But how can this be? It seems to go against all you've been saying."

Please understand that we have separated the soup-making process from the stock-making process. And when you make soup by cooking in water aromatic vegetables such as leeks and one that gives body like potatoes, you are, in effect, making a full-bodied stock. With the addition of milk or cream and elegant seasoning, you may have a masterpiece of a soup. (See Guide at the end of the chapter for Cream of Leek-Potato-Apple-Turnip-Caraway-Marjoram Soup with Chives.)

3. Thickened Soups. Soups may be thickened in many ways. One method, which includes an entire range of soups, is to add a vegetable purée.

That's what you get when you put a vegetable that has softened during cooking through a food mill or colander (making sure you scrape up all the vegetable matter clinging to the bottom). You can also use a blender for puréeing; the texture will be a bit "slicker." When chicken stock or milk or water is added, it automatically becomes that particular vegetable soup, thickened somewhat by the purée.

Example. Purée some cooked cauliflower by sending it through one of the above-mentioned implements. Add chicken stock and simmer. You get cauliflower soup! If you add milk or cream or half-and-half, you get cream of cauliflower soup.

(When referring to soups, *cream* can mean any of these. In fact, soup thickened just with flour, or butter and flour — that is, a roux — are also called cream soups.) Cream of cauliflower soup is improved by first sautéing some onion slices in butter before adding the cooked, mushed-up cauliflower and the chicken stock. And remember that cauliflower and a touch of *nutmeg,* especially in cream of cauliflower soup, make magic together. Incidentally, certain vegetables that are stringy, like cauliflower — or seedy, like tomatoes — do need to be strained (as we did when we puréed) before being mushed into soup.

For a clean-tasting spinach or watercress soup, the onion may be too heavy, don't you think? Well, is it summer or winter?

Another thickener, traditional and rich, is egg yolks. The method here embodies the important cooking technique most often applied to egg yolks: the Big into Small into Big Technique. The egg yolks are beaten lightly. A little of the hot (not boiling) liquid is poured *into the egg yolks,* about ¼ cup for 2 yolks (just guess). These are blended; then the entire mixture *is poured back into the soup* (or sauce, if that's what you're making). Sometimes *a little cold cream* is first beaten into the yolks before this procedure. The point is that the yolks are very delicate in relation to heat. If the soup (or sauce) boils, the eggs will curdle. (In fact, they will curdle at 155°.) One egg yolk will thicken about 1 cup of soup.

*Note:* Sour cream and yogurt can approach nearer the boiling point without curdling. But if they do curdle, it affects only the appearance of the dish, not the flavor. Cream, if not especially fresh, will curdle if boiled and, fresh or not, will most likely do so if there are acidic ingredients present, like tomatoes, wine, or vinegar.

Another way to produce a cream soup is by first making a roux and turning this into a thin white sauce (a tablespoon of flour to thicken a cup of soup) by adding milk, cream, soup — or half one, half another. You can even thicken the soup with flour alone. Flour can be introduced when the vegetables are being sautéed, before they go into the pot; this will give more consistency to the final soup. In fact, for some cream soups and most legume soups (beans automatically thicken soups), you will notice a certain tendency for the beans, peas, or whatever to separate from the liquid. The introduction of flour in any of the above will "bind" the soup and keep it from separating.

Moving through the grain spectrum from flour to cereal to whole grain (from fine to coarse), you can thicken a soup by tossing in a handful or two of, say, rice or barley. Simmer for about an hour. Cooked grain works also, but you have to use almost *twice* as much for an equivalent effect. In either case, make sure you have enough liquid because grain, especially uncooked grain, *absorbs*.

There are more thickeners: grate a potato into a quart of soup and let it simmer for 15 minutes (in fact, you can use *instant mashed potatoes* for a really sneaky thickener). And there are more soups: consommés, chowders . . . But you have more than enough to begin with in order to recognize that soup-making as a flexible, flowing process doesn't mean that it lacks precision. Real precision comes from the sharpening of our senses — looking, smelling, tasting — respecting them, being quiet enough in the midst of our preparations to listen to them.

### *Finally, Seasoning*
Endless, of course. But to begin, there are herbs. There are spices like celery seed (use sparingly in all stocks), caraway, allspice for beef stock, a touch of coriander for something different. Nutmeg in cream soups. Paprika, cayenne. But the main thing is SALT. It may be that all you need is a pinch of this, a sprinkle of that, and more SALT. Or maybe just more SALT. By putting in the right amount of salt, you can much more easily determine what the soup needs. So first, salt. (I know you understand that my emphasis on salt doesn't mean to oversalt.)

Other helpful additions are lemon in chicken and vegetable soups, cider vinegar for a bit of tang, Maggi in beef-based soups (by the drop).

And spirits. A couple of glugs of red wine per quart of soup is a very robust addition to a beef stock. For chicken, use sherry (allowed in beef as well), Madeira (by the small glug), even a touch of dry white wine — or red wine if it's a heartier soup. Put in shortly before serving the soup. Don't boil after adding the wine. Wine, by the way, will accentuate the salt in the soup, so take this into account.

I didn't mention that you can also add wine (in somewhat larger amounts) when *making* the stock because I knew that you would try it on your own.

### Fish Stock

Take a couple of quarts of cold water and the bones, heads, and trimmings of a mild whitish fish, like halibut or haddock, and a "pitch" (i.e., a tablespoon) of salt. Simmer in a covered pot for an hour, no longer. Strain. Use for fish soups and for poaching fish. Store for three or four days in the refrigerator. Or freeze.

Of course you can season the stock, or wait and season the soup. The seasoning for the court bouillon in Chapter 19 (page 156) is appropriate here. Something acidic, like white wine, lemon, or vinegar (or a combination), seems to be essential.

Yes, everything can be made into soup.

---

. . . . . . . . . . . . . . . . . . . . . . . . . . . . . . . . . . . . . . . . . . . . . .

GUIDE TO
**Cream of Leek-Potato-Apple-Turnip-Caraway-Marjoram Soup with Chives — and Later, the Next Day, Vichyssoise Extraordinaire***

There are *no onions in this soup.*

Put 2 pounds of mealy POTATOES, unpeeled, in two quarts of water (any good baking potato will do, such as Idaho or russet), *except,* substitute one for a medium-sized TURNIP, and one for an APPLE (this will probably leave you with two, possible three POTATOES). Add 2 tablespoons of CARAWAY SEEDS and a teaspoon of KOSHER or SEA SALT. Simmer half an hour. Remove the potatoes, turnip, and apple. Peel them and cut into small pieces and return them to the water. Cut six LEEKS into small pieces (make sure they're degritted) — only the white part; add the green pieces in their whole length.

* A "deviation" from a recipe found in *Magic in Herbs* by Leonie de Sounin.

Simmer another half-hour and remove the green leek pieces; the soup will have been boiled down to a soft purée. Strain it (a colander will do — I prefer one with big holes for this) and return it to the pot (make sure you scrape the bottom of the strainer). Add a quart of MILK and two teaspoons of FRESH MARJORAM — or slightly less of DRIED MARJORAM, another teaspoon KOSHER or SEA SALT, and a teaspoon PAPRIKA. Cook 15 minutes more.

Just before serving, add HEAVY CREAM and 2 tablespoons of finely cut PARSLEY. Add more SALT, if necessary (and possibly more MARJORAM). Scatter a few fresh CHIVES over the soup in each bowl.

You'll never believe that *you* made this soup (and not some famous chef). The next day have it cold — a vichyssoise without onions (the way it should have been created, in my opinion). There is never enough of it.

. . . . . . . . . . . . . . . . . . . . . . . . . . . . . . . . . . . . . . . . . . . . .
. . . . . . . . . . . . . . . . . . . . . . . . . . . . . . . . . . . . . . . . . . . . .

GUIDE TO
## Your Bag (of Soup)

At first, it's a mélange. But after a while it helps actually to consider what you've got in your scrap bag. Here are a few examples of good combinations:

ASPARAGUS, CELERY, ONION — or, instead of onion, SPINACH (or WATERCRESS). BASIL?

POTATOES, TOMATOES, CELERY, ONION — or, instead of onion, LEEKS. DILL?

You expected a list, didn't you? Sorry, you'll have to take it from here.

. . . . . . . . . . . . . . . . . . . . . . . . . . . . . . . . . . . . . . . . . . . . .
. . . . . . . . . . . . . . . . . . . . . . . . . . . . . . . . . . . . . . . . . . . . .

GUIDE TO
## Avocado All-Together Soup

If you're itching to use the blender you got as a wedding present (or were left with after the separation), try this.

Put all the following in the blender and blend:
1 big AVOCADO, quartered
1 cup hot CHICKEN STOCK
Juice of 1 LEMON
CURRY POWDER, but not as much as a teaspoon
About a teaspoon GRATED ONION or some ONION JUICE
A crushed GARLIC CLOVE
A tablespoon ("pitch") of SHERRY
SALT, PEPPER
Then stir in ½ cup PLAIN YOGURT. Chill.
*Second method:* Put EVERYTHING (including the YOGURT) in the blender and blend. Chill. Serve with four slices of AVOCADO on top. Or crumbled BACON and CHIVES. Or CHIVES.

. . . . . . . . . . . . . . . . . . . . . . . . . . . . . . . . . . . . . . . . . . . . . . . .
. . . . . . . . . . . . . . . . . . . . . . . . . . . . . . . . . . . . . . . . . . . . . . . .

GUIDE TO
**Improving Canned Broth**

Brands differ in flavor and quantity of salt. Some good brands are College Inn, Monarch, Swanson's, and Campbell's.

Simmer CANNED BEEF OR CHICKEN BROTH with a BOUQUET GARNI, some RED WINE (for beef) or WHITE (for chicken). You can also add the AROMATIC TRIO (ONIONS, CARROTS, CELERY).

Thirty minutes is enough. FRESH PARSLEY (or any other FRESH herb) is a great help in the soup or sauce to give the impression of freshness.

. . . . . . . . . . . . . . . . . . . . . . . . . . . . . . . . . . . . . . . . . . . . . . . .

# 31
# Casseroles, Beans, Stews, and Soups vs. Casserstews, Beanseroles, and Stewoups

Soups, stews, casseroles. It's getting too complicated. All these different kinds of things. What to do?

Begin by recognizing that all these things can be looked at in one overall way: food cooked in *liquid*. This can be mere moisture, as in some casseroles, or all liquid, as with some soups.

### Soup and Stew

It's perfectly evident that as the liquid element dwindles, a soup becomes less soupy and more stewish. Of course, this doesn't mean that "stewoup," or whatever state soup passes through on the way to being stew (or vice versa) is something you are not allowed to eat. In fact, it will probably be very tasty. But there are some other differences that are not quite so obvious.

As long as the liquid is the main element, as in a soup, we don't have to worry about the flavors from the meat, vegetables, and so on, escaping into the medium. In fact, we want them to.

But as the liquid becomes less and less central in the dish and more and more the medium in which other edibles weave and bob, following a few procedures helps these embedded items retain their individual juices and flavors.

From the standpoint of preparation, these simple stewing procedures constitute the essential differences between a soup and a stew:

1. Browning the meat, which adds flavor and seals in the juices.

2. Using just enough liquid to cover — or much less — which is boiling in the beginning and then is immediately

reduced to a simmer. (In the preparation of stock for soup, the liquid starts off cold.)

3. Not cooking the vegetables — or the meat — to pieces.

A few comments on these rules.

Slow cooking, or the very gentle simmering that is best for both soups and stews, does not give the cook a free ticket to overcook the stew. But don't worry if it happens. Stir a little sherry into it a few minutes before serving, sprinkle some parsley on each portion, and go on with your life.

*The browning.* Here's one way people have been doing it for generations. Cut the stewing beef (or any beef, for that matter) into 1½-inch cubes. If they're 2-inch cubes you still haven't ruined anything. (Ask your butcher, "Do you have any stewing beef?" Better yet, recall from Chapter 25 that **neck** or **lean chuck** makes excellent and economical stewing meat. So does **top round.** And these aren't the only ones.) Or use lamb. ("Do you have any stewing lamb?") In either case, cut off as much of the **fat** as you can without making an agonizing production out of it. (In other words, it's hard to get it all, but lamb fat and especially mutton — mature lamb — fat are the *least* desirable.) This is one of those obvious secrets frequently left out, or not sufficiently emphasized, in directions for stew. Who needs another pot of greasy stew?

(However, it's the *non*-excess fat in the meat as well as in the connective tissue that breaks down during cooking that makes the stew meat especially tender and juicy.) To skim a good part of the excess fat from a stew while it's cooking, use a lettuce leaf or paper towel, or wrap a towel around an ice cube.

By the way, veal, which happens to make a delicious stew when it is browned first, is often cooked *à blanc;* that is, without browning. (This term also refers to the white color of the vegetables that go into it. An Irish stew, in its original form of unbrowned lamb, potatoes, and onions, is a classic example.)

Dry the meat. Put some oil and butter in a shallow pan — or use pork fat or the fat from the meat if it's beef, with or without butter or oil — and heat it. It shouldn't be too hot, but the meat should sizzle a little when it hits the pan. Don't crowd the utensil. Why? Because the steam from the browning meat needs room to get out. Otherwise it moistens the meat and draws out the juices. Do only a few pieces at a time, and brown them on *all* sides. If they're swimming in too much fat, pour some of it out. Really brown them; don't fake. But don't scorch the meat. Be patient.

If you like, you can flavor the fat with a peeled garlic clove or two (remove it later) and sauté a chopped onion in the pan during the browning process — or right afterward so the liquid exuded by the onion won't interfere with the browning. Putting a bit of honey or sugar in with the onion helps develop a nice color.

Guess what? You can also brown the pieces *under the broiler* without using any additional fat at all. This gives you a tasty and crusty result. Be careful not to burn them. Incidentally, contrary to what you might imagine, lean meat browns faster (and cooks faster) than fatty meat.

For texture and deeper color, dredge (that is, coat) the pieces with flour — shaking off the excess — before browning. Or just sprinkle flour over the pieces toward the end of the browning process.

Now that you have browned and possibly floured the meat and doubtless have flavored things up with onion and garlic — and you have removed the pieces to a heavy pot or a casserole — the rest is almost common sense.

Salt and pepper the meat and add stock, a good can of beef bouillon (with tomato juice or sauce mixed in it if you want), red wine thinned with water (white wine for lighter meats), flat beer, or whatever. Even water is all right with sufficient seasoning; but there are always bouillon cubes. If by mistake some soup bones fall into the kettle, don't fish them out!

The second departure from soup making: The liquid, which at most should just cover the meat, but may come up only halfway, is usually added when boiling, then immediately reduced to a simmer. Also, during this process you should deglaze the browning pan with a little of the boiling liquid and transfer it to the stewing pot, first pouring off some of the accumulated fat in the browning pan if it feels like too much. (Really scrape the pan with, say, your rubber spatula.)

At this time, you can add another large onion, but leave the skin on. It adds color to the stew. Or you can add some small white ones; a couple of cloves can always be stuck in one of them. For a tomatoey stew, add some tomatoes cut up or a can of *Italian plum tomatoes*. In this case, reduce the other liquid accordingly. Add other seasonings. You can start with salt, peppercorns, a bay leaf, thyme (anywhere from ¼ to ½ teaspoon; just use your fingers), some parsley sprigs or, better, some chopped parsley later on. Of course, if you have some fresh thyme or marjoram, go to it.

But you also have the whole battery of herbs and spices to experiment with. Rosemary in a lamb stew, or things you may not expect — like cinnamon with lamb! Marjoram in the beef stew — or allspice. There are the savories for beans and other hearty vegetables, also good in herbal blends with meat. With tomatoes you could have basil, thyme, or marjoram (to name a few). A *little* celery seed is always good in a stew.

Now that you have the license to overseason the stew (how about flashes of ginger? or possibly nutmeg? mace? — all good — and paprika gives the touch of magic, too, but go easy), I'm going to ask you to try *not* to overseason the stew. Yes, I do suggest that beyond the onions, garlic, and other aromatics, you blend two or three seasonings — not to masquerade what's in the pot with these various essences, but to enliven, to coax forth hidden, subtle flavors. True, there is no right way to season, but there is a range (quite a wide range) where the seasoning participates pleasingly instead of being too faint-hearted or too demanding.

Cover the pot with a tight lid and let the stew cook — that is, *simmer* over low heat (*never boil*) — until the meat is just tender (test with a fork or taste), roughly 1½ hours. If the cubes are small, it may only take 1 hour or so. But it could go for 2 hours. (Lamb and veal will cook faster than beef.) At this point, if any fat has risen to the surface, skim it off with a spoon and blot what else you can with paper towels (putting an ice cube inside one may help).

You're going to cook for about 30 minutes more. Begin to add other vegetables, using Irifoy as a guide to the size of the pieces you put in — and when you should put them in.

Which vegetables, for example? Well, you certainly haven't forgotten about the aromatic trinity of onions, carrots, and celery. The onions are in, so now it's a good time for the carrots (one cut up is enough; or two; or three if you're focusing on carrots, which will make the stew rather sweet — and if you're using pork, it will probably be too sweet). And the celery (one? maybe two? and put in the leaves, too). One (and only one) turnip is a possibility. Leeks — excellent if you can get them — instead of, or along with, the onions.

Personally, I always think twice before adding potatoes. They are a definite presence in the stew, in part due to the amount of liquid they absorb. But some people can't imagine a stew without them, and that's what thinking twice is all about: "On second thought, let's leave them out." (Or ". . . let's put them in.") They're usually peeled and cut up.

These, as well as any other vegetables you might wish to put in, are helped by first sautéing or otherwise cooking them before adding; in this way, they preserve more of their flavor and individual character, which is fresh and pleasing in a stew.

Other possibilities include string beans, zucchini, Brussels sprouts (you're kidding! nope, about 10 minutes out), peas (only 5 or 10 minutes' cooking needed), asparagus! (I'll go for asparagus.) There are so many. But you can just keep it simple, putting in only a few. What do you feel like having?

This brings us to the last basic difference in preparing a stew as opposed to a soup. You do not want the vegetables (or the meat) to fall to pieces. Or, in some cases, to get stringy. Therefore, you will not overcook the stew after the vegetables have gone in. However, should the vegetables — and, heaven forfend, the meat — become disheveled and fragmented, my advice to you is: Do not worry. Your "stewoup" will still be welcomed and loved by all (as you stir sherry into it, scatter parlsey on it, and serve it in disguise over noodles).

Let the stew sit for a few minutes before serving to skim off any additional fat.

If you wish to thicken the stewing broth, hardly anything could be simpler — as effortless as salting. A standard way is to prepare a *roux* with equal parts of butter and flour; after cooking it for a while over low heat, add some of the "soup" to the *roux* and, when thickened, pour all this back into the stewing pot. This is similar to the way egg yolks are added to sauces to prevent curdling.

Then there's the "secret" method described on page 138. Simply shake up a couple of tablespoons (that is, a few "pitches") or more of flour in a jar that *already* has in it about a half-glass worth of cold broth, milk, beer, water, whatever. Shake *hard*. Taking the stew pot off the heat while you slowly pour this paste into it, stir all the while until it is blended and is as thick as you like. Put the pot back on the heat and cook for at least 5 minutes. Ten minutes won't hurt a bit. If you have browned the flour first in a pan in a 250° oven, *you'll get a richer colored stew.* In this case you'll need an extra couple of tablespoons of flour for thickening.

Since thickening broths and gravies is such a fundamental and frequent procedure, here is another quick method. Take a glob of butter and a pitch of flour and work them quickly together with your fingers. Break off bits and blend in. Let cook before you add more to see how much it thickens (*beurre manié*).

### Grains
Grains are an intriguing addition to a stew. Just add a handful or two of brown rice and/or barley 45 minutes or so before the end, or white rice and/or bulgur about 20 to 30 minutes before the end. But make sure there's plenty of liquid, because the grains will absorb more than twice their own volume. If your pot is normally soupy and you add grains, you get a perfect "stewoup."

### If You Braise or Stew, Why Not Marinate, Too?
Perhaps there's something else the dish needs, or you have found through experience that some cuts of some meat are *really* tough. Or something special is required. Then *marinate* (that is, soak) the cubes of meat before you brown them, in a mixture (not precise) of, for example, olive oil, lemon juice or wine vinegar (or wine itself), some olive oil, adding garlic, onions, parsley, peppercorns, herbs like bay, thyme, tarragon, and so on. It's sort of an elaborate vinaigrette sauce, only in reverse

— with more "tart" than oil (the oil keeps the meat from drying out). Soy sauce, whiskey, vermouth — and numberless other things — can go into a marinade. Refrigerate for at least 2 to 3 hours for any real effect; overnight is fine. If you warm the marinade after you put the herbs in, they will become even more aromatic; but cool before pouring over the meat. Use a glass, ceramic, or enameled cast iron dish, not cast iron or aluminum. You can strain the marinade and pour it into the stew pot. (Look at it. Do you think you need to strain it? Maybe you don't.)

If you're marinating larger pieces (because who said that you always have to cube the meat? Why not bigger chunks or a real hunk?), you will probably want to turn them in the marinade a few times. You will also discover that the smaller the container that holds the marinade, the less you have to use.

Be cautious about marinating for more than a day and a half. Unless it's very gamey meat (like wild boar), too much marinating may dilute or "wring out" the flavor of the meat. But don't let this stop you from doing it!

### Finally
You can't miss — but taste. Just before the end of the cooking, take stock especially of the salt situation as well as other seasonings you think might need a boost. (You've eaten before. You know what things taste like.)

You should also be informed that even though your stew is delicious the first day you make it, it is even better the next day, when all the flavors, and who knows what else, will have had a chance to "marry." (The first day, you could say they're "engaged.") Just as with soup, after chilling, covered, some fat will have risen to the surface. Remove it just before reheating. Incidentally, there's no law against mingling beef and lamb and pork. You can do it in a meat loaf and you can do it in a stew. (But too much pork may be too rich for your taste.)
**Never boil a stew!**

### Braising
You don't have to put all that liquid in there. Use the smallest pot that will accommodate the meat (otherwise too much

steam will accumulate) and put, say, ½ inch liquid into the pot, or even less, or up to 1 inch or 2. But in order not to burn the bottom of the meat, lay the cubes ("Why cubes, anyway?" You're right. Why not strips? *Or all one piece?*) **on a bed of vegetables** such as onions, carrots, celery, parsnip, or a turnip, sliced into strips or diced into cubes called **mirepoix** (remember page 148?). Or simply put the meat on a bed of onions, or on any kind of raised thing (if it's a big hunk, on a rack). Failing any of the supports, strike another blow for fearless cooking by simply setting the meat on the bottom of the pan.

Cover tightly.

If you are cooking on *low heat* and the liquid is disappearing, then put some more in. If braising one large piece, turn it once or twice for even cooking. (If you forget to turn it, it will probably still be delicious.) You can also put the pot in the oven — at about 300° — but it takes longer to cook.

It may take 2 to 4 hours if it's one big piece. (Don't try this with something over 3 or 4 pounds.) The time will depend on the size of the piece, its toughness (was it marinated?), the *amount of liquid* in the pot, and perhaps what liquid it is.

Did you know that you could use milk in braising? Or *sour cream?*

### A Summary

You can cook little pieces, big pieces. You can brown first. You don't have to brown at all. You can dredge with flour, sprinkle it over the browning pan, or not, as it pleases you. You can use liquid that covers the meat, or enough to go up, say, halfway, or almost none at all. *Mainly, do not boil. And do not overcook.* Thicken the broth if you want. Test with a fork or taste.

### Casseroles

Casseroles, like salads, can be of two sorts: mixed up (tossed) or layered (arranged). Aside from the well-known fact that *casserole* originally referred exclusively to a certain kind of cooking container, it now refers more often to what is cooked in it and has become a loosely applied term for any kind of mishmash or moist minglement simmered, braised, or baked in the oven or on top of the stove. Since we're dealing with vague usages of words, I can only report that *casserole* is a broader term that can include *stew* — and *braised dishes* — but is often assumed to be less wet than a stew: for example, noodles or rice cooked in a casserole (container) with other things. But would you believe that if you take your stew, put it in a casserole, and bake in in the oven at 300° (or 325°) for about 2 hours, everyone will say it's a casserole. (And it is.)

Certain cooking procedures are addicting. Sautéing, for example. Or "casseroling." Some people, when they discover that they can layer a lot of different things — including leftovers — or just mix it all up and have it successfully cook, like magic, inside of the mysterious oven (*in the dark*), begin to go crazy and cook every which thing like that until somebody complains (which usually takes quite a while because casseroles are good). My advice is: Don't get hooked on them too long; let them take their place. There are other forms of cooking to look into.

For simplicity, begin your casserole-making career with things already cooked.

Here's the idea behind the layered casserole: The bottom of the baking dish needs to be greased unless there is something wet or greasy in there. Then, for the first layer, put something starchy down that can absorb juices and other moisture. Potatoes, noodles, rice, or other grains — or beans.

For the next layers, pick out two or three from the following (cooked): watery, soft vegetables like onions or tomatoes (or both); firmer vegetables like string beans; meat; top with cheese (if you include cheese) and top the topping with bread crumbs (if you like).

Can you have four items? What a daring thought!

In any case, alternate what you select in layers; for instance, sliced potatoes, onions, tomatoes, zucchini, potatoes, onions (of course these could be mixed in with the potatoes; don't be too fussy), tomatoes, zucchini, and so on, ending with potatoes. You can season each layer as you go. (There's a certain amount of drama in all this.) You can grate cheese over the top. But wait! Is there enough wetness? It should have a mushiness about it (not as wet as stew, though). For liquid, you can use some tomato sauce. Or liquid you cooked some vegetables in. Or stock, including canned chicken broth. How about dairy things? Sour cream, yogurt, beaten eggs (extended with milk if need be). Milk by itself, sauces, water even.

"Do I have to be picky about these layers? I mean, what if something or other goes somewhere else, and so on?"

Do not worry. But pay the most attention to what you put on the bottom, and next, the top. The best for the latter is something that will shield what's below from drying out, especially if you bake without a cover for all or part of the time. Cheese, sauce, or a starch is typical.

For a mixed-up casserole, put everything in the pot so that it's sort of mushy, flatten out the top, and heat.

Casseroles, along with salads, are the primary means for using up leftovers. And of course you can mix leftovers with something you have just steamed or sautéed or otherwise cooked to the point of tenderness. (Eggplant?) Just as using a fresh herb in a mixture of dried ones gives a fresh character to the blend, including freshly cooked food in a casserole gives a great lift to leftovers.

Into the oven. And to remove all baking fears, just recall the magic number: 350°. If the ingredients are warm, about 30 minutes should do. If they are cold, 1 hour might be needed to heat everything through.

When you start casseroling uncooked meat (which very likely you will), brown it in a skillet first, and be sure to use uncooked vegetables as well. Remember that baking in an oven takes longer than simmering or sautéing. Pork chops, for example, with a pocket cut out and stuffed with stuffing, might need 1 hour or 1 hour and 15 minutes to bake.

"When do you cook casseroles covered and when uncovered?"

Aha! Hardly anyone tells the poor beginner about this. But you know what? It may be because no matter what happens, it's all right *unless it dries out.* **Don't let it dry out.** Add more wetness if necessary at any point. Don't be bashful.

Here's a guide to covering. When you are concerned about maintaining the shape of what you're casseroling, then you should leave the cover off; for instance, when you make lasagna. Leaving the cover on creates and entraps steam, which will cause things to become more mushed into one another. If you are making a casserole with cheese on top, or something else that wants glazing or browning, you may wish to uncover the casserole for the last 10 minutes. As soon as the cheese bubbles up and, if you like, browns a little, remove it. Bread crumbs should brown.

A note on 350°. It would be an oversimplification to say that this is always the best temperature. But it's probably the safest bet when you're in doubt. If some things like potatoes or eggs seem to be toughening up on you, reduce the heat a little. Until your own experience guides you, start out at the magic number.

If you should find that by accident you have produced, instead of a casserole, some sort of "casserostew," my advice to you is . . . Well, you already know what my advice is.

Like child's play — in the true sense of the word — casseroles are fun. Garnish, if you like (I like) maybe with some parsley, nuts, or seeds. And serve right out of — the casserole.


### Beans (Dried)

Beans really deserve a chapter by themselves. But the problem is that many people think of beans as "by themselves," as though on one side there is food and on the other side, beans. I am blending them into this discussion so that you will remember about beans more often. Besides, beans have always reminded me of a "stewerole."

Beans are as close to edible earth as any food I know of. They are mild, filling, and nutritious. They welcome dressing up.

People have various prejudices about beans. But when you begin to relish beans, especially after eating them with some regularity, you get this sort of "home" feeling about them. They seem to be a part of our nature in a quieter and more intimate way than many other foods.

And beans are simple.

Take **beans.** Pick out any little rocks and whatnots that are bound to be mixed in with them and put them in a pot. (Bean companies hire someone to make sure that at least one non-bean is included in every package so you won't feel your effort has been wasted.) Run water into it and pick the beans up, a handful at a time, and rinse them out; then discard the water and refill, covering the beans plus an inch or 2 more, and soak them uncovered overnight — or in the daytime in a cool place for about 8 hours.

The faster-cooking beans, like lentils or split peas, do not require soaking, but are a little more yielding in texture and flavor when soaked. Soaking them cuts about 20 minutes off the cooking time.

When you are ready to cook the beans, discard any duds that are floating on top, then heat the pot using the same water. If you throw out the water, some vitamins go down the drain. (However, many cooks change the water anyway. I don't.)

Don't boil the beans; they should simmer over *low heat.* Cover — or if they want to foam over the top, you can skim the foam and partially cover — but if you don't skim the foam, it gradually gets absorbed by the beans (most of the time). Cook until done — when the beans are tender, not mushy. Taste one. Or blow on the skins of one or two. If the skins crack, they're done!

**Do not add salt until at least halfway through cooking.** Beans should be soft when the salt goes in. Salt toughens the beans and will lengthen the cooking time if put in too early. I like to add salt about 10 to 15 minutes from the end of cooking. Other seasonings, however, may be added halfway through.

There are some who say that acidic seasonings, like vinegar, lemon juice, and molasses, also toughen the beans and should be put in toward the end. Really, you can do it either way. Experiment. Which works best in your pot, in your water, with your beans, in your climate?

How long should you cook beans? The times given are not exact. The older the beans, the tougher — and the longer they will take to cook. (The same for grains, and most food.) If your water is hard, it will take longer. If it's too hard, you'll have to use bottled (not distilled) water. As a guide, lentils and peas take about 20 to 45 minutes. Most others, 1½ hours. Navy beans and garbanzos (also known as chickpeas) may take 2 or even 2½ hours to cook. Soybeans, over 3 — 3½ sometimes.

The safest way to proceed with beans is to allow plenty of time for cooking. Reheating will not hurt them.

A very useful method for cooking beans without having to soak them overnight is this: Merely drop the beans into boiling water so slowly that the water does not unboil. Put a tight lid on the pot and remove from the heat for an hour or so. Then add salt and other seasonings. Bring to a boil and *simmer* till done. (However, it's only humane to inform you that some people's interiors turn into compression chambers full of gas if the beans haven't had a thorough initial soaking.)

It shouldn't surprise you to know that instead of dropping the beanlets into boiling water, you can also start them out in cold water, bring to a boil for the requisite 2 minutes, and proceed as before.

As you may have remembered, this is analogous to cooking cereal grains and pasta (also a grain). This is interesting to ponder. (It's also an excellent way to boil an egg.)

It is a reminder that much good cooking is a combination of processes: boil, then soak; blanch, then sauté; sauté, then bake; sauté, then simmer (called braising). There seems to be a certain kind of mellowing that occurs when processes are combined, which is especially suitable for older, tougher, or otherwise less yielding foods. As the cook gains experience, more and more of these combinations are appreciated. Interestingly, it enhances one's admiration for simple, direct methods as well.

Beans welcome seasonings and complements. They enjoy onions (very much), tomatoes, cheese, olives (have you tried olives?), the ancient trinity of onions/carrots/celery, along with bay and thyme. Parsley is always a friend. (It sounds just like a meat stew.) Stronger beans love oregano. Lentils are graced by vinegar or lemon juice. Cumin in pintos if you want a Mexican touch. A dash of celery seed in beans along with garlic, perhaps, and maybe another herb. Mustard, coriander, a *dash* of cayenne, are all compatible with beans. Molasses, sugar, or honey work for some occasions. Red wine (try on reddish beans), cognac, rum, Drambuie (I tried this once — not too much), have all been partners with beans. Beer.

Vegetables in endless variety. And the great meat complement to beans — pork. Try lentils with sausage or ham hocks. Or the day after you've eaten ham, cook limas with a ham bone and some leftover ham.

*Caution:* Be careful when stirring beans. They are more delicate than they look.

We shall finish this discussion with *Maggie's Multiday Beanfest.*

Maggie does not soak her beans overnight. (Incidentally, there's nothing wrong with soaking beans half-overnight, etc.) She does not soak them at all. Of course, the canny reader will observe how she gets away with it.

She takes pinto beans, picks them over, rinses them, and puts fresh water in the pot — almost but not quite twice as much as you normally would put in for beans. The amount is not critical. She covers the pot and brings it to a boil right away, then lowers the heat to a *strong* simmer. After 30 or 45 minutes, or "whenever things start to smell good," she puts in a large onion coarsely chopped, some peeled garlic cloves (maybe), perhaps a touch of oregano, or, if she wants a Mexican flavor, some cumin. (Cumin is spicy — beware!) Maybe even a chile.

She cooks the beans covered until she can take a bean between her tongue and the roof of her mouth and crush it. "It should be *mushy.*" This is because she is making a bean **soup**, and so the beans should be softer than when just making *beans themselves.* Now and only now does she add salt, turning down the heat to a low simmer for about 5 more minutes.

This is the first day. It is essentially bean broth with more — or less — beans in each bowl, depending on how people like them. It is essential to have on the side for everyone a dish of chopped tomato, chopped onion, and cilantro (which is fresh coriander, sometimes called Chinese parsley), all sprinkled or doused with lime juice. (You can also use lemon juice.) You can add a chile pepper.

On the second day, there may or may not be some broth left. By the third day, it's always down to the beans themselves.

Maggie then puts corn oil in a skillet, or bacon fat, seasons the oil with torn shreds of tortilla (bought is okay), and possibly a chile. She mashes about half the beans with a wooden utensil (a masher or a wooden spoon). She cooks them for a few minutes to a consistency that looks pleasant to eat, then puts some jack cheese in the pan in small pieces (if you use Cheddar, you will not be arrested). "It doesn't matter if the cheese is irregularly blended." Cook gently so the cheese doesn't toughen. You can also stir in some sour cream (please do, sometimes!), but don't let the mixture boil. If it does, the sour cream will curdle though it will still taste good.

**And One of Life's Doorways Will Always Remain Closed — *until you have cooked beans in beer.* ***

· · · · · · · · · · · · · · · · · · · · · · · · · · · · · · · · · · · · · · · · · · · · · · · · · · · · ·

GUIDE TO
### Lamb, Rice, Cinnamon Stick and Peppercorn Stewoup

I set out to see how hard it would be to find a "stewoup" in a cookbook. I found one.†

Take a couple of pounds of STEWING LAMB, BONE AND MEAT, and cut into bite-sized cubes, cutting off the excess fat. Put into 2½ quarts of cold water, salted with KOSHER OR SEA SALT (what I've been telling you to use in cooking), and add about 15 WHOLE BLACK PEPPERCORNS and 2 WHOLE CINNAMON STICKS. Bring to a boil and simmer for 30 minutes. Add 2 cups of WHITE RICE (washed, if necessary) and simmer for 30 minutes more. This is not a rice soup. It's a very hearty stewoup. Excellent with YOGURT. If you don't want to be surprised by one of the peppercorns, then watch out for them.

Based on our chapter, all you really had to know were the ingredients: LAMB, RICE, SALT, CINNAMON,‡ and PEPPER. May the guide act as an inspiration for you to *try it.*

· · · · · · · · · · · · · · · · · · · · · · · · · · · · · · · · · · · · · · · · · · · · · · · · · · · · ·

*The beer should be flat. Open the can at least a half hour in advance. Use half beer/half water for starters.

†*One Pot Dishes*, Rochester Folk Art Guild, 1975, page 2.

‡However, you may not have known that cinnamon *sticks* are quite strong. That's why only two of them are sufficient.

# 32
# Special Finishing Tools
# (Polishing Up with Lemon,
# Parsley, Paprika, Nutmeg . . .)

*Show me a man who never burns . . .*

Fabled and even historical tales about the origins of foods and
the causes of their ancient esteem may provide clues to how
these more subtle foods were really understood and what their
essential functions were in cooking. But in this chapter we're
going to get down to a time that's closer — in fact, as close as
possible — to the inevitable moment when a particular twen-
tieth-century meal is about to enter the serving-eating phase.

As a new, often final, addition to a dish — to differentiate it
from a correction of the seasoning already present — lemon
juice is one of the most called upon. It can be used at the end in
soups, stews, starches, and grains, on vegetables, poultry, fish,
veal, and fruit. Use a little at a time, even by drops, and (when
possible) taste the result until you begin to know without tasting what the effect will be. (You can still taste, though.) Before
cutting into a lemon to extract the juice, *always* roll it on a
hard surface, pressing down with your palm, and you'll get
much more juice. Warming it will also increase the flow. If you
only need a few drops at a time, the lemon will keep longer if
you simply score a small X — or poke a hole — in the end,
squeeze, then put away.

We're concerned here exclusively with finishing, with polishing — that is, fine tuning — zest,* and emergency work. This involves not only the taste but the appearance of the food on the plate. *Garnishing*, a final touch added just before serving, is an important factor in meal preparation.

Scallions (also known as green or spring onions), melon and other fruit, olives, artichoke hearts, watercress, the well-known lemon slices and parsley sprigs — but why go on and on? Just remember to pay attention to this part of cooking, and consider the impressive role that appearance can assume in our meals. (In addition, this will remind you to slice and arrange the garnishes in pleasing ways.)

It may seem unfair to the actual cooking process that merely some color, a few fresh, raw things, or other "illusions" put upon a plate or table could give a meal such a lift, but it's not as unjust or mindless as it seems.

---

*Zest in the general sense, not just as the grated rind of lemon or orange (just the rind, not the white pulpy part, which is bitter) that is called zest and is used to flavor baked desserts as well as some main dishes.

You need a certain vision or intention while in the kitchen to be a part of what's happening at the table. A cook can get lost in the rice pots and the baking pans while human beings out there are going to eat the food! So putting a proper garnish on a plate — not just for looks, but one whose taste and texture set off the other items on the plate — is pleasing to those at the table as well as a help to the cook.

Returning to the emphasis on flavor, the following are some common finishing tools, with only a *few* of the possible suggestions for each. It could be expanded, of course, but that would defeat its purpose. It's far better to know about a few condiments that have fairly wide use, and actually to practice using them, than to clutter everything up with an endless procession of possibilities.

There's no secret magic about how to use them except not to overdo, especially when lacing with peppers or concentrated prepared sauces. (It's important to know that there are times when you really may want to put in a lot of lemon or minced parsley, just as there are times when much more salt than you think has to be put into the soup.) The real magic is in what happens.

*Lemon.* Fish, many vegetables, casseroles, grains, chicken.
*Lime.* Fish, salads — it's sweeter than lemon.
*Vinegar,* including *apple cider vinegar.* Any liquid or semi-liquid dish that needs pepping up.

*Parsley.* For freshness and color, almost everywhere — the great rescuer.
*Chives.* Egg dishes, potatoes, salads.

*Nutmeg.* Cream dishes, stews, casseroles, spinach, rice — a perfect touch sometimes on squash or eggplant.
*Paprika.* A mild pepper with widespread use: chicken, cheese, sauces, soups, stews.

*Ginger.* Fruit dishes, also vegetables, fish, chicken, salads.
*Capers.* Bland fish, salads.

*Cayenne.* Piquant; use in tiny amounts for cheese dishes, white sauce, mushrooms, beans. A de-blandifier.

*Tabasco sauce.* Wherever you might want a red-hot pepper sauce; also, try a drop or two in scrambled eggs.

*Soy sauce* (tamari sauce is a Japanese version you may prefer). For flavoring and browning chicken and other meats in marinades; a few drops at the end in stews; with vegetables and grains, but don't always drench them.

*Maggi.* Stews, soups; a drop at a time in salad dressing.

*Butter.* Use your imagination.

*Cream.* Soups; eggs; in the pan sauce for veal.

*Bread crumbs.* A topping for noodles, casseroles, vegetables.

*Grated cheese.* Wherever you want some; often used with bread crumbs.

*Sherry.* A soup rescuer, but do not use it too often. Add right near the end — it's primarily the aroma of the sherry, not the flavor. A love match with cream of mushroom soup.

*Wine.* Add to soups 5 or 10 minutes before the end, simmering only, though it can also go in near the beginning for a more pervasive effect. An invaluable deglazer of pans in which meat or fish has been cooked, but occasionally, with ground beef or a steak, splurge with some *cognac.*

### The Great Health Food Restaurant Demonstration

There are two kinds of Health Food Restaurants. The first kind is concerned with using ingredients that if possible have been "organically grown." Since the ingredients are all of excellent quality, the owner (or the cook) is not concerned about what combination of foods are cooked or served together — or sometimes even how they're cooked. For example, the owner or cook likes raisin bread, or he or she has heard that it's nutritious or something. So when it's the "bread of the day" (and the only such), it's served with every dish on the menu regardless of how compatible it is with all these dishes. Or else you see this wonderful-looking apple pie heading your way. You bite into it, and before your very eyes, mouth, and fork, it transmogrifies into apples of marble set in a crust of concrete.

In this restaurant you can get food poisoning.

The second kind of Health Food Restaurant is also concerned

with using ingredients that if possible have been "organically grown." In this restaurant they have a feeling for food. The meals are delicious, satisfying, and memorable.

One evening I was dining in the second kind of Health Food Restaurant with a friend who admitted to little experience and even less knowledge of the art of cooking.

We both had (brown) rice on our plates. At a certain moment I saw her pick up the bottle of soy sauce that was permanently stationed on the table and begin shaking it liberally over her rice. I suddenly asked her if she would be willing to try an experiment! To just shake a few *drops* on part of the rice and mix it gently in. Then taste.

She was willing to try it — and she liked it. After quietly savoring another bite or two, she decided she preferred (or pretended to prefer) to eat the rest of her rice that same way. I was amazed. I had no idea it would work.

Of all the practical suggestions in this book, this may be the most important. If all you remember is this one thing — this little event — maybe something could happen just from that. Books will devote their pages to the preparation of various excellent dishes (certainly there's nothing wrong with that) and only mention something like this casually, or in the introduction, where nobody pays any attention to it.

Here is an experiment in which you can experience for yourself *the mystery of cooking*. It doesn't mean it's so recondite a mystery that nobody can know anything about it. No, it means that the workings of food are not wholly within our comprehension. (Some would say, not yet.) They are too quick, too fine — even for microscopes! Or maybe we have to wait for a different microscope.

Don't misunderstand me. It's okay to pour soy sauce (or tamari sauce) all over your rice like that. Who am I to tell you what to do with your rice? But do you see what happens when sometimes you use *drops*?

You can taste that the soy sauce actually "develops" the rice's own flavor without the slightest taste of soy, although there is a slightly different taste, which is the *result* of the soy yet *not* the soy.

Many things can be tried. See what opens up. Remember,

sometimes spices, herbs, and sauces are used "in the large" simply for what they are — like pan gravy on mashed potatoes, sour cream in borscht, basil in pesto sauce, curry in curried things, and so on. But this episode is about something finer; something that permeates all of cooking.

When you're done with this book, it will most likely fade away into a few thoughts, maybe a recipe or two, or some vague memories. But through a slight ungluing, a willingness to try a little something new, this story could help you participate in a certain subtle experience that you might have wondered about. It also happens to be a practice that perhaps more than anything can help you *understand recipes*.

The next thing to practice with is the lemon. Cookbooks talk about and their authors understand very well, but many cooks do *not* understand, this "soft" use of lemon.

I repeat. There are two different uses for each kind of seasoning. One, the "large" use, where lemon tastes like lemon (as in Greek avgolemono soup); and the other, where you do not taste the lemon without a special effort to do so. Like a few drops on *spinach* or *chard* during, or just after, cooking. This particular addition is perhaps even more magical — as though the lemon could charm into life some lethargic flavor spirit dozing in the midst of spring.

### When Apparent Catastrophe Strikes
*Scalding.* Stop it.

*Burning.* (1) *You* — Apply an ice cube to the area immediately and if possible keep air from getting to it (putting it in your mouth, your other hand, wherever); if you are knowing enough to have an aloe plant about, apply some of its juice. All pharmaceutical first-degree burn remedies pale before it, and of course if you grow your own it costs practically nothing. (2) *The food* — Get it off the heat immediately. What is on top may still be in good condition. Let the pot soak in a baking soda solution — if necessary, overnight.

*Collapsing.* It may still taste just fine.

*Mushing Up.* Mush it up even more, add to white sauce for cream soup — or, with butter, parsley, and maybe bread crumbs and cheese (and additional seasoning if necessary), make the renowned Wayfarer's Mush Dish (or some such thing).

*Boiling.* The sour cream has curdled. Well, since the taste is not affected in this case, you have merely created . . . (give it some French or Russian name). If the eggs have curdled, pour into a cold dish, perhaps with an ice cube, and whisk like mad. Sometimes beating in a couple of globs of sweet cream will save them.

*Boiling Over.* Get newspaper.

*Getting Real Irritated.* Pour half a glass of wine (do not measure) and sip while humming an invented Italian folk song.

*Getting Burned Up.* It will pass.

. . . and I'll show you a man who never cooks.

— Lois Lane

# PART SEVEN

# THE CALL
# FROM CHILDHOOD
# THROUGH
# THE AGES

# 33
# Baking

**Bread First**

*Wheat* — a secret awaiting rediscovery.

Once upon a time a taste existed that was appreciated by more or less everybody. It was a modest yet substantial taste, a simple yet fulfilling taste, a sweet — surprisingly sweet — yet subtle taste. It was blendable, in harmony with a rich experience of life. It never forced its way into favor. It never pushed or shoved. It never demanded a special time or place to be worshiped or required a special container. It lived the way a blade of grass lives, strong and yielding — plain, like a mountain, like sky. It was entirely itself, yet many joined themselves to it as it weaved its way into humankind for untold thousands of years.

This was wheat — that is, before every imaginable "improvement" was made on it. And like the demise of most things, it didn't begin as any sort of obvious outrage. So subtle was the beginning of this downturn to complete submersion that it went almost entirely unnoticed — and so it does still.

Wheat, one of the great staple grains on the planet, is not a dull, emasculated flavor yearning to be gooey or prettied up. It is strong, yet extraordinarily delicate. With an "outer" flavor that is somewhat bland, comfortable, and pleasant in its texture, it possesses a range of "inner" flavors — much like a fine wine, though not as obvious or with so full a spectrum — delicate flavors that are easily overwhelmed by almost anything one adds to inspire or improve it. Wheat is essentially intimate and therefore a bit shy, at least on the surface. It doesn't reveal itself or feel entirely at home when inundated by "company," though it is an excellent mixer, cheerfully adapting to most anyone or anything.

I'm not talking just about obvious additions, like nuts or raisins or herbs, or even eggs, but about *milk, honey, sugar* (including sugar for the yeast) and, yes, *salt.*

I'm certainly not saying that bread made with any of these isn't delicious and satisfying. These were the breads that used to be reserved for special days. They can be wonderful loaves, and probably they're even better than this simple bread. But it's a different kind of food.

What I'm suggesting is that you have a go at making a loaf of bread with three — only three — ingredients:

*Whole wheat flour* (not graham flour; the best is bread flour).

*Good water* (use spring or distilled water for the best possible result. But the inundation of chemicals in our tap water still takes a back seat to real bread, so don't worry overmuch).

*Yeast* (dry granules or a yeast cake).

If you've never eaten Whole Wheat Bread before (and if it's made with milk or honey or molasses or eggs or whatever else, it's *not* Whole Wheat Bread. It's Whole Wheat Milk Bread or Whole Wheat Honey Bread, etc.), you may discover that you're not that distant from other people who lived on the Earth a thousand years ago.

---

GUIDE TO
## Celtic Hearth Bread

2 cups MOUNTAIN SPRING WATER, or REALLY GOOD WATER, or JUST ANY WATER. 6 CUPS 100% WHOLE WHEAT FLOUR. YEAST. Heat ¼ cup of the water to body temperature or a little warmer. Stir briefly into it a package of active dry yeast. After some

minutes the yeast will froth up the water, which means there's life and the yeast is growing. Heat up the rest of the water only to lukewarm. Add the yeast water and about half the flour and with a big wooden spoon begin stirring the mixture. When it starts to get smooth and begins to stretch, add the remaining flour a cup at a time, all the while stirring and beating. Keep adding until the dough begins to leave the sides of the bowl even though it's still sticky. You may not use all of the 6 cups of flour.

Beat the dough in the bowl until you feel like your arm is falling off, about 5 minutes. The dough is a little resistant, but you can do it.

Then turn out the dough onto a lightly floured board and begin *kneading*. Good heavens! How do I do that? First of all, try to understand that kneading is an entire body movement, not just hands and arms. Think of it as a rocking motion using the heels of your hands, gently but firmly (your great-grandmother is right behind you, urging you on) pushing the dough forward, folding it back, turning it a quarter-turn and repeating. A very satisfying activity. But of course many people push, then turn, then fold back. I have seen people knead in what looks like a figure-eight pattern, and I have seen people knead bread like a corkscrew. They all work. Knead the bread for about 8 to 10 minutes. It should be satiny smooth, elastic, and springy. *Add only the amount of flour you need to keep it from sticking to the board. At this stage, too much flour will toughen the loaf.* When you do add flour, add it to the *board* — not to the top of the dough.

It's amazing; the dough feels magically, really magically *light*.

Oil a large bowl and put the dough into it and turn it upside down to grease both sides. Cover with a damp cloth and let stand in a warm place (not hot), free from drafts, for up to 2 hours, until the dough has *doubled in bulk*. In some kitchens, on top of the stove is a good spot — or in the unlit gas oven with the pilot light. Leave door open. *Don't let it rise too much* or you'll have a coarser loaf than you should — also yeastier. If you make a dent in the dough with your fingertips and the imprint remains, it's ready for the next stage.

*Punch it down with your fist.* Knead again in the bowl for just a minute or two. Let rise again — it won't take as long as the first time. Then turn out the dough and divide it in two loaves without shaping it yet. Let it rest for about 10 minutes while you get out the 9 by 5 by 3 inch (or some such) loaf pans. The oven should be preheated to 425° (25° less if the pans are Pyrex). Then shape the loaves, making sure each one touches the short edge of the loaf pan. Bake for 10 minutes; reduce the heat to 375° for another 20 to 30 minutes. When done, the loaves should slide easily out of the pans. Tap the bottom of the loaf. It should sound hollow. Otherwise, send it back for another 5 minutes. When done, a loaf is resilient to the touch. It's best to let it cool before serving. But if this is impossible, have a real bread knife handy or it will be a mess.

What I didn't tell you is that there's plenty of leeway. It's almost impossible to fail. Really. But the second time *may* be better than the first.

*Variations:*
Use 2 to 2½ cups whole wheat and 3 to 3½ cups unbleached white flour.

Add a glob of honey — also a pinch of sugar when proofing the yeast — and a pitch of salt.

Milk can be substituted for water.

. . . . . . . . . . . . . . . . . . . . . . . . . . . . . . . . . . . . . . . . . . . . . . . . . . .

Actually, you can take 2 cups of water, a package of yeast (you know now how to start it), flour of all kinds (see "The Fear of Baking," which follows), and other things of your choosing — there's amazing flexibility in making bread — as long as you know the "feel" of the dough and there's enough wheat flour in the mixture to make it rise. (Other flours don't have wheat flour's capacity to rise.) You can make two different loaves every day of the year without ever consulting a book (including this one).

### The Fear of Baking
Is there a Fear of Baking that is different from the Fear of Cooking?

Yes. Because in most cooking, the presence of a particular ingredient in any given dish is well understood: the chicken, the wine, the celery, the herbs. The experienced cook, merely by knowing what ingredients are to go into a dish, can estimate their relative proportions.

But in baking — that is, the baking of *batter* and *dough* — small changes in one or two ingredients can produce an entirely different result. For example, the difference between a sweet egg biscuit and a muffin is only an extra teaspoon of milk per muffin! Just as different sequences and durations of the same few notes produce thousands of different melodies, so in baking small changes in a few elements produce most of the great variety of tastable — and tasty — results.

Another dynamic factor in baking is that everything goes into a **dark oven and generally can't be monkeyed with until done.** In other words, it's "do or die."

How to overcome the Fear of Baking?

First, a brief list of some of the things you can bake with batter and dough:

*Bread* is flour and liquid leavened slowly by yeast (or unleavened).

*Quick breads* include certain cakes, also muffins and cupcakes, biscuits, popovers, and even pancakes and crepes. They are leavened by baking powder, baking soda, or only by the air beaten into eggs. The ingredients are usually combined simply and quickly and put right into the oven — or in the case of pancakes and crepes, into a hot skillet.

*Cakes* are similar to quick-bread cakes except that the combining of the ingredients is a little more drawn out with an additional procedure or two, such as creaming* the butter (often with sugar) instead of melting it. Cakes are usually leavened the same way as quick breads.

*Cookies* are actually a cake, but because they lack liquid they have a stiffer dough. The butter in cookies is usually creamed with the sugar.

*Pie pastry* requires that the shortening be "cut into"* the flour and that the dough be "rolled out."

---

*An interesting Arm and Hand Body Movement.

### You're Lost on a Desert Island Without Measuring Cups

Possessing only a muffin tin, a fork and bowl, some ingredients, and an oven (your basic desert island array), you are settling in for a (long) comfortable stay.

*Preliminaries.* Grease inside the cavities *well* with vegetable shortening or with the butter that's clinging to the butter wrapper the ship's cook threw up to you as he went under. Then melt a glob of butter over low heat.

*Preparing the basic substance.* Pour any amount of flour into the bowl — roughly, *a cup.* Pour about the same amount of milk into the bowl. (Thank heaven for coconuts!) Pour in the melted butter. Put in however much salt you think you'd like. (Should I tell *you,* a shipwreck survivor, how much salt to put on your food? But if you'd like a general indication, a couple of pinches for each cup of flour is plenty.)

Crack 2, even 3, eggs into the bowl. Or you can beat them slightly in one of those coconut shells, then add them to the bowl.

Mix all these things up with a fork until you've got a fairly smooth substance. This may take a minute or two. (You have the time.) It's better not to overmix, but it will work no matter what you do as long as the consistency is more or less right, like thin cream (or slightly heavier).

*Start baking, then head for the beach.* From variations and additions to this basic substance, called batter, you get crepes, pancakes, waffles, blintzes, and so on. You can start a restaurant (for tourists) later; now, let's pour the batter into the muffin tin cavities, *half full only* (a touch more won't hurt — but I hope the muffin tin in your shipwreck kit has fairly deep muffin holes). Turn the oven to 450°. (Preheating is permitted, but in this case it's not necessary.)

Put the tin in the oven and go for a 15- or 20-minute swim (watch out for sharks). Come back and lower the heat to 350°, then return to the beach for another 20 minutes to start your new sunbathing career. If you didn't get to turn down the heat (I know being chased by sharks isn't fun), don't get mad. In 35 minutes at 450° they'll be perfectly done anyway. The higher the heat, the crisper they'll be outside and the moister inside.

*Warning:* **Do not open the oven door during the first 30 minutes of baking — or else.**
*Ah, results.* Even if you have never made these before — or even if you have never cooked or baked anything in your life (it's a good time to begin, don't you think?) — you can tell when they're ready. (Just don't burn them!) If you don't know what they are, when you first look into the oven you will be astonished to see what happened to the batter you put into those muffin holes.

When done, if you like them drier inside, then slit the sides of each one with your Swiss Army knife (or nail clippers) to let the steam escape. Turn off the oven and leave the door ajar. If they can be easily removed from their containers, do so. You can let them rest on their sides in their little homes with the oven heat wafting over them for a few minutes so they will continue drying out. Or you can just snatch them out right away. (The air makes you hungry.)

Serve (yourself) — with almost *anything.* The obvious: butter and jam. But also chicken, cheese, whatever you can dig up, or pull down, or drag out. Go on a spree! (Actually, many such things can be put into the *batter* before it goes into the muffin tin. It's very flexible.)

For desert dessert I offer one splendid variation: Add a tablespoon — excuse me, you don't have one of those — I mean a hit, or a pitch, of cognac or your favorite brandy. (You didn't let *that* go down with the ship, did you?)

And be generous. Serve some to the rescue team, should they **pop over.**

### The Fear of Measurement — and Nonmeasurement
There is much more latitude in baking recipes than many people realize. Certainly there are some cakes and other products that require pretty precise measurement. But with measuring cups there is a limit to this precision, because when flour is more moist, for example in winter, a cup contains *less* flour than when it's dry. Professional bakers use scales for better accuracy, but here is a secret: The more experienced the baker, in most cases, the less the baker measures.

How can this be? Because in baking, not only can you tell by eye and by the feel of the weight of the flour or sugar in the scoop how much is there, you can also tell a great deal by the texture and the consistency of the dough or batter. One needs simply to know that throughout the entire range of normal, delicious breads and quick breads of almost every kind — biscuits, muffins, scones, pancakes, popovers, crepes, and even spice cakes and coffee cakes — there is enough leeway so that after you gain a little experience, much of the measuring is no longer needed.

But don't misunderstand me. Measuring is a blessed activity. Without measurement, everything in the world falls down at once. And certainly it's very satisfying to measure attentively and combine definite quantities of interesting substances like flour, baking soda, salt, and milk. The question is, what kind of measuring do we need for which things? Sometimes measuring with cups and spoons is the best way. And sometimes it isn't.

What about leavening? Perhaps you've heard that you have to be *very* careful about using substances like baking powder — or something will explode! Well, won't it?

How about this: In various cookbooks there are different directions for the amount of baking powder to put in, say, biscuits — or a coffee cake. For each 2 cups of flour, they vary all the way from 2 teaspoons to 3 or even 3½. Absurd, yes? (I've provided an experiment in the Guide to Biscuits.) In general, people use too much baking powder. Yes, there are various types of baking powder — some stronger, some weaker — but usually more is used than necessary.

### The Basic Seven, Leading to the Big Secret of Baking

There are exactly *seven* basic ingredients in baking — not "a few" or "a small number." Seven. This fact undercuts at least 90 percent of the unreasonable Fear of Baking.

Learn these in the following order, just as you would a scale: **flour, leavening, salt, sugar, butter, eggs,** and **milk.** *

---

*I find the above easier to say than the following, which admittedly is more comprehensive: **flour, leavening, salt, sweetening, shortening, eggs,** and **liquid.** Suit yourself.

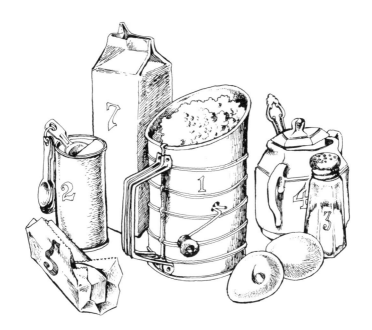

*Dry ingredients:* **flour** (the "body" of batter and dough — most often wheat) **leavening** (yeast, baking powder, baking soda) **salt.**

*Dry or semiliquid:* **sugar** (honey and a little molasses are the other common sweeteners).

*Semiliquid or liquid:* **butter** (or vegetable shortening, margarine, vegetable oil, lard), **eggs, milk** (water, buttermilk, sour cream, yogurt, fruit juice, or fruit pulp).

Additional flavorings such as vanilla or a liqueur can be considered as a liquid ("milk") ingredient, though they enter in very small amounts. Other additions, such as nuts and seasonings, if they don't contribute to the "body" (i.e., the "flour"), are not essential to the *structure* of the bread, quick bread, cake, cookie, or whatever. (There are some tarts, however, made only with filberts and eggs.)

**The big secret of baking:** Every bread, quick bread, and so on, is a result of combining two or more of the Basic Seven and applying *heat* (fire).

As soon as you know these ingredients, you will be able to "unravel" any recipe by *ordering* it along this scale. You will undoubtedly observe that many recipes purporting to be different have merely scrambled the ingredients in the written recipe and changed cinnamon to cloves or something. By ordering the ingredients you will make sense out of a baking recipe, and see how it compares with other recipes you have used, or at least unraveled. (Very soon you can take it all in at a glance.)

Having a definite number of basic ingredients makes them easy to remember; it appeals to our sense of order — as well as our sense of wonder — and it makes the new baker feel secure. But before we come to a more detailed look at the Basic Seven, you should be familiar with the most fundamental *relationship* in baking:

### The Creation of Batter and Dough — The Relationship of Flour to Liquid

This is what determines the kind of product we are making, whether a pancake, a coffee cake, a biscuit, bread, or pie crust. Don't memorize anything. Just get the basic idea.

A **pour batter** makes pancakes, popovers, crepes. Approximately 1 part flour to 1 part liquid.

A **drop batter** makes muffins, drop biscuits, and some cakes (but other cakes may be closer to a pour batter). About 2 parts flour to 1 part liquid.

**Dough** makes bread, biscuits, and scones. About 3 parts flour (some breads, 4) to 1 part liquid.

A **stiff dough** makes pastry, pie crust. About 6 to 8 parts flour to 1 part liquid.

Having a sense of this, along with a closer examination of the Basic Seven, we can begin to devise our own baking recipes. (That's terrifying. I mean anything might happen. A 30-foot plum cake!)

### Flour

Wheat flour is the only flour with sufficient gluten for rising. It comes essentially in three forms: whole wheat, regular white, and cake flour.

*One hundred percent whole wheat bread flour* is a hard, winter wheat, the best for bread but not always easy to find. Its toughness makes it less satisfactory for other baked products. There is perfectly fine *100 percent whole wheat* that is more adaptable.

*All-purpose (bleached) white* flour is the most common and can be used for almost anything. It's a mixture of hard and soft wheats. But why not use *unbleached* white flour instead? It's fuller bodied, richer, and softer than bleached, though slightly heavier. (Nutritionists favor it as well.) Wheat bread is often made with both whole wheat and white flours in order to achieve a lighter loaf than one using whole wheat alone.

*Cake flour* is a soft, bleached wheat flour that is good for making light cakes. You can substitute all-purpose or un- bleached flour for cake flour, yielding a heavier texture, but in some cases it's really not desirable. Use about 2 teaspoons *less* of all-purpose than cake flour. (This is the same as seven eighths of the amount of cake flour in the recipe, which may be easier to remember.) *Whole wheat pastry flour* is a 100 per- cent whole wheat suitable for pastry and many cakes (giv- ing a characteristic wheatier taste and a somewhat heavier texture).

All wheat flours can be freely intermixed.

Other grains are good with wheat and may be substituted for part of the wheat flour. Begin using a couple of tablespoons (pitches, remember?) of the new flour for an equivalent amount of wheat flour. This way you'll know how the new flour tastes and feels, yet you can be reasonably sure that nothing disas- trous will happen.

Examples: barley flour, potato flour, rice flour, and corn meal, rye flour (oops! an exception — rye can always be added up to at least a third of the wheat flour, sometimes half). To avoid lumps and excessive graininess in *rice flour* and *corn meal*, add these first to the liquid, bring to a boil, cool, then add to the other ingredients. Cracked wheat, wheat germ, and hulled millet are not actually flours, but they can also be added to bread dough.

### Leavening

Bread is leavened by *yeast,* which actually consists of living organisms that grow in warm, wet places before our very eyes (too small to pick out individuals, though). In its feeding process, yeast creates a gas (carbon dioxide) that pushes against the gluten of the wheat, which is sufficiently elastic to permit stretching, and that's how dough rises. Well, more or less. (Of course, many of the world's hardy and enduring civilizations existed on *unleavened* bread; it wasn't just Moses in the wilderness.)

Dry yeast granules (in packages) are the most common, but many experienced bakers prefer yeast in cake form. You can make delicious bread with either. There is a definite range of the proportion of yeast to flour. You can always use a little more, which will speed the rising time, but it won't make it rise any higher. Too much yeast will give the bread a yeasty taste (a little of this is usually fine). But most often an unpleasant, heavy yeasty taste is caused by *too much rising.*

The temperature for yeast to proof (that is, start to grow) is slightly hotter than lukewarm, but not hot. Once you experience the temperature, you'll always know it. Use your elbow as a measuring place — or your wrist. Very hot water from the tap is usually too hot, and if it's too hot, you kill the yeast; too cold, and it won't work. Somewhere between 95° and 110° is best. There is latitude.

With regard to leavenings for most butter cakes and quick breads, the most common is *baking powder,* which is 1 part baking soda and 2 parts some acidic ingredient (like tartaric acid) blended in an inert base that, when subjected to heat, creates the magical carbon dioxide, and this, just as with the yeast, stretches the gluten in the dough. When there is already an acid present, such as buttermilk, sour cream, yogurt, fruit pulp, orange juice, or molasses, *baking soda* (or *soda,* to help distinguish it from baking powder) is substituted for some of the baking powder. When there is a lot of acid present — for example, in the Kitchen-in-Ruins-Baking-School Banana Bread (page 324), where both sour cream and banana pulp make up the liquid — soda may constitute *all* of the leavening (with the help of a couple of eggs). Soda generally gives a more tender product, with a somewhat lighter crust (though sufficient sweetening will brown the crust).

*Eggs* also act as a leavener by trapping air during the beating process, and in contact with heat produce expanding steam.

Soda needs more careful measurement than baking powder because it's used in smaller amounts, so there's less leeway. And excess soda tastes even more unpleasant than excess baking powder.

There are *three simple proportions* you need to know in improvising with chemical leavenings. These are rarely, if ever, set down clearly and consecutively.

*Warning:* What follows will involve **mathematics** (shudder).

*Proportion 1.* One to 1¼ teaspoons of double-acting *baking powder* will raise 1 cup of flour. Use the higher amount when there is relatively more butter, nuts, and other heavier ingredients. (Older recipes were often written for single-acting baking powder, which requires nearly twice the amount of the modern, double-acting kind.)

*Proportion 2. (The Baking Soda Rule.)* For every cup of an acid ingredient in the recipe such as sour cream, yogurt, buttermilk, or fruit pulp, you need ½ teaspoon *soda* to neutralize it. This ½ teaspoon is also exactly what's needed to raise 1 cup of flour. **If there is baking powder in the original recipe, subtract** (don't keel over) 1½ teaspoons of the baking powder for every ½ teaspoon of soda that you add to the recipe. (It's simply that baking powder has a lot of soda in it.) If you only subtract a teaspoon of baking powder, you haven't ruined anything.

*Proportion 3:* An *egg* (beaten) is equivalent in leavening power to ½ teaspoon *baking powder*, but you need 2 or 3 eggs before this seems to have an appreciable effect on the rising.

### Salt

About ¼ teaspoon per cup of flour is average. That means about 1 teaspoon per loaf of bread. If you don't want to use salt, don't. Salt will tend to slow the action of the yeast in bread (sugar will speed it up), and it provides some structural support to the loaf — but don't worry about it. Use the amount of salt you want to use. *Caution:* baking soda (sodium) tastes salty, so go easy on the salt when using it.

So far, we've talked about flour, leavening, and salt — all dry ingredients. Once you have a little experience with these (and you already understand about salt) you're in an excellent position to experiment, because these proportions are pretty much fixed throughout most of baking. This means that by and large you have only to concern yourself with the other, more variable ingredients in the composition. And you know that the amount of liquid to flour is what determines the stiffness of the batter or dough — and this can be determined by feel. You see how it all comes together?

I am speaking especially about quick breads and regular yeast bread, *not about the many fine and delicate cakes that do need more exact measurements.* In the former two, there is room for substituting, for adding or subtracting honey or sugar, increasing or decreasing the butter or other shortening, and adding 1 or even 2 eggs. Of course, noticeable differences of amounts of these will give you somewhat different results. But that's what's interesting. You can experiment and see (and taste) for yourself without the Fear of Ruin.

### Sugar or Honey

In bread, it's usually honey. Use a mild honey if you don't want it to overpower the taste. (Generally, the lighter the honey, the more mild it is.) Sugar or honey is not just for a sweet taste. They will give a more moist and tender loaf with a browner crust, a more refined texture (sugar more than honey), and both will increase the keeping time of baked products. A little sugar or honey in the water where the yeast begins to grow will speed the microorganisms' activity (though too much will actually retard its growth). In general, sugar or honey can be reduced or increased in a recipe by a modest amount without a disaster, but the resulting texture will be (with some experience, quite predictably) a little coarser or finer, as the case may be.

Honey can always be substituted for sugar, but honey is

somewhat sweeter, so use a little less. (Try a third less.) You'll have to experiment because not all honeys are alike. When you're adding honey, you're adding *liquid*. But look at it. It doesn't flow like a liquid. So consider a cup equivalent to about ¼ cup of "regular" liquid. Therefore, subtract about a quarter of the regular liquid when adding honey to a recipe. Irifoy.

Molasses is rarely wholly substituted in an existing recipe for all of the sugar or honey; it's too strong. Try about half and half. A little molasses alone, however, is a good thing in many breads and cookies — whole wheat has an affinity for this sweetener — but too much really is a disaster. (I know this for a fact.) For those quick breads leavened by baking powder, you'll have to add a bit more soda than the pinch you might have needed to add (sometimes, even a big pinch) for the honey. Molasses is acidic; some strong honeys are about half as acidic. Most are even less so. Brown sugar, which has some molasses in it, is not considered much of an acid, but a pinch of soda if there's a lot of brown sugar present is not a bad idea.

### Butter

A code word for shortening in general: vegetable shortening, margarine, etc. For what it does to the flavor, texture, and appearance (F.T.A.), butter is my preference for most baked things, but vegetable oil can give excellent results (and cheaper ones) in some quick breads. Shortening makes things richer and more tender and moist, which also increases the keeping qualities. You can use from a glob to half a stick of butter for each loaf of bread, quick bread, or batch of biscuits or muffins. As with sugar or honey, you can usually be very flexible about how much to use. And just as with honey, when adding oil or melted butter, if you add at least half a stick you're adding a noticeable amount of liquid.

*Warning:* Just because butter does good things doesn't mean you should add too much. It will make your results depressingly heavy.

### Eggs

Amazing eggs! They do about everything, including leavening things. Five eggs alone will raise a sponge cake; 2 (per cup of flour and liquid) will raise popovers. (For some reason, on desert islands, I use 3.) By the way, once you begin beating eggs, *carry it through*. Don't let them sit around half-beaten.

Eggs make things richer, "yellowier," and more flavorful, just as shortening does, and, in addition, they toughen weak flour, such as a cake flour, giving it more firmness. You can fearlessly add at least 1 egg to any bread or quick bread. Remember, you're adding some liquid.

### Liquid

The most overlooked variable. Again, it's common sense. If I say that water makes bread *crisper* than milk, you understand — because milk is "softer" than water. Irifoy. And buttermilk, by the same token, is softer, more "tender," than sweet milk. Water tends to bring out the wheat taste in wheat bread. Milk makes bread more velvety and moist, so it keeps longer. ("Keeping," when referring to baked things, doesn't mean resisting mold; it means how long something will endure before *drying out*. Of course, when bread is homemade, it doesn't last very long!)

You can use your favorite fruit juice in quick breads (some chicken broth! in biscuits, sometimes — or *orange juice* in *pancakes*) and other flavorings. Quick breads almost always favor milk over water. But I think water in biscuits is just fine occasionally, depending on how you *season* them (yes, biscuits can be seasoned) and what you're eating them with. (Dill in water biscuits with a chicken lunch.)

### Flavorings and Additions

Your imagination is the limit. Raisins, dates, herbs (for example, fennel, caraway, sage, nutmeg, dill), and fruits. (Dust fruits — dates, etc. — with a little flour so they won't glom together in the dough. Add them at the end, just before baking.) A teaspoon or two of vanilla for sweeter breads. Sprinkle the top with sesame seeds or poppy seeds. In bread, especially, you can put in millet.

There is much flexibility, but the first thing in breads and quick breads is to keep the proportion of flour to liquid more or less the same. This you learn by looking, touching, and by feel . . . and you learn it fast. You don't have to have baked for twenty years to know how biscuit dough should feel, or how easily (or not easily) muffin batter should drop from the spoon. After just a few experiences, you can even tell something from tasting the cake batter.

### Some Common Temperatures in Baking
Biscuits and rolls: 425°
Bread: 375° (often 425° for the first 15 minutes)
Pies: 350° (usually 425° for the first 10 minutes)
Cookies: 350°–375°
Cakes and batter breads: 350°

See a pattern? The stiffer doughs generally require higher heat. (In general, when in doubt about your oven temperature, it's best to bake at a lower heat. An accurate oven thermometer can help you.)

### Arm and Hand Body Movements Common in Baking
Kneading, folding, beating, stirring, handling lightly, cutting, creaming, separating eggs, whisking egg whites, rolling out, shaping, stealing bits of dough and sneaking fingers into the batter with the excuse of "correcting" something.

If you're familiar with these few procedures, fear will never prevent you from baking wonderfully good and tasty things.

### Some Baking Secrets and Tips
Oven heat is often higher in baking (batter and dough) than in other kinds of cooking.

*On sifting.* There is no reason to sift flour for bread or most quick breads, except that when you measure a cup of sifted flour, it will contain about ⅛ cup (2 tablespoons or pitches) *less* than unsifted flour because the unsifted flour is more packed down. Many recipes call for sifted flour, so if you're following such a recipe, either take this into account by sifting — or by not sifting, and using less flour. Only for very light cakes does sifting seem to be useful. It also helps assure that all the dry ingredients are evenly combined, but you can achieve this by stirring just as well.

*Whole wheat flour is never sifted, only stirred.* Whole wheat flour may be cut with white flour, usually ⅔ whole wheat to ⅓ white — or the opposite — to give a lighter result.

*Quick breads.* Biscuit dough should be handled lightly.

Muffin batter should be mixed very little. Even less than little.

You can vary quick breads by adding or subtracting sugar, honey, butter, an egg, flavorings — and by varying the liquid medium.

For quick breads it's better to use less baking powder (and soda) than too much. But you do need enough! Two cups of flour will take 2 to 3 teaspoons baking powder, or about ¾ to 1 teaspoon soda. One common combination is ½ teaspoon soda and 1 or 1½ teaspoons baking powder.

In making quick breads, once you mix the batter or dough, you are supposed to put it in the oven without waiting too long. In spite of this traditional warning, I have noticed that biscuits, cakes, and pancakes made with *soda* mixed into the dough or some other thick substance like sour cream seem to benefit from a short rest *before* being put into the hot oven, during which the dough rises a little or the sour cream starts foaming up. (See the Guide to Banana Bread, for example.)

*Baking powder* loses its leavening power after a (long) time. Keep the lid on when not in use. To test its action from time to time, put a teaspoon of powder into ½ cup of warm water. It should fizz up vigorously.

*To sour milk*, add a tablespoon of white vinegar or lemon juice to a glass of warm milk, and let it sit for 10 minutes or so. (Suppose you're out of baking powder, you have some soda, and you want to make biscuits: sour the milk and use soda.)

*Cakes.* Beginning bakers almost never cream the butter with the sugar long enough when making cakes. Creaming the butter insufficiently (it should be light and fluffy, not greasy) is one of the major causes of inferior cakes. It takes minutes — maybe 5, but go longer.

*Cutting in butter in quick breads, cakes, and pastry.* It is easiest to cut butter into quick bread, cakes, and pastry when it is slightly colder than room temperature. However, for *pastry*, the results are better if the butter is even colder, though it's a little less convenient for cutting in. (You can use a pastry blender, two butter knives, or your fingers.)

### The Beginning
The Basic Seven, the amount of leavening and salt in relation to the flour (a fairly constant proportion), the relative stiffness of doughs and batters, and being hungry — what can stop you? (A 30-foot plum cake will probably have to be assembled outside.)

Of course, baking is not just breads and quick breads. As an introduction to future masterpieces, I have included in the Guides a simple cake leavened only with eggs.

---
. . . . . . . . . . . . . . . . . . . . . . . . . . . . . . . . . . . . . . . . . . . . . . . . .

GUIDE TO
### Of All Things, Measurements!

There's nothing wrong with a cookbook that encourages you to measure with your God-given faculties. But there's no reason to develop the Fear of Measurement. Most cookbooks give so many different equivalences that beginners (and even non-beginners) get discouraged. Here are the really few important ones to know in baking:

*1 TABLESPOON = 3 TEASPOONS. 4 TABLESPOONS = ¼ CUP. (This is very handy to know without stopping to figure it out.) 1 CUP = 8 OUNCES (A COFFEE CUP is considered to be only 6 OUNCES.) 1 PINT = 2 CUPS and 1 QUART, 4 CUPS. (You know these already.)

*The main substance to know about in connection with measuring is, first and foremost, BUTTER. You already know that 1 STICK = ¼ POUND; BUT IT ALSO = ½ CUP. (Learn this right now. It will save you *years* of confusion.) So 2 STICKS = ½ POUND or 1 CUP. FOUR STICKS, of course, make 1 POUND.

It helps to know that 1 CUP SIFTED FLOUR = ⅞ UNSIFTED, which means that 2 CUPS SIFTED FLOUR = 1¾ CUPS UNSIFTED

---
*I have starred the two most important — in fact, essential — paragraphs.

(which, for some, is easier to remember). And the opposite: 1 CUP UNSIFTED FLOUR = 1⅛ cups SIFTED, and therefore 2 CUPS UNSIFTED FLOUR = 2¼ CUPS SIFTED. (Pick one of these to remember, and the rest will follow automatically. Sifted flour takes up more room than unsifted.) If you substitute ALL-PURPOSE FLOUR for CAKE FLOUR, consider the CAKE FLOUR like *sifted* (lighter) and the ALL-PURPOSE like *unsifted* (heavier) and apply the above ratios.

FIVE LARGE EGGS = about 1 CUP LIQUID.

. . . . . . . . . . . . . . . . . . . . . . . . . . . . . . . . . . . . . . . . . . . . . . .
. . . . . . . . . . . . . . . . . . . . . . . . . . . . . . . . . . . . . . . . . . . . . .

GUIDE TO
## Kitchen-in-Ruins-Baking-School Banana Bread

This is more like a cake than a bread, and it illustrates how measurement needs to be more precise the more the product is refined. For example, you may reduce the sugar by a tablespoon or two and the resulting texture is not that different. If you reduce it by ¼ cup (4 tablespoons), the texture is noticeably coarser. But the bread is still delicious.

To give you the experience of working with recipes that ask you to *sift* the flour before measuring, I'm going to suggest that you sift the flour here. (Sift onto waxed paper or aluminum foil for easier cleaning up.) And since I ask you to measure various things with measuring implements, you may not be able to make this incredible banana bread until you've finished the book and obtained such items. (But this is really not true. I can actually make it by using ordinary cups and spoons and *eyeing* the fractional amounts; the results will be fine. In this case, though, it *may* not be as special as the original. (Or it may be more special — *but will you ever have that recipe again?*) Anyone can make perfect banana bread. It requires only a little organization.

You will need CAKE FLOUR, BANANAS, SOUR CREAM, EGGS, BUTTER, SUGAR, BAKING SODA, VANILLA, and SALT.

Begin to melt 1 STICK BUTTER (slowly). Then lightly stir 1 LEVEL TEASPOON BAKING SODA into ¼ CUP (4 TABLESPOONS) SOUR CREAM. Let it sit while you do something else. Add to the melted butter 1¼ CUPS SUGAR and 2 EGGS beaten lightly. Then add the SOUR CREAM with the SODA. (It should have sat for about 15 to 20 minutes. The sour cream will be a little frothy when you add it to the mixture.) Beat everything together well. Then add 1 CUP MASHED BANANA (roughly, three bananas) — that is, PULP. It is essential to use bananas that are so (over)ripe that they are *black*. (Seriously.) Mash them to liquid pulp with a fork. Be patient; it will take a little longer than you think. (Do this while the soda is still sitting in the sour cream.) Then add 1½ CUPS SIFTED CAKE FLOUR (for the right texture, it has to be cake flour — though it still tastes good with all-purpose) and ¼ TEASPOON SALT. (Baking soda tastes saltier than baking powder, so things made with a lot of soda usually require a little less salt.) Add 1 TABLESPOON VANILLA. (*Only* if it's very strong vanilla, use a teaspoon.) Mix well, but not too much. When you have a fairly smooth (or smooth) batter, it's ready.

Put into a *well-greased* (you can use vegetable shortening, like Crisco, or butter) 9-by-5-by-3-inch baking dish and place on the middle rack of a preheated 350° oven. Bake for 60 to 70 minutes. Test by inserting a toothpick in the center. If it comes out clean, it's done. Turn it out to cool on a wire rack for about 20 minutes before slicing.

. . . . . . . . . . . . . . . . . . . . . . . . . . . . . . . . . . . . . . . . . . . . . . . . .
. . . . . . . . . . . . . . . . . . . . . . . . . . . . . . . . . . . . . . . . . . . . . . . . .

GUIDE TO
## Biscuit Experiment

You will need FLOUR, SALT, LEAVENING, BUTTER, and MILK.
FLOUR — 2 cups, or a little less, unsifted. SALT — just shake some in. LEAVENING — well, most cookbooks try to frighten you into fussy exactitude. But look, they say different things! One tells you 2½ teaspoons of baking powder; another says 3 teaspoons for the same recipe. What does this mean? It means that (1) it's not that precise, and (2) some baking powders are stronger than others so you don't need to use as much. For example, I find that Calumet is slightly more potent than Clabber Girl (*"Clabber Girl?"*). So let's do an experiment.

Whatever opinions one has about measurement, there is

definitely a time when exact measurements are needed in baking — for example, when you're experimenting with a new recipe and you want to compare the results of some relatively fine distinctions. So, MAKE TWO BATCHES OF BISCUITS USING DOUBLE-ACTING BAKING POWDER. (Or just take my word for it and make only one batch.) Make one using 1¾ cups of unsifted flour (that's the same as 2 cups sifted) and 2 teaspoons of baking powder; another using 2½ teaspoons. Borrow the measuring implements from your neighbor, telling her or him that it's in the interest of science. Put in ½ teaspoon SALT.

Mix these dry ingredients together. Cut in the BUTTER (preferably cool) with cold floured fingers (remember, you can run cold water on the main artery of your wrist) or use two butter knives or a pastry blender.

Make a well in the center of the flour and pour in ⅔ cup MILK — you may need a little more if the flour is very dry. Take a fork at "12 o'clock," run it to "6 o'clock," then in a circle around the edge of the bowl. Don't stir longer than 15 or 20 seconds. At this point the dough should just barely hang together. It's all right if it looks messy. At this stage, it *will* look messy. Turn the dough out onto a lightly floured surface — almost anyplace clean. It will not be a perfectly round ball. As a matter of fact, its shape will be indescribable by science. Gather it up somehow and *knead.* (See Guide to Celtic Hearth Bread, page 306.) *Handle very, very lightly.* Use the heels of your hands, or if it's too much pressure for the little bit of dough, try the fingers. Either way, push, turn, fold back — at most eight or ten times, and do it quickly — no more than 20, 30 seconds. *Do not beat up on the dough or you'll be sorry.*

Pat it down with your hands, making it about ½ inch thick. If, at the end, you fold it over before patting it down, it will . . . well, try it yourself and see. Using a small drinking glass dipped in flour (or a biscuit cutter if you happen to have one), cut out round pieces with a firm, straight-down motion. For an even rise, try not to twist; but if you do, no one will notice. The leftover dough between the circles can be patted into any shapes you like. (Kids like unicorns and buffalos.) Do not knead again.

Gently place the roundlets and unicorns of dough about ½

inch apart on a baking sheet. (If you don't have one, a baking sheet is an inverted roasting pan or skillet.) Bake 12 to 15 minutes. (Don't open the oven during the first 5 minutes or so because that's when the rising takes place.) By the way, if you want crustier biscuits, separate them by a good inch on the baking sheet.

After your experiment, try substitutions and additions if you like. *You can add an egg.* You can sprinkle things in or on top of the dough, like cinnamon, parsley, or dill. A half-cup of grated cheese, nuts, grated orange peel with a little sugar . . . and so on. (If you put a teaspoon of sugar into the dry ingredients, you probably won't notice its taste, but it gives a nice brown shade to a finished biscuit.) Sour cream can be used (remember the baking soda rule, page 317). You can make cheese and bacon biscuits. Parsley and garlic biscuits?! Cashew butter biscuits? Maple sugar biscuits? Forget the toast tomorrow morning. Or do the baking powder experiment. The question is: Do I need 2 — or 3 — teaspoons (a tablespoon) of baking powder? Put this way, it seems to be a silly question. But recognize that at this very moment, tens of millions may be putting too much baking powder into biscuits and other quick breads. It may not be that silly.

*Note:* To reheat biscuits and other breads, put into a damp brown paper bag and into a 300° oven for about 5 minutes. This really helps.

. . . . . . . . . . . . . . . . . . . . . . . . . . . . . . . . . . . . . . . . . . . . .
. . . . . . . . . . . . . . . . . . . . . . . . . . . . . . . . . . . . . . . . . . .

GUIDE TO
## Spirited Pound Cake

2 sticks BUTTER, 1½–1¾ cups SUGAR (or BROWN SUGAR), 1 teaspoon MACE, ¼ teaspoon SALT (measuring not required), 5 EGGS, 1¾ cups *unsifted* FLOUR, 1 teaspoon VANILLA, 2 teaspoons CALVADOS (French apple brandy).

Cream the butter, pressing the back of your wooden spoon back and forth against the bowl, adding the sugar gradually. This should take many minutes. *Cream well.* Add the mace and salt while creaming.

Crack 4 eggs, one at a time, right into the bowl and beat with the butter-sugar mixture. Then stir in the flour gradually, mixing well after each addition. Beat in the remaining egg, then blend in the vanilla and the Calvados. The batter should be smooth, but don't mix too much.

Put into a 9-by-5-by-3-inch loaf pan with the bottom greased well with butter (use what's left on a butter wrapper, smearing it around with your fingers); scatter some flour over the butter and shake it out (over the sink), leaving a light coating. Place in a *cold oven;* set to 300° and bake for 1 hour or until a TOOTH-PICK inserted in the center comes out clean. Cool in the pan for 20 minutes. Turn out onto a wire rack, where it will finish cooling. To store, put in a cake box with a tight lid. It keeps and keeps. And gets better and better and better.

. . . . . . . . . . . . . . . . . . . . . . . . . . . . . . . . . . . . . . . . .
. . . . . . . . . . . . . . . . . . . . . . . . . . . . . . . . . . . . . . . . .

GUIDE TO
**Basic Apple Pie**

Take 6 TART APPLES (tartness is especially important here — use Northern Spy, Pippin, Jonathan, Granny Smith, and many others, but not Rome Beauties, which are, however, excellent for Baked Apples; ask a good grocer about this), peeled, cored, and sliced as you like them; 1 to 2 teaspoons of LEMON JUICE; a couple pinches of SALT; a teaspoon or less of CINNAMON; a pinch or more of NUTMEG; ¾ cup (about) BROWN SUGAR — or half and half with WHITE SUGAR; 2 tablespoons (globs) of BUT-TER; 1 tablespoon (pitch) or more of FLOUR is optional (it will thicken things a little — so, do you want some?).

Why is everything so vague? Because you have to taste the apples. You may need more sugar or less; you may not need any flour; adjust the lemon juice to your taste. The first time you make this, you won't know exactly how it's going to come out. But instead of just automatically putting this much of that in there, see what things are like before you bake — and then after. The next time, you'll have a much better sense of how things will taste. Believe it or not, this is a shortcut to learning.

(Remember, most shortcuts start with a fence that you have to climb over.)

Mix everything together except the butter, adding the lemon juice last, to taste. If the apples are tasty, you won't need very much. Put the mixture in a PASTRY CRUST (see page 235) and dot with BUTTER. Put the top crust on, crimping the edges and making three or four gashes in it.

Bake in a 425° preheated oven for 10 minutes; then lower the heat to 350° for 35 or 40 minutes. The crust should be browned.

. . . . . . . . . . . . . . . . . . . . . . . . . . . . . . . . . . . . . . . . . . . . . . .
. . . . . . . . . . . . . . . . . . . . . . . . . . . . . . . . . . . . . . . . . . . . . . .

GUIDE TO
## The Basic Idea of Cookies

Cookies are a rich and flowing world you can explore. There are bakers who make cookies like musicians improvise melodies — never exactly the same. Of course, there are many things to find out about eventually, but I'm just going to start you off.

A basic ratio is BUTTER — say, ½ cup (often more); TWICE AS MUCH SUGAR — 1 cup (at the most); this can be brown sugar, honey, etc.; TWICE AS MUCH FLOUR (BY VOLUME) AS SUGAR — 2 cups; 1 EGG; maybe 1 teaspoon VANILLA; some SALT; maybe some WATER or MILK or other LIQUID; BAKING SPICES; often LEAVENING: for each cup of flour, about a teaspoon of baking powder or ¼ to ½ teaspoon baking soda if sour ingredients are used, including fruits or a relatively large amount of spices. Don't be fussy with cookies; use one kind of leavening or the other, not both.

This is meant only to give some order where confusion often reigns. SHORTBREAD: Since it is "short" — that is, more buttery — it reverses the sugar/butter ratio; e.g., ¼ cup SUGAR, ½ cup (1 stick) BUTTER, 2 cups FLOUR. *Often much less flour* is used, and sometimes other items such as nuts enter into the body. BAKING SODA is a common leavening for cookies — especially when molasses or lots of spices or nuts are used.

There is a basic cookie construction that begins with *cream* the butter; gradually add the sugar (continuing to cream); beat in an egg, then add the vanilla and other liquid. Then add the flour. (Yes, sometimes the vanilla is creamed initially with the butter, etc.) What does this remind you of? A CAKE. Right, a cookie is a member of the cake family.

The best pans for cookie making are *hard, shiny, flat,* and *just large enough to accommodate whatever number of cookies you're making.* If the dough doesn't have a lot of shortening, grease the pan lightly with a crumpled (preferably, SWEET) BUTTER WRAPPER. The usual range for oven heat is 350° to 375°; start out at 365°. If there are lots of sticky things like chocolate or molasses, try 350° to avoid burning. It's best to bake only one pan at a time. If you're making drop cookies, the dough should "plop" when dropped from a spoon. When adding the flour, do not overmix or it will make things tough. You can tell if the amount of flour is right if your finger doesn't stick to the dough. But don't add too much. To flatten cookie dough, use your wet fingers. Cookies can take anywhere from 7 to 25 minutes, depending on the cookie. Most important: *watch carefully,* because when they're done (browned nicely) they should be removed immediately.

This may be difficult to swallow (I hope that doesn't turn out to be a pun), but *I'm not going to give you a recipe.* Isn't it exciting just to plunge in and invent your own personal cookie? That's right. This guide stops here.

. . . . . . . . . . . . . . . . . . . . . . . . . . . . . . . . . . . . . . . . . . . . . . . . . .

# 34
# We Won't Dessert
# a Chapter on Need
# (Short and Sweet)

> Desserts yesterday, desserts tomorrow, and
> desserts today!
>
> — The Mad Hatter

Is dessert just a rounding off of the meal, a way to signal the organism that food service is temporarily suspended and will you please get up so someone can clear the dishes?

Certainly it is these essential things. But dessert also dramatizes and civilizes the meal. Every cook has experienced the presentation and preparation of a meal as a miniature (and sometimes not so miniature) drama. It has a beginning, a middle, and an *end*. *Dessert* is derived from a word that means "to clear the table."

Without a proper space of time after the main course, however, the dessert may be just another (often sweet) dish served on a smaller plate than the meat. The pause before dessert is a special time in any meal. After the main dishes are removed, we begin to enter more totally into the experience of the meal — the food, the surroundings, the people. The conversation becomes more lively; articulate observations (and uproarious ones) are freely exchanged; liaisons are strengthened — and loosened; friendships deepened; real attitudes (wine helps) reveal themselves. Our lives, unfolding.

Finally, the dessert is served. Upon its arrival a hush, if ever so brief, and the characters we were playing out a moment ago recede, as our attention is called back to the meal at hand and the anticipation, and satisfaction, of another perfect finish.

Desserts, through all of our days.

. . . . . . . . . . . . . . . . . . . . . . . . . . . . . . . . . . . . . . . . . . . . .

GUIDE TO
**Strawberries in Heaven**

Large STRAWBERRIES sliced, or small whole ones, dipped in a bowl of SOUR CREAM mixed with BROWN SUGAR (*at least* twice as much sour cream as sugar — start out with three times as

much and add more sugar if you need it) are almost unbelievable.

Depending upon your religious beliefs, you may consider
adding a "spirit" to the blend.

. . . . . . . . . . . . . . . . . . . . . . . . . . . . . . . . . . . . . . . . . . . . . . . . . . .
. . . . . . . . . . . . . . . . . . . . . . . . . . . . . . . . . . . . . . . . . . . . . . . . . . .

GUIDE TO
**Apples Underneath**

Tart APPLES (Northern Spy, Pippin, Jonathan, Granny Smith
and many others — ask your grocer), peeled, cored, and sliced.
BROWN SUGAR, a goodly amount — or HONEY (or both), SOUR
CREAM or YOGURT (really, put some in). A little LEMON JUICE.
FLOUR, well sprinkled. Some VANILLA, if you like. Some CINNA-
MON, and a pinch or so of NUTMEG. A little SALT may be
needed. Put half-globs of BUTTER all over.

Do it in layers, or don't. Put them in different orders, more of
this, less of that. But put the APPLES UNDERNEATH.

Place uncovered in 350° oven — for 30, 35 minutes?

Perhaps now you'd like to "graduate" to a more specific procedure — and something most delicious (next page).

. . . . . . . . . . . . . . . . . . . . . . . . . . . . . . . . . . . . . . . . . . . . . . . . . . .
. . . . . . . . . . . . . . . . . . . . . . . . . . . . . . . . . . . . . . . . . . . . . . . . . . .

GUIDE TO
**A Single-Nut-Crust Apple Pie**

Place 3 or 4 tart APPLES, peeled and sliced the way you'd like
to have them in a pie, in a 10-inch pie plate (glass is fine). Add
¾ cup LIGHT BROWN SUGAR and spread over the apples. Cut 1
stick BUTTER into 1 cup WHITE FLOUR with another ¾ cup
LIGHT BROWN SUGAR and ¼ teaspoon SALT. Mix these together
thoroughly, and add ½ cup chopped PECANS and ¼ cup
blanched, toasted ALMONDS and mix well for a doughy consistency.

Spread the mixture with a broad knife (or some other way)
over the apples, covering them evenly, and pinch the dough
down all around the edge of the plate.

Bake for 1 hour in a 350° oven or until done and the crust edge is lightly browned. Serve with EASY HARD SAUCE (next).

. . . . . . . . . . . . . . . . . . . . . . . . . . . . . . . . . . . . . . . . . . . .
. . . . . . . . . . . . . . . . . . . . . . . . . . . . . . . . . . . . . . . . . . . .

GUIDE TO
**Easy Hard Sauce**

Cream some BUTTER until soft. Quite a bit of SUGAR, added gradually, creamed with butter. Add SALT, VANILLA (or RUM, or BRANDY). Blend in.
Chill, covered.
You can put over Apples Underneath, if you want.

. . . . . . . . . . . . . . . . . . . . . . . . . . . . . . . . . . . . . . . . . . . .
. . . . . . . . . . . . . . . . . . . . . . . . . . . . . . . . . . . . . . . . . . . .

GUIDE TO
**Light and Wonderful Chocolate Mousse**

There are richer MOUSSES (what a funny word), but for simplicity of preparation and refreshing satisfaction, this one is hard to surpass.
Melt 4 ounces of SEMISWEET CHOCOLATE SQUARES (or BITS) over *low heat* in a *heavy-bottomed pan* with 1 tablespoon of BLACK COFFEE. (If you measure this, you have missed an important point.) Stir to prevent burning and to make smooth. Remove from heat and as it cools a little, separate 3 EGGS. Beat the yolks lightly. Stir the chocolate into the yolks (not the reverse) and blend thoroughly. If you want VANILLA, put in about a teaspoon now. Beat the whites until stiff but not dry, and fold in, a little at a time, until *completely* blended. Spoon into a serving dish and chill, covered, for at least 8 hours.
You can make the mousse eggier or less eggy simply by adding or subtracting an egg. You can omit the vanilla; you can also add some other spirit of your choice.
Do a mousse.

. . . . . . . . . . . . . . . . . . . . . . . . . . . . . . . . . . . . . . . . . . . .

. . . . . . . . . . . . . . . . . . . . . . . . . . . . . . . . . . . . . . . . .

GUIDE TO
**Idiot Custard**

Various books tell you to combine things different ways. I've never had any problem making delicious CUSTARD by stirring — not beating — 3 EGGS (or, for a more tender product, 2 EGGS and 2 EGG YOLKS), 2 cups MILK, about ⅓ cup of SUGAR — or use HONEY — more than a teaspoon VANILLA, a good pinch SALT — even a pinch FLOUR, sometimes. *I mix it all together without worrying.* I put it in one big dish (you can also pour it into individual custard cups, which will cook in half the time) and put that in a larger pan that has about an inch of hot water in it to "buffer" the custard from the oven heat. Bake in a slow oven, 325°, for at least an hour. Insert a knife blade near the edge; if it comes out clean, remove from oven (and other pan) and let stand to cool and finish cooking (the center doesn't cook as fast). Chill before serving. It's excellent over or under BERRIES — or all alone.

Instead of vanilla, dissolve some MELTED CHOCOLATE into it (slowly, gently). The list of possibilities could go on and on.

Custards should always be kept refrigerated.

. . . . . . . . . . . . . . . . . . . . . . . . . . . . . . . . . . . . . . . . .
. . . . . . . . . . . . . . . . . . . . . . . . . . . . . . . . . . . . . . . . .

GUIDE TO
**Childhood Chocolate Icebox Cake**

This is an unfair dessert. Why? Because no dessert I know provides such profound dessert-fantasy fulfillment compared to the ease of preparation.

Go to the STORE and BUY a product called CHOCOLATE ICEBOX WAFERS. These are nondescript, thin, pale brown cookies that taste absolutely like nothing special whatsoever.

Go HOME and make WHIPPED CREAM with a bit of SUGAR. Take a loaf pan and alternate putting cookies on their edges with slabs of whipped cream and fill up the dish.

336 • The Call from Childhood Through the Ages

Put in the refrigerator overnight. Everything will soak together into the most delicious dessert. Cut across the cake at
an angle so you don't separate the layers. Just hanging out
around the icebox while it's chilling in there is a thrill.

. . . . . . . . . . . . . . . . . . . . . . . . . . . . . . . . . . . . . . . . . . . . . . . .
. . . . . . . . . . . . . . . . . . . . . . . . . . . . . . . . . . . . . . . . . . . . . . . .

GUIDE TO
**Flaming Bananas**

Slice thin slabs of BANANA and sauté them in BUTTER over
fairly high heat, about a minute on each side. Scatter BROWN
SUGAR over the slices and when it just begins to melt, remove
it from heat and pour *warm* RUM or COGNAC over and *light it. It
goes up in flames!* (After this, it tastes great.)

. . . . . . . . . . . . . . . . . . . . . . . . . . . . . . . . . . . . . . . . . . . . . . . .

# OVERVIEW

# 35
# Vital Aspects

Amore sol la mi fa remirare, la sol mi fa collecita. *(Love alone makes me remember, it alone keeps me alert.)*
— Leonardo da Vinci

Maybe you think that a recipe is like one of those chemical formulas you mixed up in school, a clearly definable process. You measure properly, follow the instructions, don't make any mistakes, and you produce the best possible results.

Right?

Wrong.

Cooking is like chemistry only if you are picturing the chemist as delightfully mad. Not only are the movements and rhythms of cooking different from those of chemistry, but the entire framework is also broader, richer, and more subtle; yet if one tries to describe it in words, it just seems foolish and overstated. Countless things are taken into account in cooking: the weather, the season, the cook's disposition and mood, the quality and state of the ingredients, and so on.

*An experiment.* Take a snapshot and ask some capable artist *to draw a likeness from the snapshot.* Then ask the artist to draw the same subject from life.

What's the basic difference?

No matter how good the photo is, in rendering from life the artist has an immensely larger field that he can hardly avoid relating to: three dimensions (at least), his other senses, changes in the atmosphere, vibrations, and who knows what else. In other words, the framework in which he observes the subject is richer, more encompassing, and more complex, and he cannot help but take much more into account.

Similarly, cooking exists in a much wider framework than, for example, chemical science — at least the way in which we presently conceive of chemistry. For the particular genius of science is that its framework is intentionally restricted to known and repeatable conditions, to verbal or mathematical formulations, and thus results can be reproduced "exactly" — the concept of exactness in science being "exactly" describable (well, in a way).

But in the process of cooking there are many factors that never are and never can be itemized in a recipe. The issue is not that of a lack of precision but of a different kind of precision, a precision that has known boundaries of leeway (known not necessarily in the intellect) like a navigator coming into port or a tightrope walker balancing in the wind. Many of the elements in cooking are subtle and elusive, influencing the process in ways we don't yet fully appreciate.

For example, the world at large impinges, and what's wrong with letting it in? Suppose it's raining. You could start simply with: What would be nice to eat on a rainy day?

> If you would like to investigate sauce béarnaise further, much can be done. I was impressed by how little quantitative control I had over the experiments. For example, the eggs were nonuniform and all measurements were unnervingly imprecise for a physicist. A thorough quantitative, controlled experiment is needed. — Jearl Walker, "The Physics and Chemistry of a Failed Sauce Béarnaise," *Scientific American*, December 1979.

The process of cooking. Many are inclined to think that cooking is a procedure to be performed, but actually it's a process that, at best, we manage. Every cook knows that the most active part of the cooking process goes on all over the world inside pots, saucepans, skillets, on grills and skewers, in baskets and leaves, and that it needs a certain kind of care and attention that is hard to describe because it doesn't involve at every moment a physical activity or task.

These are practical matters, for as our awareness broadens

and deepens, our understanding of what we are working with and how we are working with it changes and substantially influences the results. Becoming aware — sometimes in the very midst of the activity of cooking — of the larger world within which we prepare our meals helps us to experience cooking not just as a linear set of procedures (which it also involves), but directly as a *living* process; and a simple wonder at the reality of all this food roasting and simmering and steaming keeps the cook alert and contributes to an atmosphere in which something subtle and wonderful can occur — noticeable in the quality of the food that ultimately appears on the plates.

Of course, there is a science of food preparation just as there is a science of drawing, of writing, of being a businessman, or of gardening — but there is more. What do we really mean when we say that he or she cooks with love? Is it just a figure of speech? Is it just the excellence of technique? Or is it something else? Isn't it true that most of us *know* that it's something else?

We know now that plants, for example, are in some way sensitive to other forms of life about them, including humans (which, of course, is not surprising to anyone truly familiar with plants).

So what about food? Eggs, for instance, as cooks know, are extraordinarily sensitive to how they're treated with regard to beating, heating, timing, etc. Maybe they're also sensitive to how *we* are toward *them*. You think this is absurd? Perhaps it is, but you could ask some of your friends, including a scientist or two *after* he has doffed his or her "official" pose and goes into the kitchen to cook! Or ask a potter about clay being "dead" or a weaver about wool. Their responses don't make any of this true, but they could give one room for thought.

It's not that science verifies things that are wrong; it's just that a particular science may be too limited, too old-fashioned. So, heavier balls used to fall faster than lighter balls (seems reasonable, come to think of it) and today, if the question were put, the response from some quarters might well be that Food Is Dead. In other words, *life* is just a molecular phenomenon. It doesn't matter what cooks say about all this — or whether they believe it or even think about it; it's to what extent they put it into practice that matters.

Whether you believe that foods "respond," or that with more care we are helped to be better prepared, quicker, and more responsive in the kitchen, since this is a practical manual and not a place to settle ancient controversies, we'll leave the matter here. But there is something more.

Chemistry as a paradigm for cooking, though sometimes helpful, may give rise to a basic misunderstanding that many never get free of no matter how much time they put into cooking.

This doesn't mean that chemical research and discoveries about the cooking process are not useful or welcome. It simply takes issue with the naive concept that chemistry (at least the stage to which we have been able to bring it in the twentieth century) is comprehensive, quick, and fine enough to stand as a model for the comprehensive, flowing, profound reality that is cooking.

If a chemical description of what is going on in the kitchen is what you wanted, you know by now that this is the wrong book! (A chemical description of asparagus will never taste like asparagus.)

The reader who wishes to pursue this could begin by inspecting the article in *Scientific American* quoted earlier in which a scientist attempts to analyze a failed sauce béarnaise. A valiant and informative attempt — if you are a chemist. If you are a cook, unless you have a bent for chemistry, it's all rather peculiar. And that failure is inevitable is quite reasonable to anyone who has observed that in certain domains we are more sensitive than any of our instruments.

Walker goes on to say:

> Since preparing the sauce involves rather inexact measurements of ingredients that can vary considerably in their composition, I cannot be more definite about what is responsible for the stability of the sauce or about which remedy is best every time. I cannot even say with certainty that the sauce is either a lyophobic or a lyophilic suspension or whether its stability is due to electric repulsions between diffuse layers or to protective coatings of bound water. In

short, the preparation of sauce béarnaise remains more an art than a science.

But instead of despairing and calling it an art, a word that here means "not understood by science," perhaps it is better to recognize that even when cooking is pursued as a *science*, it is necessary to welcome the participation of the one instrument we know of that is capable of assessing very subtle qualitative changes (perhaps even in domains not officially deemed to exist), an instrument that modern science in its investigations rigorously tries to exclude.

Ourselves.

# 36
# How to Invent Food:
# The ABC's of Cooking

"Aooga!"
— The Invention of the Wheel (also, the horn)

"How do you Invent Food, Part Three?"

It's as simple as A, B, C.

"What's A?"

A is what you want to cook — you know, veal scallops, mustard greens, rutabagas, pork chops, noodles, onions, oysters, endive, leg of lamb, carrots, lobster, asparagus, boysenberries . . .

"Some of those are pretty weird."

Okay, how about beefsteak, russet potatoes, string beans, mushrooms, turkey, spinach, cornmeal, tomatoes, Gruyère cheese, tapioca, blowfish, and apples?

"*Blowfish?* Anyhow, I got what A is. What's B?"

B is what makes the A's go, what pushes, pulls, and changes them into edible food. Naturally, there are the basic processes like braising, baking, and so on. Then you've got essentials like butter, oil, shortening, water, stock, flour, and salt (when used in the cooking), *which are intimately bound up in the basic processes*, often conducting the heat to the main ingredients. They're easily recognized because they're major factors in cooking, substances that occur again and again, or their variations. For instance, you don't simmer something without a liquid to simmer it in; but it may not be water — it may be milk.

"That's pretty obvious."

The whole thing's obvious. That's the point: it's so obvious that a lot of people starting out don't know anything about it.

"What about C?"

C's are what modify the main ingredients, the A's. Different flavors, nuances, greater intensity or depth — like seasoning, sauces, garnishes, or even foods that in other dishes might serve as main ingredients. And it's the C's on which depend the usual "inventing" that people think of, at least in the beginning.

"How's that?"

Before I answer, I must tell you that in the next chapter we're going to expand the ABC method just a little, and —

"Next *chapter*? Are you writing a book or something?"

Don't you — oh, never mind. Anyway, the point of the C's is that they can be easily *changed,* and the changes are somewhat different in character than when you change the B's.

"Okay, different flavors, different shadings, various touches — whatever — right?"

Right. Of course, you can also change the B's. But as I said, the effects are a little different. The distinction between B's and C's may seem picayune, but it can be a very useful one.

"In reality, though, it's not always so hard and fast, is it?"

Well, no, it's just a guide. Let's look at an example.

"It's about time."

For instance, wine with chicken might be a B (if it's cooked mostly in wine) or a C (if wine is added, say, to the pan juices at the end), but never an A; that is, it's not the main dish, unless you're having a glass of wine with a piece of chicken floating in it.

"Bizarre."

Certainly the B's flavor the dish, too. But the cook *has* to have a B to make the entire process happen (in a roast, for example, the only B might be *the heat*), whereas a C is always expendable. I know it sounds complicated, but it's really simple. The point of the ABC method is just to have an idea of which things are A, which are B, and which are C. Or even just to realize that there *are* — roughly — these three different categories of ingredients in most every dish.

"Okay, that's helpful."

Again, to cooks this is obvious, but to the beginner it may not be. For example, how is it cooked? Liquid, fat, dry, or combination? Check out the B (or B's). What do you need? Butter, oil, chicken broth? Suppose you're sautéing in butter and you don't have any butter, or not enough, so you'll put in some oil; depending on the A that you're cooking, or what you like, or what you have around, it might be olive or corn or some other.

Also, there are those ingredients that are so pervasive in a particular kind of cuisine — such as garlic, oregano, olive oil, and lemon in Southern Italian or Greek cooking; soy and ginger in Chinese; shallots, sweet butter and wine, in French; coconut milk in Caribbean cooking; tomatoes and chile peppers in Mexican — that they must be considered a B, or even an A. But *not* a C. That is, if they're in the recipe and if you eliminate one of them, you may stray too far from the basic dish. (But remember, it's not always so inflexible. Shallots can sometimes be onions or garlic, etc.)

The old hand knows all about these things, but the new cook is bewildered. Yet just *knowing* that there are three kinds of ingredients in any recipe, in any dish, can simplify everything and give you a basic foothold.

(However, it's different in baking. Each of the B's, like milk, butter, or eggs, can also be considered — like flour — one of the A's!)

"Hey, I have an idea. Going back to what you were talking about before. Can't you just say: Look, in every recipe, in every dish, you've got a certain amount of leeway. Obviously, if you're cooking turkey, you can't just switch it with halibut and get away with it. But in terms of the basic cooking processes, you know that certain things are required for each, like oil, salt, stock, maybe vinegar or something. So you know enough about them to be able to substitute what you have to, or even what you want to, to make it come out fine.

"Then there are the seasonings, the accompaniments, the

stuff that goes into the cavity of the bird, or the sauce, and whatever else. You can try different things. It doesn't have to be oranges; it can be peaches. You can put oysters in it if you want to. At first, I suppose this is what 'creative' cooking seems to be. But after a while you discover another way through varying the cooking processes themselves along with the substances that enable them to work."

Maybe you should take over.

. . . . . . . . . . . . . . . . . . . . . . . . . . . . . . . . . . . . . . . . . .

GUIDE TO
## The ABC's of Cooking

Here are things that make cooking "go," from cooking liquids to subtle flavorings, but all are so important that they are set down as part of the basic panorama. Included are those items in writing and common parlance that often stand for an entire category of ingredients; for example, *flour* can represent *thickeners* in general.

Oh, great universal *water!* LIQUID.
*Pots*, blessed cooking heroes, often unsung. CONTAINERS.
*Hands and knives* — *sine quae non.* IMPLEMENTS.
*Oil, butter.* FAT.
*Cream.* DAIRY PRODUCTS.
*Flour.* THICKENERS.
*Dough.* ALL BAKED THINGS.
*Yeast.* LEAVENERS.
*Stock.* PROFUNDITY, SOUP.
*Salt.* SPICES.
*Parsley.* HERBS.
*Sugar.* SWEETENERS.
*Wine.* SPIRITS.
*Salt, pepper, and lemon.* SHARPENERS.
*Garlic, shallots.* A SEASONING CLASS BY THEMSELVES.
*Onions, carrots, and celery.* AROMATIC SEASONINGS.
*Eggs.* RICHNESS, UNIQUENESS, COMPLETENESS.
*Tomatoes.* COLOR.
*Cinnamon and nutmeg.* BAKING SPICES.

*Chombas, nuts.* EXCELLENT EXTRAS.
*Onions sautéed in butter.* BEGINNING TO COOK.
*Lemon wedges and parsley sprigs.* GARNISH.
*Oil, onions, garlic, lemon, and parsley.* TIRELESS MAGICIANS.

Of course, it's just my opinion. Different cultures will produce different lists.

And what are we cooking? MEAT, STARCH, VEGETABLES, BEANS, DAIRY PRODUCTS (including EGGS), NUTS, and FRUIT.

· · · · · · · · · · · · · · · · · · · · · · · · · · · · · · · · · · · · · · · · · · · · · · · · · · ·

# 37
# How to Sightread Cookbooks

*In print, everything seems more important.*

When I wanted to make Beef Stroganoff for the first time, about
all I was sure of was that it contained beef, sour cream, and
mushrooms. This was because I've never had two Beef
Stroganoffs that were alike.

And when I started looking in cookbooks, I found the same
thing. Recipes that used wine, recipes that used vinegar, recipes that used tomato paste, recipes that forbade tomato paste,
even one recipe without the mushrooms that I thought were
essential. (I still think they're essential.)

And as for cooking, although most insisted on a quick cooking time for the beef strips, some had you simmering these
little striplets for half an hour!

But none of them told you the most important thing; obviously they assumed you knew it already. The beef has to be
tender (I told you to make friends with your butcher), and if it
isn't tender, you have to do something to it.*

Cookbooks are, after all, just the favorite recipes of someone
or other — at best. For convincing proof, look up any recipe —
Beef Stroganoff, for example — in eight different cookbooks. I
*guarantee* you that, with few exceptions, you'll find eight different recipes. The exceptions generally occur where one cook

---

*What do you think you need, a "Beef Stroganoff Food Manipulator"? Pound it
with something. With anything. A plate!

has plagiarized from the other. And that's as it should be. No blame. But why not, as excellent cooks more often used to, and occasionally still do today, write the books in such a way that you know and feel that that is *their* method, not *the* method. *The* method just produces nervous cooks who can't do anything without consulting a written formula.

Or, if that requires too expansive a style, still, why does one always have to give all these nervous measurements? An eighth teaspoon paprika? What cook pays any attention to that! Can you picture it? Some poor beginning cook fiddling with the measuring spoons ("But there *aren't* any ⅛ ones!) while the meat is scorching or the sour cream is curdling. It's hilarious — except that it isn't. Why not call a pinch a pinch? (Most cookbook authors do it occasionally, possibly to remind their readers that they really *do* cook.)

Anyway, you might as well start out reading cookbooks the way most people read them, and have doubtless always read them: by the ABC method. If you've cooked much — or even a little — you won't find anything surprising in what follows.

You need three cookbooks. In fact, all you *ever* need is three cookbooks. (But you can have more if you want, or less. Or none.) Look up the desired recipe in one of your cookbooks and survey the ingredients.

Look in another one. See what's in there. By now, you've got a fair idea of what the dish really is. You know, for example, that the currants in the first recipe are probably just a personal touch. (But it could be that in the second book, leaving them *out* was the "personal touch.") Anyway, one more cookbook will really lay it out for you. (If you like, or think you'd like, currants with your glazed pork chops, then go to it. Not me!)

### *ABCDHKQRYZ*

Remember what C's were? The seasonings and accompanying food flavors in whatever dish you're cooking. Well, there are those that are essential to the accepted tradition of a particular dish — like the tomato and cheese in pizza, the leeks in vichyssoise, the chicken in paella — and there are those that aren't, though they may be just what you want or what you'd like to try this time — like mushrooms in pizza, onions in leek soup, and things you will discover for yourself. And there are definitely ambiguous cases — like nutmeg in eggnog.

But once you've acquired the means to differentiate the various categories of ingredients *just by looking at the recipes,* something makes plain to you what the dish is really about. And chances are, at least as far as you're concerned, that it's not exactly like any one of the recipes you looked at.

And except for all this ABC stuff, this is how almost everybody reads cookbooks most of the time. They look at a few, get a basic notion of the dish, then cook.

### Sightreading Recipes (Another Way to Look at It)

Let's suppose you are able to sightread a popular song. That is, you can play something straight off from the written music, looking at it for the first time. You can then sightread many other popular songs. You are not just reading note by note, vertically and horizontally, on the sheet music staves; it means you have learned to see in *patterns,* to take in at a glance the structures that simplify the work.

Something analogous occurs in reading cookbooks. Once you can see the patterns, you can "sightread" recipes. Then the entire cooking procedure becomes more fluent *even if you're cooking something you've never cooked before.*

And sightreading in cooking is easier to learn than in music. For we can draw on other experiences and processes that we already know about: certainly the simple things we've all learned to do in making food ready contribute — like boiling water, buttering bread, shaking out salt — in fact, everything connected with the activity of eating.

Suppose you've sautéed, baked, boiled, braised, or whatever — even just once or twice — any particular kind of meat, fish, vegetable, etc. You then have the wherewithal to sightread not only a recipe, but also the "food" itself. That is, if you've sautéed onions, you can sauté carrots. If you've baked lamb, you can bake chicken. And so on. You can just proceed with cooking whatever there is to be cooked.

Well, here's how I do it — Beef Stroganoff — and this includes a few secrets.

. . . . . . . . . . . . . . . . . . . . . . . . . . . . . . . . . . . . . . . . . . .

GUIDE TO
### Peter the Great Went to China to Learn How to Cook *Beef Stroganoff* Properly Because All His Chefs Turned It into Horrible Bland Stuff

BEEF STROGANOFF is supposed to be made from the TENDER-LOIN or FILLET pounded thin, but it can also be made (and it's good) from the FLANK, frozen for an hour for carving easily thin, diagonal slices across the grain (just as for LONDON BROIL), and these can be cut thin enough so pounding is unnecessary. Cut into strips roughly 2 inches by ½ inch.

Instead of cooking these until dead, consider it similar to a Chinese stir-fry. Mince some ONION and cook it in BUTTER until transparent. Turn up the heat and add the meat, turning, browning on all sides for a few minutes. Do a little at a time; they will brown more easily. Remove the beef. Put in MUSH-ROOMS, sliced, and more BUTTER and cook for a few minutes. Add the beef, SALT, PEPPER, a pinch of NUTMEG, and heat. Add a little DRY WHITE WINE (or RED WINE) and maybe three or four times as much YOGURT (someone took the SOUR CREAM! and used it in Apples Underneath), but SOUR CREAM is not to be sneered at. The yogurt (or sour cream) should be added at room temperature and quickly stirred in. Heat through, but absolutely do not boil or it will curdle. If it does curdle, it will taste fine anyway. In this case you will have made Peter the Great's Three-in-the-Morning Stroganoff.

. . . . . . . . . . . . . . . . . . . . . . . . . . . . . . . . . . . . . . . . . . .

# 38
# The Boundaries of Cooking

There's something new every time you cook. You can't
even write down all the questions and possibilities that
open up once you begin. Hundreds, thousands, millions, of different substances, bubbling, simmering,
changing, melting, shrinking, expanding . . . Cooking is
not an art. Cooking isn't a science. Cooking is a living
reality.

*Composition*

With few exceptions, there needs to be a main course, a
center of attraction around which other foods take their place.

This prominent dish has **nothing** to do with being either the
most elaborate, the tastiest, the most subtle, the cook's favorite, or the one everyone likes the best. It may be any or all of
these, or none. It may, for example, be a simple and hearty
meat dish, while the accompanying rice wrapped in palm
leaves or the celery-almond combination may prove to be the
most interesting or elegant.

Aside from being another field for artistry and experimentation, this part of cooking is a very important one. Many who
start out, caught up in the enthusiasm of producing individual
dishes, fail to consider enough the composition of the meal.
For example, the main course can rarely support two main
dishes. (Be an illusionist! Blend them. Turn one into an hors
d'oeuvre. Cut one up in small pieces, or serve it in little portions. Or hold one of them off till tomorrow.)

The basic approach to a balanced meal is to consider Variety (no unintelligent repetition), Weight (care with regard to Heaviness and Fatness), and Color. This is really Flavor, Texture, and Appearance from a somewhat different angle.

*Variety.* If you have cream of asparagus or potato soup in the beginning, you won't serve asparagus or potatoes later on. This is obvious — as long as the cook looks at *the meal as a whole.* Variety in texture should be considered here as well.

*Heaviness and Fatness.* These are akin. A meal with a heavy meat such as pork, or a hearty roast, or with steaks or chops should not be surrounded by heavy or fatty dishes such as cream soups or excessively rich cakes or pies; even a (substantial) custard may be too heavy to finish off such a meal. A fruit dessert, perhaps with a fine wafer ("eleganto" for cookie), a pound cake, a *small* serving of Brie or Camembert or Stilton, or a lemon ice with an excellent coffee would be appropriate.

A meal that contains a substantial fatty dish like a lasagna, or any starchy food cooked in oil, is helped by something astringent like a light salad with lemon juice or vinegar in the dressing, tomatoes, fruit, and of course wine. This is one of the reasons certain fruits are often served with meats: pears, prunes (why not peaches?) with lamb, apples or pineapple with pork (how about cranberries?). Experimentation (with pretasting) is allowed.

*Color.* Again, if one just takes the time to consider this factor, the normal sensitivity we are all blessed with will prevent the presentation of a plate of mashed potatoes, white onions, and white chicken breast. If you need help, a few of the common colors to keep in mind are *green, orange, red, yellow.* (*Note on yellow:* yellow squash, corn, lemon slices, some sauces with egg yolks — even a butter lump! — might qualify once in a while.)

### Imagination Practice

Try to imagine a lunch, then a dinner. Play with it a little. Be free to choose. It won't cost you anything at this stage. If you need a push, then complete the following lunch: a corn tortilla, rice (brown or white?) cooked with spinach (Was the spinach chopped? How would you like it?) with yogurt or sour cream put on afterward. (Do you want some meat? What else?)

Or imagine at dinner you are having some pan-broiled lamb chops and a salad composed of green leaf lettuce and *shrimp*, seasoned with dill in a dressing of lemon juice alone. (It may sound like a peculiar combination, but the salad sets off the meat beautifully.) What are you having with it?

Or start from scratch.

### Quantity

Another area of meal planning and serving that is frequently, and quite naturally, misunderstood is reflected in the serving of *too much food*. We all have within us a joyous host, a bountiful grandfather, who wishes to provide in abundance food that satisfies, refreshes, and nourishes family and friends. I'm not talking about a good robust meal, but the inundation of dishes that beginners often succumb to in order to stave off the Fear of Hungry Guests.

The only real cure I know of for this common failing is just to go ahead and serve an inappropriate gargantuan meal or two and see for yourself how unnecessary it all is, how a deluge of dishes can detract from the quality of the meal, and even cause unpleasantness for the digestion later on.

Ideally, the cook should take these aspects of "food science" — composition and quantity — well into account early on, so that eventually they can enter into their proper and central role in planning and cooking meals.

### Serving

Are you always just going to heap things up on one big plate? No. When you can, get some tiny little dishes, even "cute" ones; they won't come over that way when you load them properly. It is a remarkable phenomenon that placing some of the food in little dishes and saucers serves to heighten the effect, encouraging the eater to focus on what he is eating.

Cookbooks don't say too much about the effect of cutting up things to be served into various shapes. They'll tell you to do it, and just assume that you realize the enormous effect this little action can have on the eater's anticipation and on his sense of care and goodness concerning the meal. Well, you probably do realize it. But in case you have a memory lapse, remember that you can enliven a meal by slicing, dicing, slivering, rounding, ovaling, or otherwising. Sometimes a simple, careful act can save a so-called failure that has fallen apart or in some way become undesirable to serve up in its present state.

It's not that we're talking about "appearance" as apart from "reality." Appearance *is* a reality.

Now certainly, if everything is always cut up in weird little pieces, or is always being fragmented into funny little bowls and things, it can be exhausting — not only to prepare, but to look at. Sometimes Yankee simplicity sets the tone.

### Energy

Two suggestions for your revitalization program if you need one. The first is to cook with another person — or two or more. It's a great tonic, but one caution. Most of us find that it's best if one person is, at least nominally, in charge. Otherwise, unsafe procedures, personality conflicts (that you never thought were there), or chaos can make it a quite different experience than you might have wished — and they may anyway. Even so, it will probably provide you with some welcome relief the next day, when you get to cook without all those crazy people in your kitchen.

Another reason, and a very good reason, for cooking with others is that you are practically bound to learn something. By this I mean specific, describable things. You see, there is so much going on in cooking, and so many approaches to everything, that each cook finds her or his own way to finesse unnecessary difficulties, to quicken some small part of the work, to fold things, to squush things, to touch things (and what to touch and when to touch), to chop things, to poke things, to turn things, to test the readiness of something better, to lighten this, to strengthen that, or to combine a step here with one there, and so on and so on.

When people talk about cooking, many of these details never get into the conversation because either people don't know that they do them (!) or they don't consider them important enough to talk about. Or they consider them too important to talk about.

For example, when Sally told Mike how to make her particular version of Irresistible Southern Fried Chicken, she at first neglected to tell him two things that were essential in her procedure: that the pot should be left uncovered, and that the chicken pieces should be *crammed* in there (not the usual practice); and she forgot to tell him one thing essential to almost any really good fried chicken: that the chicken should be young, tender, and small — 2½ pounds or less. (There's a Guide to Utterly Simple Fried Chicken in Appendix II.)

Another rejuvenating experience is to avail oneself of all the wonderful things that are, or can be, all over the place — in fields, yards, markets, on windowsills.

If you have a yard or a windowsill that gets light, why not have some vegetables or herbs? Not how *wonderful* to have some. That just puts it out of reach for those who consider it a luxury. But how ridiculous *not* to have some!

### Light

How to think of what to do, how to get "inspired."

Look at the ingredients in the Index. Compound these with the number of basic processes and their possible combinations, not to mention *ways of preparing* the ingredients (remember, for example, what you can do to a single clove of garlic?). If you like, as a help in starting you to move, you could think of some A's, B's, and C's of cooking (Chapter 36).

You're in the planning, the composing stage. You can envision all these combinations without yet going through the process of cooking them. And what a field, what a wide meadow, what a vast kingdom to go composing in! Who can't get inspired by all that! I mean, what is this about the tedium of the kitchen? The monotony of it. We're the monotony. Anybody who's bored in the kitchen is probably going to be bored somewhere else. Now no one denies that there's honest toil in cooking. But it doesn't have to be *wretched.*

I realize that there are exceptions. There are persons who really are repelled by the kitchen, but intrinsically, I suspect, there are very few. It's like being tone deaf. You can meet many who insist that they are, but hardly anyone actually is. Generally, it's simply a lack of use and, where needed, proper guidance.

Other exceptions include those affected by kitchens with bad air or kitchens with *bad light*. Probably the main reason some people believe that cooking is awful drudgery is that their kitchens have *bad light*. I don't necessarily mean "dim" light, but "ugly" light. (You don't believe me? Why not look into it?)

### Why Do We Need Recipes?

Straight off, we must acknowledge that we do need recipes. But why? It is not because cooks are helpless without them or even that they make things easier. If you didn't know before, and if you've come this far in the book (without skipping too much), you know how fundamentally unnecessary recipes are.

Once one learns to do without recipes, a strange thing happens; in fact, two things. The first is the realization that one *really* doesn't need recipes!

The second is that one has even more appreciation for a *good* recipe. But since the cook can now make up wonderful dishes on his or her own, as the spirit moves or the circumstances indicate, what's the point? Partly, it's sharing; and partly, the delight in something different, something we wouldn't have thought of by ourselves.

But a recipe is also an attempt, through a working knowledge of (real) chemistry, to gather up and distill something more permanent in the stream of life. Good recipes are like condensations, visible and tangible records created and fashioned during moments of simple communion with foods and a finer concentration. They serve as gathering places where people congregate and partake. They conform without fuss, yet they will elude every attempt at standardization. They range over the whole of life — from the fortuitous shelter in the storm to the earthy picnic in the lovers' glen, from the gathering by the cozy wood stove to the formal dinner in jeweled candlelight. And under the power of a meal, especially of a meal taken together, a noisy, heavier life recedes, while a quiet, quicker

one comes forth, and we are filled with a restoring energy to go
on cooking, eating, developing, growing — in short, living.

. . . . . . . . . . . . . . . . . . . . . . . . . . . . . . . . . . . . . . . . . . . . . . . . .

GUIDE TO
## Sherwood Forest Lamb (Braised Lamb Shanks\*)

This dish — or feast, rather — represents a meal that can be
cooked for hours and hours (and hours). Why not discover another time existing within our own? Sherwood Forest is only
hours away. (Tuck! What's the aluminum foil doing under
these blasted nettles?)
The description is in two parts: Beginning and Middle.
The End is the Eating, and this is not (at least, not obviously)
a book on Eating.

*Beginning*
One SHANK per person. Have butcher crack them once.
Deeply puncture each one in a few places with a sharp knife
and put GARLIC SLIVERS in there and in a few other nooks. You
may rub a CUT GARLIC CLOVE over the lamb as well.
Rub the shanks all over with FRESH THYME.
Roll in FLOUR. Gently shake off any excess.
Put in a roasting pan with the bottom flooded with OLIVE
OIL. Brown them at 400° to 500°, turning once or twice (more, if
necessary), for about 30 to 50 minutes.†
You can cook these very successfully at 300° to 350°, which
is what most modern cookbooks tell you to do. But there is
simply no comparison to slower cooking — 180° to 220°, say —
depending on how much time you have.

\*Too bad they aren't *Poached* Lamb Shanks . . . what a delicious pun!
†If you're going to brown meat, you have to *brown* it. Just making it look
gray or something has nothing to do with it. It takes time. Now if you're
sautéing something quickly, it obviously doesn't have to be as thoroughly
browned, because the juices that escape through the surface of unbrowned
meat don't have that much time to get away. In this case, *searing* the meat is
sufficient. But when you're cooking something longer, brown it for real; this
means if it's a thick cut, brown it on the edges as well.

There is certainly room for argument about whether simmered chicken should fall off the bone, but there is *no room* for
argument about Braised Lamb Shanks. They must be falling off
the bone. Otherwise, at best, they're satisfactory, and might
even taste too "gamey."

This temperature thing is very flexible as long as you don't
cook the shanks too fast. After browning, let about 1½ to 2
hours at 325° be your minimum cooking time. The maximum
is however long you want. Just use a lower temperature. The
last time I cooked these, I had them on 180° to 200° for about 5
or 6 hours. Uh-oh, here come the guests. I raised the heat to
350° for the last hour. ("Good thinking," said Friar Tuck. "I am
hungry," said Little John.)

After browning the shanks, put enough WEAK CHICKEN
BOUILLON in the pan to come at least a third of the way up the
lamb. Definitely pour in a few glugs of DRY WHITE WINE if you
have some. Don't overdo it. Add some SALT (if possible, kosher
or sea salt) and FRESHLY GRATED PEPPER (the chicken bouillon
also has salt in it).

*Cover the whole affair with foil.* Cover again each time you
add things. *Throughout the cooking, check the shanks now
and then* (mostly then). *If they seem to be getting too dry, put
oil on them* (with your hands). When you do this for the last
time, say about ½ to 1 hour before the end, use BUTTER. Just
glop it on. Also, you may add more stock at any time, if necessary.

If you're new at cooking, try to get the point of what follows;
it's more important than the individual ingredients.* Once you
"get it," you're free to add, subtract, multiply, divide — and
even take square roots (and cook them!).

*Middle*

This is not a recipe; it's a record put down *after* the meal.
Concerning quantities: You don't have to refer to a recipe or

---

*But if it's really Sherwood Forest Lamb you want — in all of its illustrious,
full, and subtle splendor — Maid Marion suggests you not leave out the
PRUNES, PEARS, PARSLEY, GARLIC, ROSEMARY, or THYME.

chart to know how many onions, carrots, etc., to put in something. As I recall, this is what I did for this particular meal.

14 LAMB SHANKS (14 diners)

*For each person,* 3 little, WHITE BOILING ONIONS — about a third of them had two CLOVES stuck into them — peeled, unsliced (peel by dropping them into boiling water for a minute)

1½ SMALL, RUSSET POTATOES, peeled and sliced

⅓ TURNIP, peeled and sliced

½ large CARROT, lightly peeled, cut into thick rounds or chunks

½ PEAR, cored, peeled, sliced

3 or 4 PRUNES, soaked (marinated*) for 2 to 3 hours in a bowl of MADEIRA. (Save almost everything. I used the prune-soaked Madeira afterward to soak the NECTARINES that were used as a garnish.) And though not mandatory, try to avoid canned prunes. If possible, get unpitted pure PRUNES without any weird additives in them. Either kind will work, but you will notice the difference. I took the pits out (it takes time).

FRESH PARSLEY, coarsely chopped, enough to cover the entire top of the pan(s)† and also to poke around in between.

The following is pure Irifoy:

About 1½ to 2½ hours before the end (well, the end of the middle — sorry about that), put in the onions; 1 to 2 hours before the end, put in the potatoes (the time variation depends on the temperature you're using); turnips — what would you say? a little less than the potatoes, maybe; carrots are harder, but they're cut a little smaller. (Suppose you forgot the carrots until later. Well, then you'd cut them even smaller, wouldn't you?) So just after putting in the turnips, put in the carrots; about 45 minutes to an hour before the end, the pears — wait! Don't forget about an hour before the end to:

Spread FRESH SPRIGS OF ROSEMARY and THYME over everything. (Some more garlic slivers at this point are optional.)

Okay, where were we? The pears. In they go. (Of course, you're not just slipping these various things in. You're making

*Marinate* is an Arm and Hand Body Movement.
†I was using three pans.

sure they're more or less distributed. Without making a precise production out of it, you will have to do some pushing and poking with your fingers.) Prunes, just after the pears, about 45 minutes before the end; and 15 minutes before, cover the now greater amount of everything with the PARSLEY . . . which brings to life visually the wonder, the absolute wonder, of Sherwood Forest Lamb.*

On each plate were two or three black Moroccan olives and a few small cubes of fresh nectarine (or peach) that had been soaking for a while in the Madeira that the prunes had soaked in for an hour or two or three.

Served with bulgur wheat (cooked like Rice à Gauche, page 82) and pine nuts, which were so expensive that each person got a maximum of two.

I won't go into the rest of the meal, but it qualified as a Basic Feast.

---

*While you're *ooh*-ing and *ah*-ing, pour off any obvious excess fat from the pan juices (a basic principle in cooking meat) — unless you did it early on.

. . . . . . . . . . . . . . . . . . . . . . . . . . . . . . . . . . . . . . . . . . . . . . . .

# Conclusion
## At the End, the Beginning

The hardest thing sometimes is to begin.
If all else fails try starting with food.
Isn't someone hungry? At the heart of
The recipe are the ingredients:
Butternut squash, chopped walnuts, basil, butter,
Maybe onions . . . and a dash cayenne.
Alive, they speak to us, they call to us
From the heart of Earth. They are friends. I know,
You say you don't like squash. But are you sure?

Almost every time I cook there are more things to wonder about, to try. I can't just write on and on, so I'll stop here.

It's hard to go against it all, and I confess that I didn't go far enough. Reader, help me out of this bind, the bind that comes from the Fear of Having Written This Book. For it's words, just words, and cooking isn't any of these words. It's you and me among the saucepans and the fires, the sounds, the odors, the crackling and bubbling of life, the bouillabaisse, simmering and steaming through centuries, through millennia.

And as we cook, standing there in front of our modern stoves, surrounded by juice squeezers and electric blenders, eventually we, too, shall pass into legend and become one among the ancient cooks. And there were those before us, and there will be those who come after us who will discover where the real cooking goes on amid the pots and bowls.

Now go out and get a set of measuring spoons and cups — metal or plastic ones for dry ingredients and a 2-cup glass one for liquids. (How could you possibly cook without measuring cups?)

And remember, I didn't promise you a cozy, old-fashioned train ride full of subtle, exquisite impressions of bountiful meals; instead, you got a journey, rather bumpy, through the train itself.

How striking the contrast between the quiet rhythms of the countryside, flowing by like a waking dream, and the intensity of those in the coal car!

> Ancient the pots and the saucepans,
> but farther back still
> is Fire.

# APPENDIX I
*On Owning Cookbooks*

# APPENDIX II
*Additional Guides*

# APPENDIX III
*Survey / Review*

# INDEX

# Appendix I
# On Owning Cookbooks

> DRIED PEAS
> Boil the peas. When the froth has been skimmed off put
> in leeks, coriander, and cumin. Pound pepper, lovage,
> caraway, dill, fresh basil, moisten with *liquamen*,*
> blend with wine and *liquamen* (add to the peas), bring
> to the boil. When it boils stir. If something is wanting,
> add, and then serve.
> — Apicius, *The Roman Cookery Book* (1st century)

It may seem to the reader that I have been unduly harsh on
cookbooks. But this is a cookbook too.

It's not that cookbooks (that is, their authors) don't know
enough. The problem often is, they know too *much*.

But now that you've gotten this far, you can really benefit
from cookbooks because you know how to use them. Someone
who just skips to this chapter may think he knows, but this is
*our* secret.

So if you struggled with me and you made it to here — or
nearly, or you tried to — *go get a cookbook.*

And you can follow a recipe now if you recognize that to
follow one the way it was intended is *not* just a mechanical
measuring procedure. You need to follow it with a certain
amount of joy; or rather, if you just try it, the joy will come.
But when it isn't there, you've got your next best friend.
Fear.

There are many cookbooks to suit your taste, with type face,

---

*Liquamen*, which was usually produced in factories, was used by the Romans in lieu of salt. It is an extract of fish and salt.

design, organization, writing style, pictures — whatever helps you *feel* like cooking. Yours won't be the same as mine. And either you'll look for a cookbook that suits you, or you'll just go out and get the "best" cookbook in print. But there is no "best." The best is, first of all, what gets *you* to cook.

I've recommended a few well-known, easily obtainable cookbooks for the beginner, but there's absolutely nothing comprehensive, authoritative, or impartial about this selection. Every good book has a unique "something." I think each of these has.

*Joy of Cooking,* by Irma S. Rombauer and Marion Rombauer Becker

The encyclopedic American cookbook of our day and a rich reference on many cooking matters. It is a broad compendium of American cooking routines, with many "secrets" and so much information — and cross references — that some beginners find it overwhelming. (But it isn't, really.) The recipes are discriminating and straightforward, and usually leave plenty of room for the cook who wants to modify them (although some cooks don't realize this).

*The James Beard Cookbook,* by James Beard

It's like having your favorite Uncle James in the kitchen, who not only knows how to cook, but how to eat! Sharing his experience and knowledge with you in a readable, flowing style, he is so expert you almost forget that he is. As you go on cooking and trying different things, you may disagree with him on various points, but so what?

The following is the opening paragraph from *James Beard's Theory and Practice of Good Cooking:*

> Cooking starts with your hands, the most important and basic of all implements. They were the earliest tools for the preparation of food, and they have remained one of the most efficient, sensitive, and versatile. Hands can beat, cream, fold, knead, pat, press, form, toss, tear, and pound. They are so sensitive that the instant your fingers touch or feel something, they transmit messages to your brain about texture and temperature. Just by touching a broiled steak or a roast, you can learn to tell when the meat is done to your

liking. To test the temperature of a sauce, a soup, a stew, or a vegetable purée, just dip your finger in. Then touch your finger to your tongue, and you'll know whether the seasoning and flavoring are right or need some adjustment. There are prissy people who think sticking fingers in food is dirty, but there's nothing disgraceful about touching food if your hands are clean, and don't let anyone tell you there is . . . I can think of no more rewarding and sensuous a pleasure than plunging one's hands into a batter or dough and mixing or kneading away.

What else is there to say?

*The Fannie Farmer Cookbook*, 12th edition, revised by Marion Cunningham with Jeri Laber

Another comprehensive cookbook, worth looking into for its culinary wisdom, its spacious and appealing design, and its superb compression of style, all of which make such a work more approachable. Some who think they are in the know claim that Fannie Farmer was responsible for overcodifying cooking routines with fussy measurements. But if you take the trouble to peruse one of her own early editions, you will quickly recognize an author with a profound understanding of food — cooking being only one of its aspects — and a great sensitivity to its preparation.

The present revision was obviously not made to imitate, but to reach an accord with the spirit of this early-twentieth-century bible of American cooking.

*The New York Times Cookbook*, by Craig Claiborne

Authoritative, empathetic to the cook with a wide range of interests, and considering the author's vast knowledge of culinary subjects, generously helpful even to the novice. For your one cookbook on a desert island, not a bad choice.

*Tassajara Cooking*, by Edward Espe Brown

A model of a book. The approach to cooking is sure and refreshing, with the soul of Cooking as close to the surface as you will ever find in a cookbook. Obviously I'm not a vegetarian, yet as a learner's guide to *cooking* — though it may not appeal to everyone — it would be hard to surpass.

*Magic in Herbs,* by Leonie de Sounin

A rare spirit breathes through this little book as the author warms to her subject in a most individual way. Some have probably complained that all the dishes described in it are cooked with herbs, that nothing is left plain. But it's a book on *herbs.*

The author knows something, from deep and way back.

*Mediterranean Food,* by Elizabeth David

This small volume, an early one by this well-known author, is a first-rate example of how to say more with less. Part of its deep charm is due to the perfect marriage of its subject matter with the type face, illustrations, layout, and all-around feel. And like any good cookbook about the food of another place, in simply telling you about it, it takes you there.

*Mastering the Art of French Cooking,* Volume 1, by Simone Beck, Louisette Bertholle, and Julia Child

Clear and precise. But you better watch Julia cook so you don't get the wrong idea.

*Moosewood Cookbook,* by Mollie Katzen

You may or may not like a vegetarian cookbook with home-style calligraphy. Either way, it's one of the most usable recipe books available, written by a most knowledgeable and articulate cook.

*Laurel's Kitchen,* by Laurel Robertson, Carol Flinders, and Brownwen Godfrey

For the nutrition-minded cook as well as the vegetarian, this volume is very informative, as its many readers will affirm. But in a book where such pains were taken (successfully) to be genuine and to use real food, why not recommend *real* garlic? I can't believe that Laurel is afraid of garlic.

*The Unabridged Vegetable Book,* by Nika Hazelton

For lovers, or haters, of vegetables and everyone in between. Comprehensive, with an organization that is simple, pleasing, and practical.

*The Sixty-Minute Gourmet,* by Pierre Franey
One of our finest chefs has written one of the decade's finest and most serviceable cookbooks. Knowledgeable, succinct, yet warmly personal. The book designer should also take a bow — simple, fresh, remarkably effective.

Of course one could go on filling pages up. I shall only add that at the earliest opportunity you should go to a library and look at some old cookery books — books at least one or two hundred years old, but how about a thousand (or two thousand) years old?
Then ask yourself: What is progress?

# Appendix II
# Additional Guides

Now that you understand better about "measurements" in cooking, I have given a few; but in many cases I have made it difficult — no, impossible — for you to follow slavishly any of these without relating to your own needs or those for whom you're cooking in order to decide how much of what to put in.

These guides have been especially selected to build confidence and at the same time to satisfy normal yearnings for good tasting food.

I have not always indicated salt and pepper. It depends on you.

· · · · · · · · · · · · · · · · · · · · · · · · · · · · · · · · · · · · · · · · · · · ·

GUIDE TO
**Utterly Simple Fried Chicken**

The CHICKEN should be young, tender, and small — 2½ pounds or less.

Shake in a bag with FLOUR or CORNMEAL, seasoned with SALT, PEPPER — maybe PAPRIKA.

Place FAT, about ⅛ to ¼ inch, in the pan.

When it's hot, put the chicken in. Turn. Cook for 20 to 25 minutes.

Drain on absorbent paper. Pour off all but a little of the fat for gravy.

· · · · · · · · · · · · · · · · · · · · · · · · · · · · · · · · · · · · · · · · · · · ·

GUIDE TO
**Salad Niçoise**

Rub a salad bowl with a cut GARLIC CLOVE. Add bite-size
pieces of any one or two: BIBB, BOSTON, or ROMAINE LETTUCE.
Now here is your chance to really *arrange* something — but
guess what? If you just add the ingredients and toss with a good
VINAIGRETTE, you will have a most refreshing salad.

The basic ingredients are ANCHOVIES, drained (maybe a can),
chopped coarsely — or, for arranging, leave as is — a good
number of BLACK OLIVES (a dozen?), a couple of TOMATOES,
quartered, and either (or both) a few HARD-BOILED EGGS, quartered and/or BOILED NEW POTATOES, sliced. Some excellent op-
tions are slightly undercooked GREEN BEANS (cut), peeled
CUCUMBER ROUNDS, ONION SLICES, and CAPERS. If you need to
extend the anchovies (or if you don't like them), you can use
TUNAFISH. TARRAGON is good with this, or BASIL.

Toss with the dressing, or arrange and pour over.

GUIDE TO
**Non-Chinese Black Mushroom Scrambled Eggs (or an
Omelet) Using Chinese Black Mushrooms**

DRIED CHINESE BLACK MUSHROOMS are something every cook
should know about. But just because they're one of the essentials in Chinese cooking doesn't mean they have to be used
exclusively that way. First and foremost, they're EARTH MUSH-
ROOMS, not Chinese or Italian or American. So feel free.

Put the dried black Chinese mushrooms in a bowl of hot or
boiling water and let them soak for 15 to 30 minutes. (They're
expensive, but as you will see, even *one mushroom* expands a
great deal when it absorbs water. They keep almost in-
definitely in a cool dry place, in a bag.) They will get *huge.*
Squeeze or pat them dry. The juice can be saved for stock.
Sliver them up and sauté them in BUTTER for 3 or 4 minutes,

seasoning them with, say, MARJORAM. Add more butter, put in beaten EGGS with SALT and PEPPER, and scr(i)a(u)mble (see Chapter 7 if you have doubts about how to do this).

Find out what it's like if you put them (cooked) in an OMELET and add SOUR CREAM at the end. Whatever you do, the mushrooms will really appreciate some MINCED PARSLEY.

Check out something called DRIED BLACK TREE FUNGUS. If that frightens you, you can also call them WOOD EARS. They have much less flavor than the mushrooms, but a little more body. Treat them the same way. Or mix the two of them.

. . . . . . . . . . . . . . . . . . . . . . . . . . . . . . . . . . . . . . . . . . . . .
. . . . . . . . . . . . . . . . . . . . . . . . . . . . . . . . . . . . . . . . . . . . .

GUIDE TO
## Cauliflower and Mushroom Togetherment

Boil or steam a head of CAULIFLOWER — do not overcook. As it nears doneness, sauté some MUSHROOMS in BUTTER with BASIL or TARRAGON for 5 or 10 minutes. If they really cook down, it's fine. Break up the cauliflower in smallish pieces and add them to the sauté with some LEMON JUICE, and cook briefly until mingled. Add a grating of NUTMEG or two. (If you're out of nutmeg, you can put in a pinch of CAYENNE.)

Serve with, for example, chicken.

. . . . . . . . . . . . . . . . . . . . . . . . . . . . . . . . . . . . . . . . . . . . .
. . . . . . . . . . . . . . . . . . . . . . . . . . . . . . . . . . . . . . . . . . . . .

GUIDE TO
## Tabbouleh

TABBOULEH is another generic name for a delicious salad prepared any number of ways. The constants are BULGUR WHEAT (cooked, or uncooked — in which case it is technically "CRACKED WHEAT"), MINT, PARSLEY, TOMATOES, and LEMON JUICE. Good OIL is usually added — about half and half with the lemon juice, or up to twice as much lemon juice as oil to make a lemony dressing. Minced ONION is often added and so is minced GARLIC. Minced GREEN PEPPER?

I find the best way to prepare the BULGUR (or CRACKED

WHEAT) is to let it stand in twice as much boiling WATER for an hour or two. Some like to use CHICKEN BROTH, but I think it masks the flavor of some of the other ingredients. But you may not agree.

Fluff up with a fork and add everything except the dressing. Then toss with lemon and oil — salt and pepper, too, if desired.

For a cup of bulgur, a tablespoon (pitch) of dried mint (or about three times as much fresh), is good to begin with. Adjust to your own taste. *Much* more parsley can be added, minced fine. Tomatoes are coarsely chopped; onion and garlic are minced.

. . . . . . . . . . . . . . . . . . . . . . . . . . . . . . . . . . . . . . . . . . . . . . .
. . . . . . . . . . . . . . . . . . . . . . . . . . . . . . . . . . . . . . . . . . . . . . .

GUIDE TO
## Tofu

I just want you to look at some TOFU. Aside from its high protein and calcium content, it is one of the world's most unutilized foods. It is a true "receiver," capable of being used in many ways. What I would like you to do is to get some (at least once) and sauté it with something. Use your *imagination.* You know what I mean. (For example, recall some things like cut-up broccoli, a little garlic, soy sauce, a touch of sherry, some water if needed — and sautéing.)

. . . . . . . . . . . . . . . . . . . . . . . . . . . . . . . . . . . . . . . . . . . . . . .
. . . . . . . . . . . . . . . . . . . . . . . . . . . . . . . . . . . . . . . . . . . . . . .

GUIDE TO
## Illegal, Elegant Macaroni

Instead of using the usual macaroni, use MASTOCCIOLLI or some other imposing pasta. After cooking the pasta (see Chapter 28, where it will tell you to begin the cooking with a 3-minute boil for larger pasta) and draining it, you can put it back in the same emptied-out pot on top of the stove (don't let your guests see you do this — they think macaroni is always made in the oven). Grate CHEDDAR CHEESE and for a particularly nice touch, a little grated GRUYÈRE. Add some SALT, PEPPER, and

MILK. Toss and cook for a while. You can serve it without putting it in the oven at all. Or grate more cheese over it, and just as one of your guests comes into the kitchen to say hello, put it in the oven (you may need to turn it into another dish) until the cheese is lightly browned and bubbly. Where's the PARSLEY?

Of course you can use WHITE SAUCE WITH CHEESE instead of grated cheese and milk.

. . . . . . . . . . . . . . . . . . . . . . . . . . . . . . . . . . . . . . . . . . . . . . . . . .
. . . . . . . . . . . . . . . . . . . . . . . . . . . . . . . . . . . . . . . . . . . . . . . . .

GUIDE TO
**French Onion Soup à la Ellen**

Sauté a mass of THINLY SLICED ONIONS in BUTTER until limp — about 5 minutes or so. Add BEEF STOCK or BOUILLON — the onions should come about halfway up — and A SMALL BAY LEAF. Simmer for 45 minutes. About 10 or 15 minutes before the end, add THYME and a little ROSEMARY. About 5 minutes or so from the end, add 2 capfuls of BRANDY.

When finished cooking, put rounds of FRENCH BREAD on top and top these with GRUYÈRE CHEESE. Put under the broiler in ovenproof soup bowls (3 to 4 inches from the heat) just until brown — or in the soup pot in a moderately hot oven.

It is imperative that this be eaten immediately. The worst possible thing is for the cheese to get cold and tough. Indigestible onion soup.

. . . . . . . . . . . . . . . . . . . . . . . . . . . . . . . . . . . . . . . . . . . . . . . . . .
. . . . . . . . . . . . . . . . . . . . . . . . . . . . . . . . . . . . . . . . . . . . . . . . .

GUIDE TO
**One of the Hundred Thousand and One Tunafish Salads That There Are**

Drained TUNA, finely chopped CELERY (or CUCUMBER), some minced SCALLIONS, MUSTARD, CELERY SEED, much LEMON JUICE (a must). Garnish with WATERCRESS.

. . . . . . . . . . . . . . . . . . . . . . . . . . . . . . . . . . . . . . . . . . . . . . . . . .

. . . . . . . . . . . . . . . . . . . . . . . . . . . . . . . . . . . . . . . .

GUIDE TO
## Sautéed Scallops (Also Broiled)

Rinse off, like all fish, some SCALLOPS. Sauté in BUTTER over high heat — a minute per side should be enough if they're small. Don't overcook. Some prefer to dry them and roll them in FLOUR first. Like other seafood, they favor being blessed with WHITE WINE (a good way to deglaze the pan). LEMON WEDGES for garnish, please.

If you don't cook these with minced GARLIC at least half the time, consider doing so. Especially when wine or VERMOUTH is involved (vermouth is good with fish).

Scallops are good *broiled*, too. Nothing could be easier. Dry them, dip them in butter, broil them, say, 4 inches from the heat for about 5 minutes. Don't even turn them. (What if there's AN HERB in the butter? A daredevil!)

. . . . . . . . . . . . . . . . . . . . . . . . . . . . . . . . . . . . . . . .
. . . . . . . . . . . . . . . . . . . . . . . . . . . . . . . . . . . . . . . .

GUIDE TO
## Irresistible Moules (Mussels)

Some people have never eaten MUSSELS. Too bad! Scrub them with a stiff brush and pull away or snip off any weird things protruding from the shells. The mussels should all be tightly closed; discard any whose shells are open. Let them stand in cold, salted water for about half an hour.

I like these steamed with wine and herbs. Melt some BUTTER in a deep kettle and add GARLIC (or SHALLOTS), ONION, BAY LEAF, THYME, some PEPPERCORNS (bruise them a little) — that sort of thing. Cook these together for a minute or two. For a couple dozen mussels, add about a cup of WHITE WINE. Cover and steam over good heat. Look in after 6 minutes and remove any whose shells have opened. Look in again 2 minutes later and remove any other good ones. Those whose shells didn't open were dead to begin with. Discard. The broth can be served with the mussels. Stir in PARSLEY.

Another delicious way to serve them is to remove only the upper shells and arrange them on a plate. Reduce the broth by a half by fierce boiling and drain through a few thicknesses of cheesecloth. For an optional enrichment, add ½ cup CREAM; heat but don't boil. Stir in PARSLEY. Spoon over the mussels.

Or put some of AN ULTIMATE GARLIC SAUCE (page 249) over them. If you had some finely chopped BREAD CRUMBS, what could you do with them?

. . . . . . . . . . . . . . . . . . . . . . . . . . . . . . . . . . . . . . . . . . . .
. . . . . . . . . . . . . . . . . . . . . . . . . . . . . . . . . . . . . . . . . . . .

GUIDE TO
## Never-Dry Swordfish (or Halibut) Steak

SWORDFISH and HALIBUT are excellent fare, but often they are cooked too dry. (Everyone knows what I mean.)

How will you prevent this? Lackluster measures may not work. I leave it to you. So this is not a "guide," it's a "goad." (Spread MAYONNAISE on the fish before broiling?)

. . . . . . . . . . . . . . . . . . . . . . . . . . . . . . . . . . . . . . . . . . . .
. . . . . . . . . . . . . . . . . . . . . . . . . . . . . . . . . . . . . . . . . . . .

GUIDE TO
## Sautéed Chicken Livers

Sauté MUSHROOMS (optional) in BUTTER, add CHICKEN LIVERS and, for each person served, a finely chopped SHALLOT, more BUTTER if necessary, *or* (you may not have considered this, but it's good) a fair amount of BEEF BROTH. Include some minced GREEN ONIONS if you have some on hand and LEMON JUICE. When the chicken livers go in, turn up the heat and cook for 3 or 4 minutes, tossing about. Do not overcook or they'll be tough. They should be browned on the outside and (the way I like them) pink on the inside.

How will you garnish? How will you serve them? Over rice? On toast? In an omelet? And seasoning . . . TARRAGON, ROSEMARY, or BASIL . . . PARSLEY, and A TOUCH OF NUTMEG. Or maybe just a SMILE.

. . . . . . . . . . . . . . . . . . . . . . . . . . . . . . . . . . . . . . . . . . . .

GUIDE TO
## Above All Roast Chicken

So simple, and so juicy. SALT the cavity of a 3½- to 4-pound CHICKEN with your fist. Put an ONION and, if desired, a CELERY STALK in there — but definitely include 2 or 3 ORANGES chopped up into 1-inch cubes. Truss up the legs and wings with some twine. No big production; just pretend it's a package.

For this roast, a V-rack is easiest, but you can improvise with saucers, potatoes, or whatever. The idea is to cook the chicken first *breast down*, then *on each wing*, then *breast up* — about 20 minutes for each. Start in a preheated 400° oven; after 20 minutes, reduce it to 325°. You may, in the very beginning, rub the chicken with SOY SAUCE — if you have a yen to do that.

No basting is required. You won't believe how good and juicy it is.

GUIDE TO
## A Continuing Sour Cream and Veal Story

Brown ONIONS in BUTTER, slowly. Add SALT and IMPORTED HUNGARIAN PAPRIKA (about a tablespoon) instead of pepper. Gradually stir in a cup of SOUR CREAM (at room temperature) and then cubes of VEAL. A little CHICKEN BROTH can go in as well. Cover and *simmer* until tender. It shouldn't take an hour. This can all be done in a heavy skillet with a tight lid.

GUIDE TO
## Roast Leg of Lamb on a Muffin Tin (or What Have You)

This may sound frivolous, but it was first rate. Some friends and I were roasting a LEG OF LAMB in a kitchen that didn't have an oven rack. Looking in various cupboards and niches, we found — a muffin tin! Various chefs will tell you that you don't have to baste or do anything at all to a roast leg of lamb, and they are right. With one exception. If you really want to, just do it and see what (or taste what) happens.

The leg has a "fell" covering it, which is a tough, plastic-like membrane that, if left on, tends to make the lamb taste "gamey." I prefer removing it (the butcher will do it). Preheat the oven to 325°. Rub olive oil all over the leg. Cut off as much excess fat as you conveniently can. Rub A CUT CLOVE OF GARLIC all over the lamb, and some FRESH (if possible) or dried THYME. You can also make deep incisions (about an inch) here and there and insert SLIVERS OF GARLIC in them. (We did.) If you put little pieces of PEAR in there also, it won't hurt. Pour DRY WHITE WINE in the muffin cavities, about halfway up each one that will be more or less under the lamb. Put some FRESH SPRIGS OF ROSEMARY over the muffin tin (or, if you don't have any, rub some dried over the lamb), put the leg on it, and lay a sprig or two on top. Roast. (You can sear at 450° first for 15 minutes, then reduce the heat. This gives a nice crust, with more well-done meat on the outside.) But please don't cook the leg well done. It should be, in my opinion, somewhat pink. Start checking it after an hour and 15 minutes to an hour and a half. Cut into it and look, if you like, at any reasonable time. Toward the end, add a little more rosemary if you didn't use fresh. Do you think it needs more garlic? About 5 minutes before the end, chop up AN ENORMOUS AMOUNT OF PARSLEY — at least a whole bunch — and spread it all over the lamb.

Pour off any excess fat from the muffin cavities (you can chill it in a tall container while the lamb rests for about 15 minutes before carving, and that will help). The juices from the carving will fall into the drippings into which you have put some of the parsley (some fell in, anyway). That's all the gravy you'll need — not very much, but so concentratedly delicious that it will go a long way.

Fortunately for us, other friends arrived just in time (in the middle of the roasting) for us to take the PARBOILED NEW POTATOES (they had been cooking for about 10 minutes) and the PARBOILED LITTLE WHITE ONIONS (the same) and put them in the *large* ovenproof *skillet* they brought (which also was big enough to accommodate the muffin tin), surrounding the lamb as it roasted for about 45 minutes to an hour. I'm sure we could have found some other way to do it if we had had to.

SALT and PEPPER before roasting — or afterward, whichever you like.

. . . . . . . . . . . . . . . . . . . . . . . . . . . . . . . . . . . . . . . . . . . . . . . . .
. . . . . . . . . . . . . . . . . . . . . . . . . . . . . . . . . . . . . . . . . . . . . . . .

GUIDE TO
## Thomas Smith's Sweet Potato Pudding

A 5-pound bag of *frozen* (or fresh) SWEET POTATOES
6–8 EGGS
1 stick MARGARINE (yes — or BUTTER)
1⅓ cups ALL-PURPOSE FLOUR
2 cups white SUGAR
1 cup MILK
1 cup WATER
LEMON or VANILLA extract to taste
If you need dessert for a lot of people, try this.
Mix the dry (first five) ingredients together, then add the milk and water. Stir well.
Stir in the vanilla or lemon extract.
Pour the mixture into a baking pan 15 by 12 by 2½ inches.
Bake at 300° to 350° for 30 to 40 minutes.
Let cool, then slice.
It is *good.*

. . . . . . . . . . . . . . . . . . . . . . . . . . . . . . . . . . . . . . . . . . . . . . . . .
. . . . . . . . . . . . . . . . . . . . . . . . . . . . . . . . . . . . . . . . . . . . . . . .

GUIDE TO
## Baked Apple Memories (Also Pears)

Remove the core — but don't cut through the bottom — and cut away an inch or two of the peel from the stem end of an APPLE. (Any good cooking apple will work. Rome Beauties are especially good for this, but not, in my opinion, for pies.) Now, think back to early days. What were all those things put in the middle? BROWN SUGAR, CINNAMON, LEMON RIND, A BIT OF LEMON JUICE, RAISINS, ALMONDS, BREAD CRUMBS, and so on. Pick one or two or three. Dab some BUTTER on the top. Put in a baking dish with about ½ inch of water and bake in a 350° oven for about half an hour, until tender but not too soft. Basting now and then is a good thing. But I have also baked apples without putting any water in the dish, covering it, cooking it for just a little less — about 25 minutes — until not quite tender, and letting it stand for another 15 or 20 minutes.

Serve with CREAM or HARD SAUCE (see page 334).

To bake PEARS, halve them, core them, add BROWN SUGAR and, say, GINGER and CARDAMOM (or CORIANDER), or just a couple of CLOVES. If you put a few WALNUTS in, no one will report you. Bake longer and slower — at 325° for maybe an hour — well, when they're done. CREAM (or SOUR CREAM) is all you need.

. . . . . . . . . . . . . . . . . . . . . . . . . . . . . . . . . . . . . . . . . . .
. . . . . . . . . . . . . . . . . . . . . . . . . . . . . . . . . . . . . . . . . .

GUIDE TO
**Dooka**

DOOKA (a phonetic mangling of a Persian word) is a very refreshing drink popular in many parts of the Middle East and India. Another idea for a nationwide chain.

YOGURT plus ICE CUBES plus CLUB SODA (!) plus MINT (preferably fresh) plus SALT and PEPPER. Blend in a blender or by hand. *Drink.*

. . . . . . . . . . . . . . . . . . . . . . . . . . . . . . . . . . . . . . . . . . .
. . . . . . . . . . . . . . . . . . . . . . . . . . . . . . . . . . . . . . . . . .

GUIDE TO
**Lemon (or Lime) Ice**

ICE, a classic dessert. So easy. A cup of WATER boiled with ½ cup of SUGAR. Cook about 5 minutes. Cool and blend in the JUICE OF 2 LEMONS (or a bit less) and grate about a teaspoon of the RIND into the mixture.

Put into foil-covered ICE CUBE TRAYS in the freezing compartment of your icebox, with the setting at maximum coldness. After half an hour — it should be mushy — turn it into a metal bowl and beat till smooth (you can stir it around in the tray, but it's easier the other way). Return to the freezer. In a couple of hours it should be done. It's nice to "warm" them in the regular part of your refrigerator for about 15 minutes before serving.

Maybe you have some nice things to put the ICE in for the table (made of glass?). A WAFER (an elegant COOKIE; store-bought is fashionable) would be an appropriate and classical accompaniment.

. . . . . . . . . . . . . . . . . . . . . . . . . . . . . . . . . . . . . . . . . . . . . . . .

# Appendix III
## Survey / Review

HUNGER, then EATING and TASTING. ALL COOKING comes from this.

YOU ARE THE COOK, not the EQUIPMENT — but respect the equipment: GOOD KNIVES: no dinky, flimsy POTS; HEAVY-GAUGE UTENSILS with TIGHT LIDS.

THE INGREDIENTS underlie the meal the way words do a language.

COMPOSE THE MEAL AS A WHOLE.

"GLUP" IS REAL. Get on with it.

VARIETY — what is cooked, how it's cooked, and what it goes with.

FLAVOR, TEXTURE, APPEARANCE (F.T.A.) — a pocket guide to cooking.

THE OMELET LAW — the first time you try someone else's recipe for an omelet, it won't work.

DEVELOP a COOKING SYSTEM in which it is convenient to save PERFECTLY GOOD VEGETABLE PEELINGS and LIQUIDS (STOCK) in which MEAT, POULTRY, and VEGETABLES are cooked — if you're cooking a lot every day.

MAKE FRIENDS WITH YOUR BUTCHER AND YOUR CHEESE PERSON.

KNOW YOUR MARKET.

COOKING PROCESSES:

Tender meat is usually cooked with dry heat.

Tough stringy meat (which is generally more flavorful) usually requires moist heat and prolonged cooking. Very thin cuts can be quickly sautéed.

EGGS, SOUR CREAM, YOGURT — and CREAM (especially when acidic ingredients like wine or tomatoes are present) — will *curdle* if boiled. (Except for EGGS, this will not affect the taste.)

BOILING often means SIMMERING. But in cooking pasta, rapid boiling is called for. When wine or a sauce is being *reduced* (unless it contains *eggs, sour cream, yogurt,* or *cream*), rapid boiling in an open pan is called for.

CHOMBAS will help you remember some possible additions to things: CHEESE, ONIONS, MUSHROOMS, BACON, ALMONDS, and SESAME SEEDS.

F.E.C. stands for FLOUR first, then lightly beaten EGG, then BREAD CRUMBS. A common coating for deep-fried foods to keep them dry.

IRIFOY (It's Right in Front of You) is sometimes better than an explanation.

MANAGING THE HEAT IS MANAGING THE COOKING. Learn to check food *before* it's overcooked.

OVERCOOKING is a misunderstanding, or a substitute for lack of attentiveness. Undercooking is not the solution.

THE COOKING CURVE shows that the MOMENT OF DONENESS sometimes seems to come OUT OF NOWHERE, especially with delicate foods like eggs and fish.

DRYING OUT IS TO BE GUARDED AGAINST, but excess liquid is not the answer.

ONIONS, LEMON, PARSLEY, GARLIC, and OIL — tireless helpers in the earth's kitchens.

PRETASTING can be exercised and developed.

SAUCES ARE ACCESSIBLE TO EVERYONE. And don't forget THE INVISIBLE SAUCE. (Smile over the food.)

IN SAUCES and DRESSINGS, generally, no particular ingredient should stand out.

THE GINGER PRINCIPLE: Putting in *too much* of something will *guide you* unerringly toward *perfection*.

WOODEN SPOONS should be in an upright container, handy to the stove.

PREHEAT the OVEN; WARM the PLATES.

APPEARANCE IS A REALITY: *the plate, the table, the service, the atmosphere,* and *the meal as a whole.*

FINISHING UP means CARING A LITTLE EXTRA AT THE END.

# Index

ABC's of cooking, the, 347–48
almonds
   in chombas, 183
   *See also* nuts and seeds
Amaretto, 153
anchovies. *See* fish
anchovy paste. *See* sauces
appearance: a reality in cooking,
   162, 355–56, 385
apples
   apple-cucumber salad, 205
   apples underneath, 333
   baked apple memories, 381–82
   basic apple pie, 328–29
   sautéed (in guide to beginner's
     duck), 103
   single-nut-crust pie, 333–34
Arm and Hand Body Move-
     ments, 31–36
   in baking, 33, 235, 307, 321,
     322
aromatic trinity, the, 120–21
   in soup, 264
artichoke, 178
   dip for, 139
asparagus, 178
   alone in salad, 202

asparagus tips–jicama salad,
   196
au gratin, 167
avocado
   avocado all-together soup,
     277–78
   avocado-grapefruit salad, 200
   to ripen quickly, 208n

bacon, 255
   in chombas, 183
   in spinach salad, 204
baking powder, 316–17, 325
baking soda, 316–17, 322
   rule, 317
   in sour cream in baking, 324–
     25
bananas
   banana bread, 324–25
   flaming, 336
   marriage of cranberries and
     bananas, the, 259
   rice going bananas with anise,
     258
barley, 242
   as a soup thickener, 275

Basic Seven, the, ingredients in baking, 312–14
baste, 33–35, 42, 149
batter: pour, drop (definition), 314
beans, cooking, 290–94
  in beer, 294n
  multiday beanfest, 293–94
  seasoning, 292
  *See also* green beans, lima beans
beef, 211–22
  beef scallops, 223–24, 226–27
  beef stroganoff, Peter the Great's, 352
  broth, improving canned, 136
  eye à la veal, 223–4
  eye-cooked beef, 226–27
  London broil, 275–76
  salad, 196
beer, cooking beans in, 294n
beets, 178–79
*beurre manié*, 135, 285
*beurre noir. See* sauces
big secret of baking, the, 312–14
biscuits, 325–27
blanching, 35
boiling (often means simmering), 168, 385
boil/steam method of cooking, the
  beans, 292
  cereal, 5, 243–44
  eggs (soft-boiled), 203
  pasta, 246–47
bok choy, 180
bouillon cubes as stock substitute, 95, 239
bread, 305–8
  banana bread, 324–25

Celtic hearth bread, 306–7
definition of, 309
garlic bread, 144–45, 152, 159
kneading, 307
leavening (yeast), 307
whole wheat bread (and variations), 305–9
bread crumbs, 298
  in casseroles, 290
  in chombas, B.C., 183
  in deep-fat frying, 175
broccoli, 145–46
  broccoli-onion minglement, 158
  parboiling, 170–71, 195–96
  steamed, 170, 182
broth. *See* chicken broth
Brussels sprouts, 61–62, 127, 181
buckwheat (kasha), 241, 242
bulgur
  à gauche, 95
  in tabbouleh, 374–75
burns: what to do, 300
butter
  in baking, 319
  butter-lemon-mustard sauce, 149–51, 158
  cutting in, 235, 322–23
  finish to eggs, 50
  herb butter, 98, 128, 158–59
  as sauce and sauce enrichment, 128, 129
  sautéing with, 85–86, 170–71
  sweet preferred, 85–86
buttermilk
  in baking, 316, 320
  buttermilk conversion, the great, 233
  in *crème fraîche*, 104

cabbage, 181–82
  spinach cooked in curly-leaf
    cabbage water, 270
cake
  chocolate ice-box cake, 335–
    36
  definition of, 309
  failures, 322
  spirited pound cake, 327–28
capers, 121
  on fish, 129, 153
  in salads, 297
carrots, 179
  in the aromatic trinity, 120–
    21, 264
  country carrots, 188–89
casseroles, 287–90
  on covering, 289–90
catastrophes, apparent, 300–301
cauliflower, 182
  cauliflower-mushroom to-
    getherment, 374
  cream of cauliflower soup,
    273–74
  parboiling, 195–96
cayenne pepper, 108–21 *passim*,
  297
celery
  in the aromatic trinity, 120–
    21, 264
  curling stalks for salad, 195
celery root, 187
celery seed, 82
cereal
  cold (granola), 6
  cooking cereal grains, 243–44
  hot, 4–5
chard. *See* Swiss chard

cheese
  in casseroles, 288–90
  in chombas, 183
  make your own, 236
  in omelets, 62
  storage, 232
chicken
  boiled, 268
  cutting up, 88
  doneness of, 75
  fried chicken, utterly simple,
    372
  poached. *See* chicken rustique
  roast chicken, above all, 379
  rustique, 73–75, 81–82
  salad, 204
  stock, 267
  washing before cooking, 88
chicken broth
  improving canned, 136
  with lemon in salad dressing,
    202
  in quick breads, 320
  in sauces, 134
chicken livers, sautéed, 378
chocolate ice-box cake, 335–36
chocolate mousse, 334
chombas, 183, 385
clam and sausage fettuccine, 259
coffee, 67–70
cognac, deglazing pan with, 298
cookbooks, 11–12, 367–71
cookies
  definition of, 309
  making, 329–30
cooking
  chemistry in, 339–43, 358–59
  composition of meal, 353–54

cooking curve, 47–48, 141, 385
innovative, 253–59
light on, 357–58
meal as a whole, the, 353–62
processes, 86–87, 175–76, 254, 257–58, 292, 351. *See also* meat, vegetables
revitalizing, 356–58
survey-review of basic principles, 384–85
system, 177–78, 186, 268–70
tasting (when important), 151
timing, 141–42, 146–47, 151–52
coriander: children's bedtime drink, 115–16
cornmeal, 244
polenta, 244
cornstarch: as thickener, 138–39
court bouillon, 156
cranberries and bananas, the marriage of, 259
cream
to avoid curdling, 128, 274, 385
as finishing touch, 298
whipped, 159
cream, to
butter (with or without sugar), 33
herb butter (with or without lemon), 128
*crème fraîche*, 104, 129
cucumber
in salad, 195
cucumber-apple salad, 205
curdling, to avoid, 128, 204, 385

custard, idiot, 335
cut in, butter and shortening, to, 33, 235, 322–23

dates, in baking, 320
deep-fat frying, 175–76
deglazing, 35–36, 126, 298
dooka, 382
dough, definition of, 314
duck, beginner's, with rosemary and *crème fraîche*, 102

egg(s)
in baking, 319–20
cracking, 40–41
to avoid curdling, 274
dechilling, 47
in deep-fry coating, 175
eggs Guinevere (sautéed), 40–44
hard-boiled, 203
herb omelet, 53–56
nonlinear, 51–52
omelets, 53–59
as receivers, 96, 109
scrambled, 46–52
separating, 133
soft-boiled, 203
egg yolks
as leavening, 317, 319–20
heat test for, 129
as thickeners in soup, 129–132
uses for, 130
eggplant, 179

fat
rendering, 217

fat (*cont.*)
  skimming, 281 (during cook-
    ing), 266 (when chilled)
  uses for different kinds of, 217
F.E.C. (flour, egg, bread crumbs),
    coating for deep frying, 175
fines herbes, 112
finishing touches, 295–301
fish
  baking, 149, 155
  broiling, poaching, sautéing,
    steaming, 156–57
  court bouillon, 156
  doneness, 151–52
  forms in which you buy, 155
  halibut, my actual great-grand-
    mother Eva's poached, 157
  halibut, never-dry (broiled),
    157
  salmon salad, 205
  swordfish, never-dry (broiled),
    157
  tunafish salad, 376
flake, to, 33
flour
  about, 314–15
  to brown, 138
  in deep-fry coating, 175
  sifting, 321, 323, 324
  as a thickener, 131, 133–35,
    138–39
fold, to, 33
fruit(s)
  in baking, 320
  caution in combining fruits
    and vegetables, 257
  discoloration when sliced, 185
  fruit salad, 205
  with meat, 354

  to ripen quickly, 208n
  *See also individual fruits*
frying, fear of, 175–76
F.T.A. (flavor, texture, appear-
    ance), 161–63, 353–56

garlic, 91–93
  bread, 144–45, 152, 159
  sauce, 249
garnishing, 271, 296, 362
ginger principle, the, 154, 385
"glob," definition of, 41n
grain(s)
  about, 237–44
  cereal vs. whole grain, 239
  cooking cereals, 243–44;
    whole grains, 241–42
  seasoning, 243
  should "rest" after cooking, 5,
    80
  as a thickener in soups, 274–
    75; in stews, 284–85
granola, great, 6
grapefruit-avocado salad, 200
gravy. *See* sauces
green beans, 179
  alone in salad, 202
  and deceptive cooking time,
    142
  parboiling, 170–71

ham hock cooked with lima
    beans, 255
hard sauce, easy, 334
health food restaurant demon-
    stration, the great, 298–300
heat testing
  for egg yolks, 129
  lasagna, 250

heat testing (*cont.*)
  water drop in skillet for frying, 54
herbs
  blends, 119–20
  bouquet garni, 120
  to have on hand, 27–29
  relative strength of, 118–19
  for salad, 199
hollandaise. *See* sauces
honey, in baking, 318–19
hors d'oeuvres, 61–62
hunger, 7

ice, lemon, lime, 382–83
ingredients
  the Basic Seven in baking, 312
  staples in other cultures, 346
Irifoy, 141–42, 385
  in buying produce, 206
  vegetable cooking with, 169

Jerusalem artichoke and Swiss chard salad, a, 187–88
jicama, 179
  with asparagus tips in salad, 196

kasha. *See* buckwheat
kitchen equipment, 12–27
  in baking, 26–27
kneading, 307
knives, 14–17

labels, reading, 209
lamb, 224–25
  braised lamb shanks (Sherwood Forest lamb), 359–62
  lamb, rice, cinnamon stick and peppercorn stewup, 294
  roast leg of lamb, 379–81

Sherwood Forest lamb (braised lamb shanks), 359–62
lasagna, Billy's restoration, 249–50
leavening, 306–7, 316, 322
leek(s)
  in soups, 268–69
  cream of leek-potato-apple-turnip-caraway-majoram soup with chives, 276–77
  vichyssoise extraordinaire, 276–77
leftovers
  in casseroles, 289
  in salads, 195
lemon, 121, 297
  butter-lemon-mustard sauce, 149–51, 158
  ice, 382–83
  to prevent discoloration of fruits and vegetables, 185
  in salad dressing, 197, 202, 203–4
  as salt alternative, 121
  in shrimp salad, 355
  "soft" use of, 300
lentil salad, 205. *See also* beans
lettuce, 97
  in salad, 193–94
  sautéed, 174–75
lima beans, 179, 255
lime ice, 382–83
liqueurs, in cooking, 91
liquids
  in baking, 320
  in cooking, 91
London broil, 225–26

macaroni, illegal elegant, 375–76

Maggi, 28, 298
marinate, to, 36, 285–86
mayonnaise. *See* sauces
measurements
  in baking, 311–12, 317, 318
  to remember, 323–24
  utensils for, 363
  without utensils, 30, 65, 218–19
meat
  braising, 286–87
  broiling, pan broiling, sautéing, 220–22
  browning, for stew, 280–82
  buying, 212–16
  cuts, descriptions and uses of each, 213–17
  doneness of, 218–19
  meat loaf, 226
  roasting, 100, 217, 219–20
  seasoning, 222, 223, 225
  storage, 212–13
  *See also* beef, lamb, pork, sausage, stew, veal
method of Noah, the, 151–52
milk
  in baking, 320
  cooking fish in, 157
  cooking vegetables in, 169
  to sour, 322
millet
  to cook, 239, 242
  cooked with brown rice, 237
*mirepoix*, 148–49, 287
molasses
  in baking, 319
muffins, mixing batter for, 322
mushrooms, 62, 180–81
  black mushrooms, 373

cauliflower and mushroom togetherment, 374
  in chombas, 183
  in omelets, 62
mussels, steamed (irresistible moules), 377
mustard
  butter-lemon-mustard sauce, 149–51, 158
  powdered, in salad dressing, 198–99
  in salad dressing, 198–99
  sour cream/mustard emergency sauce, 139

nectarine, 153
Noah and Noah's wife, 151–52
nut loaf, 192
nutmeg: as finishing touch, 297
nuts and seeds
  almonds (in chombas), 183, (skinning), 94
  nuts toasted with grains, 243
  sesame seeds, in chombas, 183

oatmeal, packaged, 4–5, 192
oats, rolled, 243–44
oil, 197
  olive and other kinds, 86
  sautéing with, 85–86, 170–73
omelet(s)
  herbal, 53–56
  stuffings (including cheese), 62
omelet law, the, 56, 385
onion
  in the aromatic trinity, 120–21, 264
  baked, 174, 380
  boiled, 144, 168–69

onion (*cont.*)
  in chombas, 183
  dicing, 17
  juice, in salad, 199
  onion-broccoli minglement,
    158
  peeling, 94, 144
  roasted, with meat, 174
  sautéing, various stages of, 94,
    174
  sliced, with orange in salad,
    197
orange juice: in baking, 316, 320
oysters, smoked (in guide to tur-
    key), 227

paprika: as finishing touch, 297
parboiling, 170–71, 195–96
parsley, 110, 120
  bed of baked, 148–49
  deep-fried, 175–76
  storing, 148–49
parsnips, in soup, 269
pasta
  homemade, 250
  lasagna, Billy's restoration,
    249–50
  macaroni, illegal elegant, 375–
    76
  sausage and clam fettuccine,
    259
pastry crust, 235–36
pears
  baked memories, 381–82
  and cheese (reminder), 258
  compatible with lamb, 380
  pears touché, 153–54, 159
peas
  dried, 367

integrity of, 78
  perfect, 78, 81, 83
pepper, 117, 198, 200
pie
  definition of, 309
  basic apple pie, 328
  pastry for, 235
  single-nut-crust apple, 333–34
"pitch," definition of, 41n
polenta. *See* cornmeal
popovers, 310–11
  eggs in, 319–20
pork, 225
  pork chops, beyond-belief,
    225
potatoes
  baked, 173–74
  boiled, 142–44, 158, 168–70
  cream of leek-potato-apple-
    turnip-caraway-marjoram
    soup with chives, 276–77
  instant mashed, as soup thick-
    ener, 275
  to "meal," 179–80
  as receiver, 96, 109, 179–80
  salad, 196
  to sauté, 171
  skins of, 142–44
  vichyssoise extraordinaire,
    276–77
poultry. *See* chicken, duck, tur-
    key
preheating, 35, 53–54
pretasting, 109–10, 120, 385
produce, how to select and buy,
    206–10
prunes, compatible with lamb,
    361
purée, 33, 126

quiche, 234–35
quick bread
  definition of, 309
  leavening for, 316, 322
  *See also* banana bread, bis-
    cuits, cookies, popovers

radishes, 195
raisins: in baking, 320
receivers, 96, 109
recipes, 11–12, 127, 358–59
reducing, 90–91, 127–28
rice, 75–78, 95–96
  brown (whole) rice, 95
  brown rice cooked with millet,
    237
  cooking, two general types of,
    96, 239–42
  à gauche (sautéed/steamed),
    75–78, 82–83
  lamb, rice, cinnamon stick and
    peppercorn stewoup, 294
  as receiver, 96
  rice going bananas with anise,
    258
  in salad, 196
rosemary tea, 113
*roux*, 131
  as stew thickener, 284–85

sage tea, 113
salad(s)
  apple-cucumber, 205
  asparagus tips and jicama, 196
  avocado-grapefruit, 200
  beef, 196
  chicken, 204
  fish (salmon), 205
  fruit, 205

Jerusalem artichoke and Swiss
    chard, 187–88
  lentil, 205
  onion-orange, 197
  potato, 196
  rice in, 196
  salad niçoise, 373
  spinach, 204
  tomato, 193
  tunafish, 376
salad dressing, 197–201
  balancing, 151, 200
  chicken broth and lemon
    juice, 94
  quick vinaigrette, 79, 80
salt
  alternatives, 121
  cooking, put in during, 41
  in cooking beans, 291
  in cooking chicken, 74
  in cooking eggs, 58n
  in soup, 275
  in cooking starch (pasta,
    potatoes, rice), 96
  in stock, 264
  kosher or sea salt preferred,
    121
  overuse of, 96–97, 121
  salad, original meaning of, 195
sauces
  anchovy paste, 129
  béarnaise, failed, 340, 342
  *beurre noir*, 129
  brown, 135
  brown butter, 129
  butter-lemon-mustard,
    149–51, 158
  clout, 147
  garlic, 147

sauces *(cont.)*
  gravy, 131, 138–39
  hard, easy, 334
  hollandaise, 130, 137
  invisible, 132–33
  mayonnaise, 137
  mornay, 134–35
  sour cream/mustard, emer-
    gency, 139
  soy, 298, 299
  spaghetti (real), 249–50
  tomato (with variations), 125
  white, 131, 133–35
  *See also* salad dressing
sausage
  and clam fettuccine, 259
  in guide to lasagna, 249
scallions
  on fish, 153
  substitute for shallots, 121
scallops, broiled, sautéed, 377
seafood. *See* clams, fish, mus-
    sels, oysters, scallops,
    shrimp
seasoning
  aromatic and other, 121
  in beans, 291–92
  in grains, 243
  herbs and spices, chapter 17
  in salads, chapter 23
  in sauces, chapter 18
  in soup, stock, 265, 267–70,
    275–76
  in vegetables, chapter 21
secret list of naked truths, the, 13
secret method of seasoning, the,
    109–10
secrets and tips in baking, 321–
    22

seeds. *See* nuts and seeds
sesame seeds in chombas, 183.
    *See also* nuts and seeds
shallots, 121
  scallions as substitute for,
    121
  staple in French cooking, 346
sherry, in soups, 298
shortening
  in baking, 319
  to cut in, 33, 235
shrimp salad with dill and lemon
    juice, 355
skillet, care of cast iron, 18–19
skins, removing, 94, 190
soup
  avocado all-together, 277–78
  court bouillon, 156
  on covering the pot, 266
  cream of leek-potato-apple-
    turnip-caraway-marjoram,
    with chives, 276–77
  cream soups, 273–75
  egg yolks as thickeners in,
    129–32
  flour as binder in, 274–75
  garnish, 271
  an infinity of, 271–75
  liqueur in, 275–76
  from stock, 271
  thickened, 273–75
  tomorrow soup, 269
  vichyssoise extraordinaire,
    276–77
  wine in, 275–76
  your bag of, 227
  *See also* chicken broth, stock
sour cream
  to avoid curdling, 274

sour cream (cont.)
sour cream/mustard emer-
gency sauce.
See also sauces
soy sauce, 298, 299
spaghetti sauce, real, 249–50
spices
relative strength of, 119
to have on hand, 28–29
spinach, 180
cooked in curly-leaf cabbage
water, 270
salad, 204
stew, 279–87
browning meat for, 280–82
difference between soup and,
280–82
recommended cuts for, 281
seasoning and other additions,
283–84
thickeners for, 284–85
stewup, lamb, rice, cinnamon
stick and peppercorn, 294
stock
cooked meat vs. raw in, 263
definition, 91n
seasoning. See soup
storing, 270–71
TYPES OF
beef, 263–67
chicken, 267
fish, 276
vegetable, 269–71
See also soup
strawberries, in heaven, 332–
33
sugar
in baking, 318–19

sunchokes. See Jerusalem artichokes
sweet potato pudding, Thomas
Smith's, 381
Swiss chard, 180
Jerusalem artichoke and Swiss
chard salad, 187–88

tabbouleh, 374
tea, 68
disposing of leaves, 69
rosemary, sage tea, 113
water at boil for (in contrast to
coffee), 68
temperatures, oven
breads, etc., 321
casseroles, 288–89
deep-fat frying, 175–76
fish, 140–41, 155, 156
meat, 211–28
potatoes, 173–74
thickeners
in sauces, 131
in soups, 273–75
in stews, 284–85
timing. See cooking, timing in
toast
broiled, 44n
toast Butterfield, 44–45
tofu, 112, 176
as receiver, 96
tomatoes
juice in nut loaf, 192
quick peeling, 94
in salad, 193
sauce (with variations), 125
in soup, 262
in stews, 283

trussing poultry, 36
tunafish salad, 376
turkey, 227–28
  stuffing (dressing), 227–28
turnips, 180, 182n
  parboiling, 170–71
  roasted with meat, 174
  in soup, 269

veal, 223
  à blanc, 281
  braised, 223
  braised veal with sour cream,
    379
  veal scallops, 224
vegetables
  to avoid overcooking, 183–
    84
  blending, 176–77
  chopping, slicing, etc., 17
  cooking in milk, 169
  on covering the pot, 168–
    69
  discoloration before cooking,
    178–85; after, 169–70
  purée, 33, 126
  reviving limp, 178
  roasting with meat, 174
  stock, 269–71
  storage, 185–86
  vegetable water, 126–27, 186
vermouth, in cooking fish, 157
vichyssoise. *See* soup

vinaigrette, 79, 80, 197–202
  similar to marinade, 285–86
vinegar, 197–98, 297

Walker, Jearl, 340, 342
water
  in baking, 320
  in testing pan heat, 54
  vegetable water, 126–27, 186
watercress, used for parsley,
    148–49, 153
wheat
  bulgur, 242, 374
  cracked, 242
  whole, 306
  *See also* flour
wine
  in cooking, 74–75, 90–91
  deglazing with, 35–36
  in marinade, 285–86
  in poaching fish, 153
  reducing, 90–91, 127–28
  in soups, 275–76
wood ears, 374

yeast, 306–7, 316
yogurt
  to avoid curdling, 128, 274
  with grains, 243
  substitute for sour cream, 333,
    352

zest, 296n
zucchini, sautéed, 172